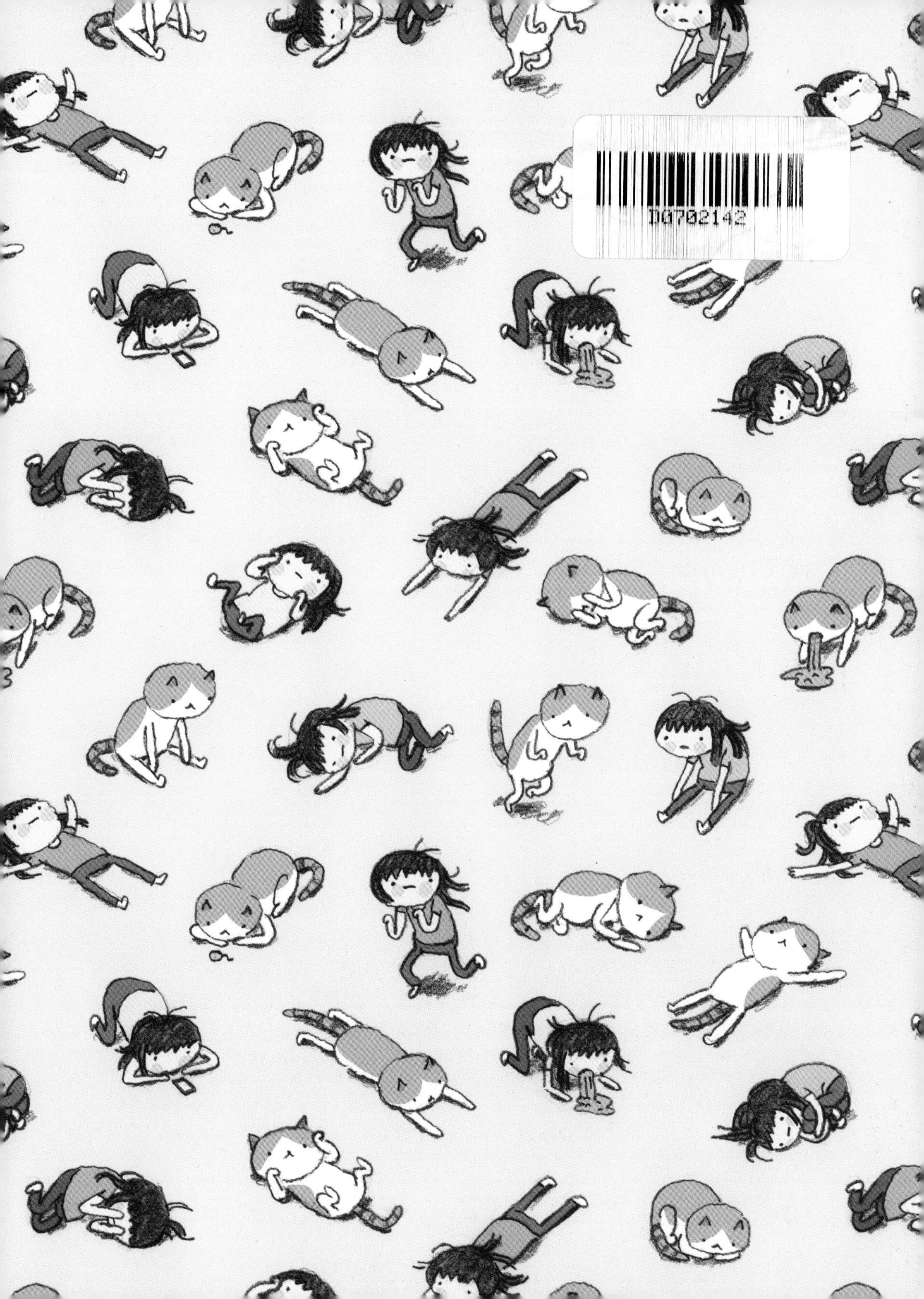

CAT PERSON   BY SEO KIM
PUBLISHED BY KOYAMA PRESS — KOYAMAPRESS.COM
ALL WORK IS © 2014 SEO KIM — SEOKIM.TUMBLR.COM
FIRST EDITION: MAY 2014   ISBN: 978-1-927668-05-4
PRINTED IN CHINA

KOYAMA PRESS GRATEFULLY ACKNOWLEDGES
THE CANADA COUNCIL FOR THE ARTS FOR THEIR
SUPPORT OF OUR PUBLISHING PROGRAM.

CAT PERSON

Seo Kim

KOYAMA PRESS

JIMMY & ME

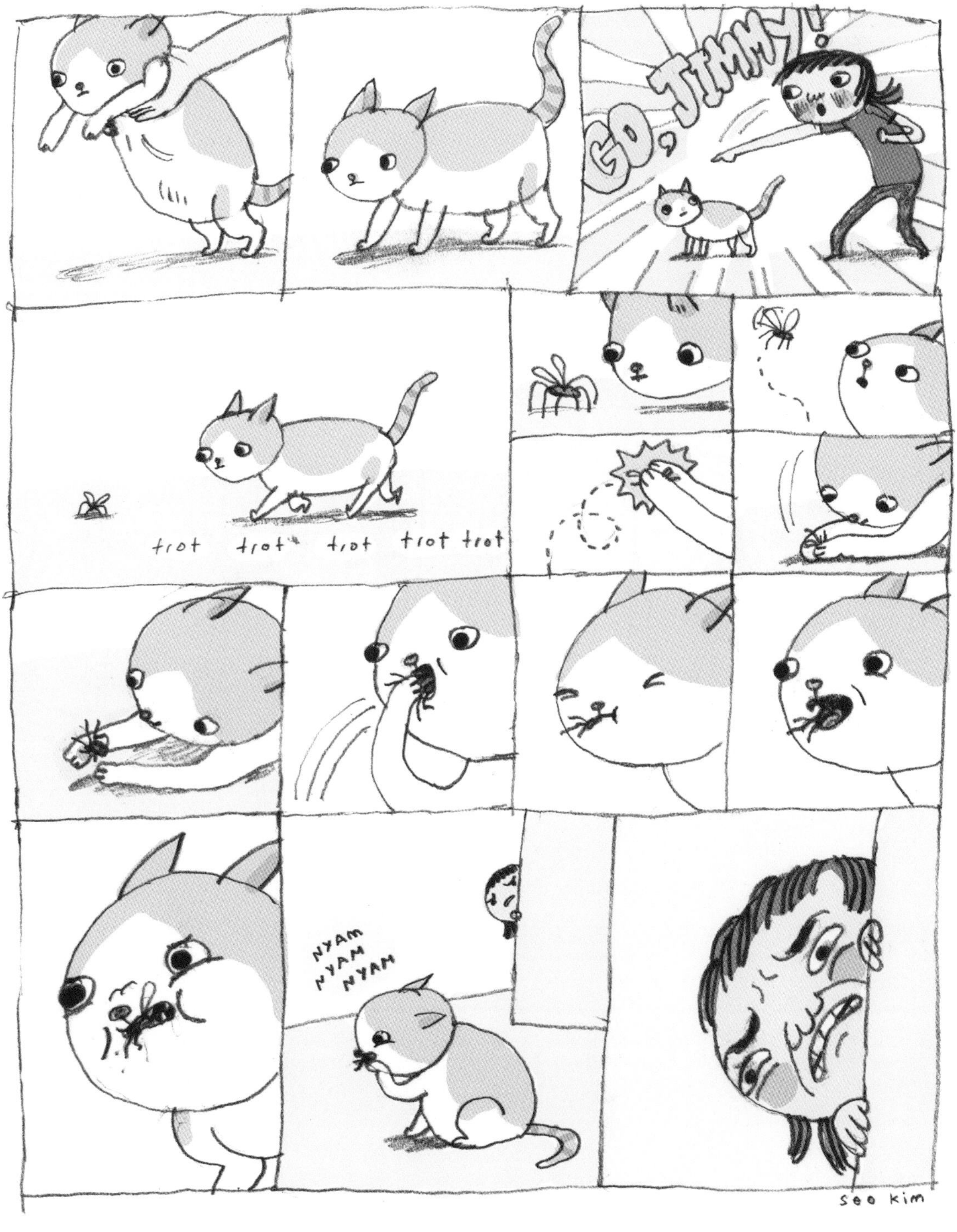
GO, JIMMY!
trot trot trot trot trot
NYAM
NYAM
NYAM
seo kim

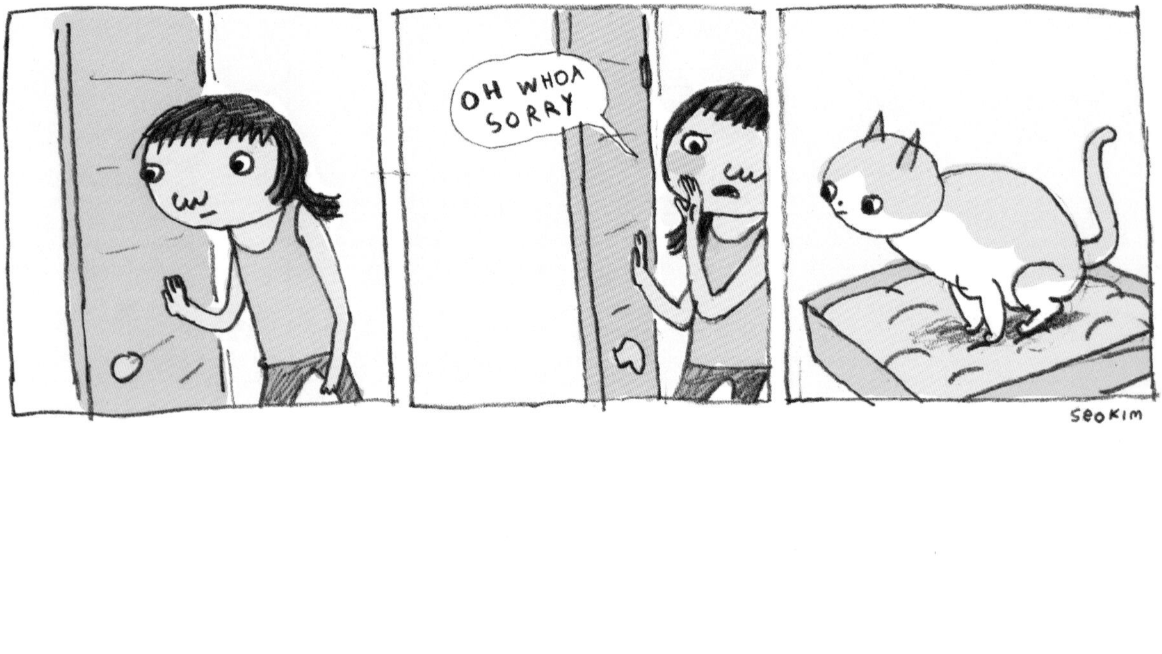
OH WHOA
SORRY
SEOKIM

human

cat

human

CAT

human

CAT

human

CAT

HUMANS AND CATS ARE THE SAME

seo kim

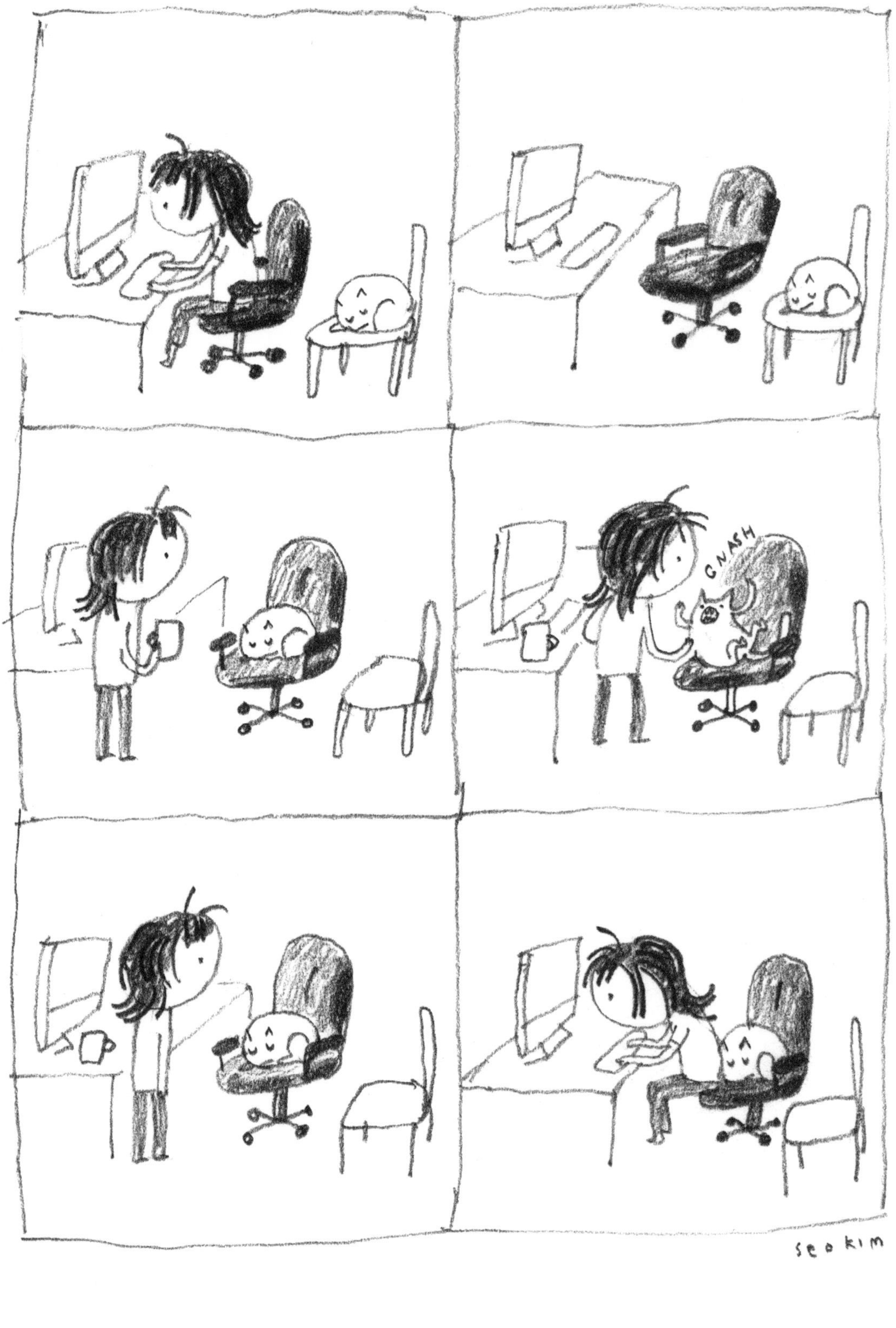
GNASH
seo kim

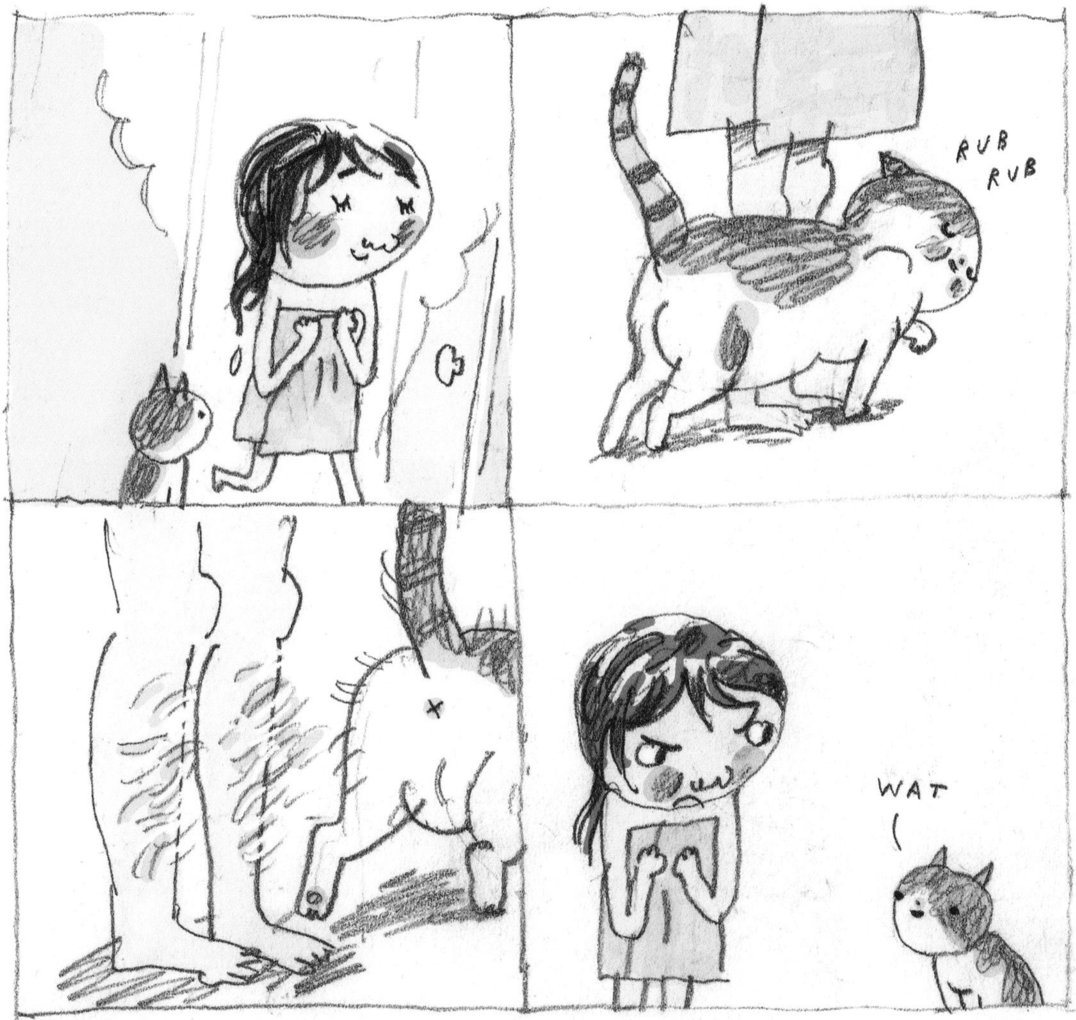
RUB RUB
WAT

SEO KIM

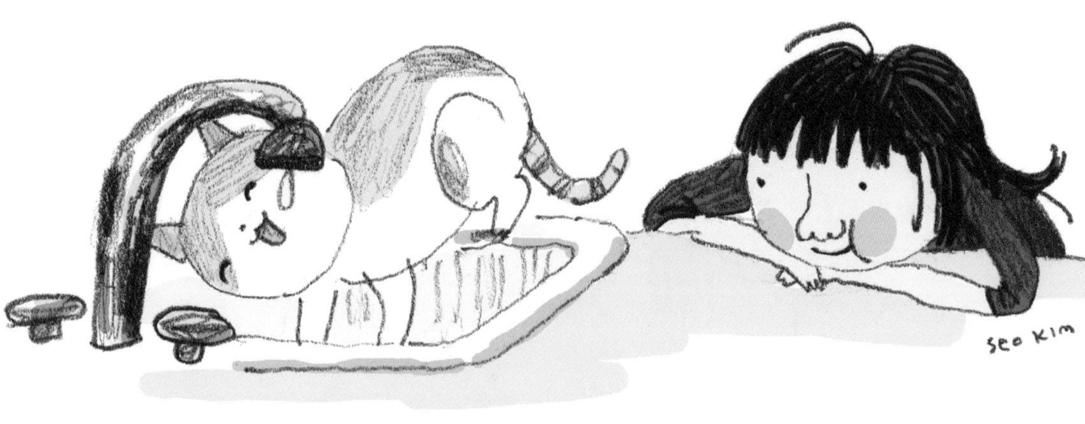
seo kim

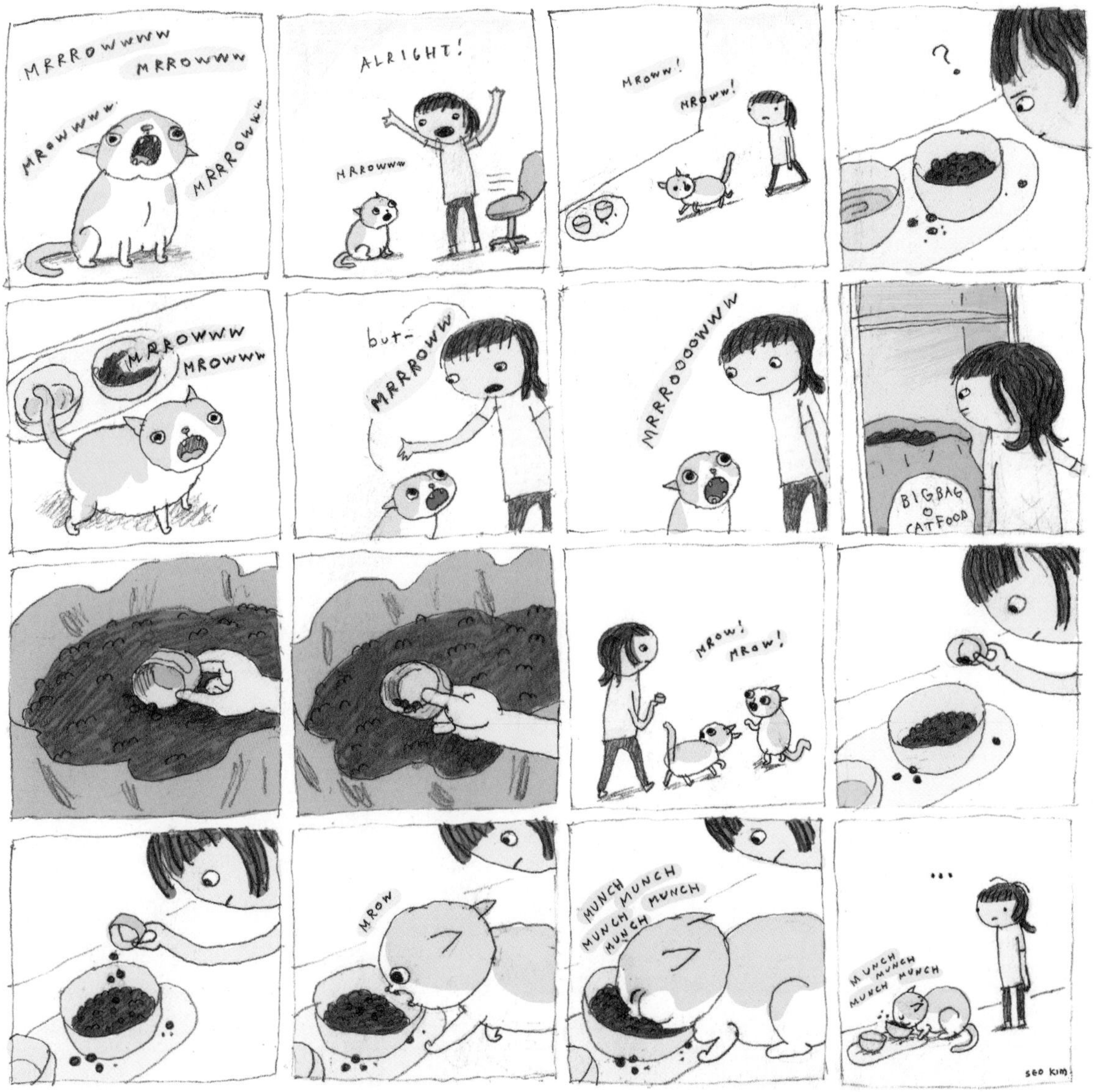
MRRROWWWW
MRROWWW
MROWWWW
MRRROWWW
ALRIGHT!
MRROWWW
MROWW!
MROWW!
?
MRROWWW
MROWWW
but-
MRRROWW
MRRROOOWWW
BIG BAG O CATFOOD
MROW!
MROW!
MROW
MUNCH MUNCH MUNCH MUNCH MUNCH
...
MUNCH MUNCH MUNCH MUNCH
seo kim

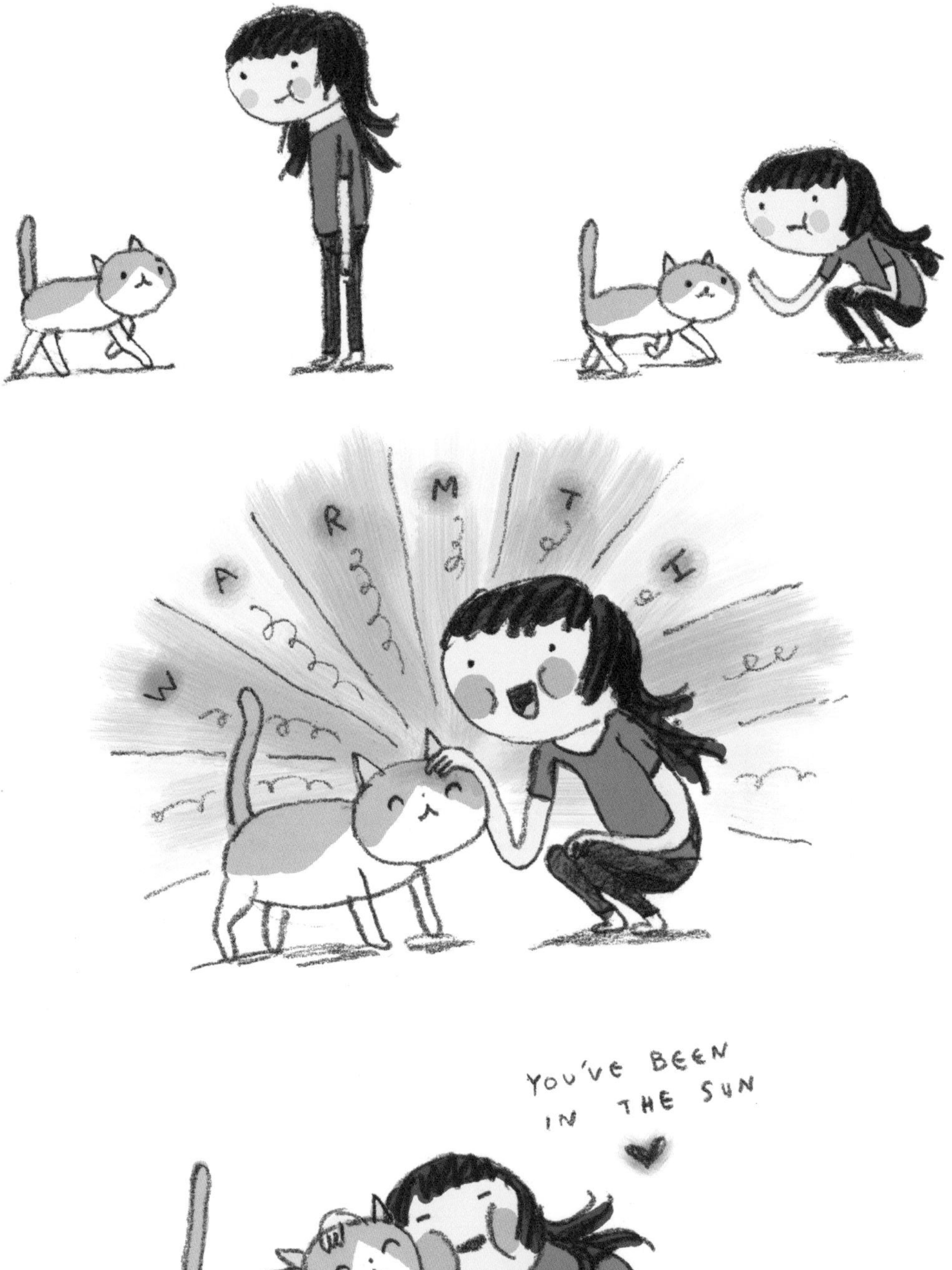
YOU'VE BEEN IN THE SUN
SEO KIM

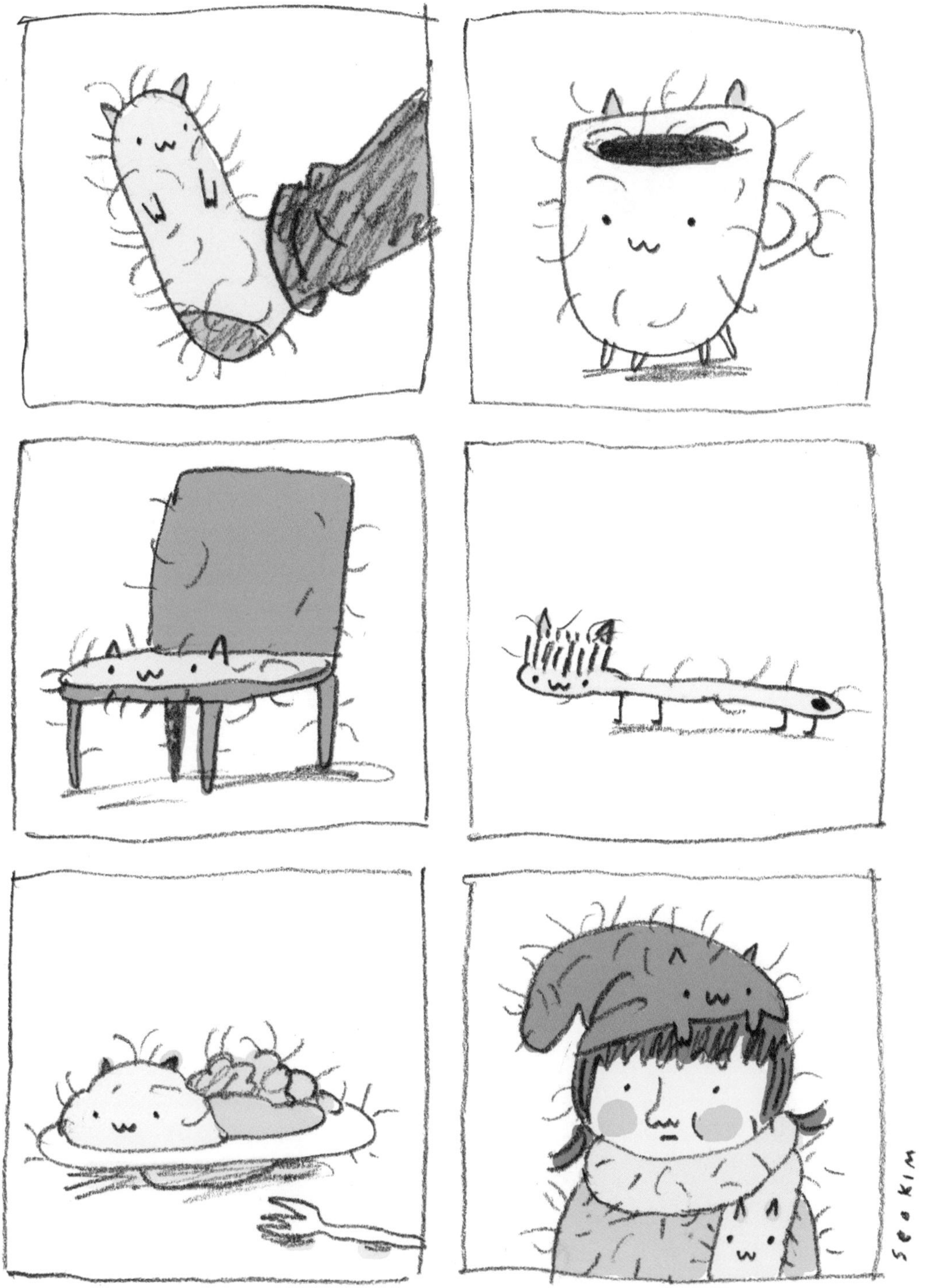
SEOKIM

Everything is a cat when you have a cat

BONK

Seo Kim

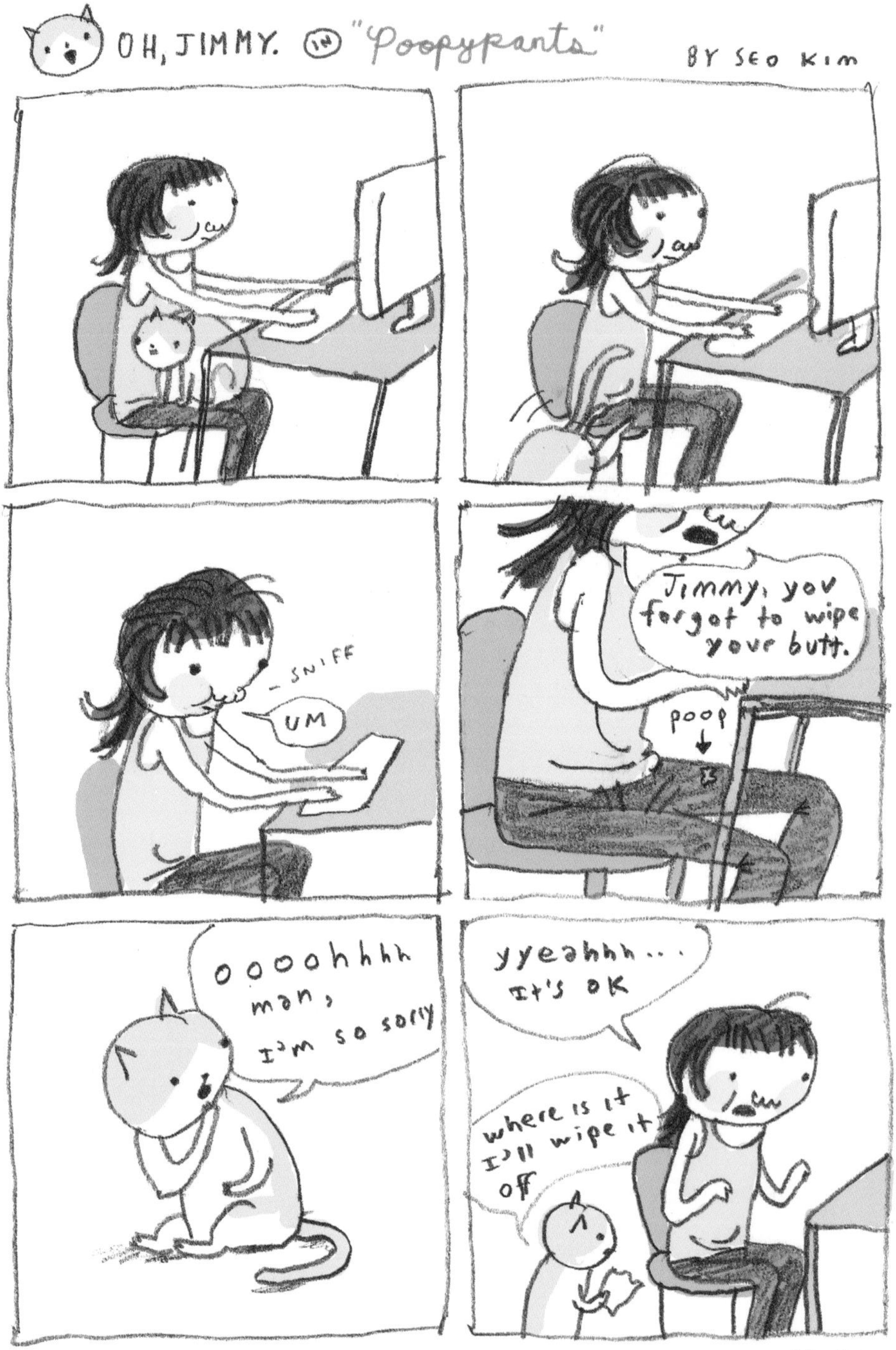
OH, JIMMY. IN "Poopypants"
BY SEO KIM
-SNIFF
UM
Jimmy, you forgot to wipe your butt.
poop
ooooohhhh man, I'm so sorry
yyeahhh... It's OK
where is it I'll wipe it off
SEO KIM

Oh, Jimmy.

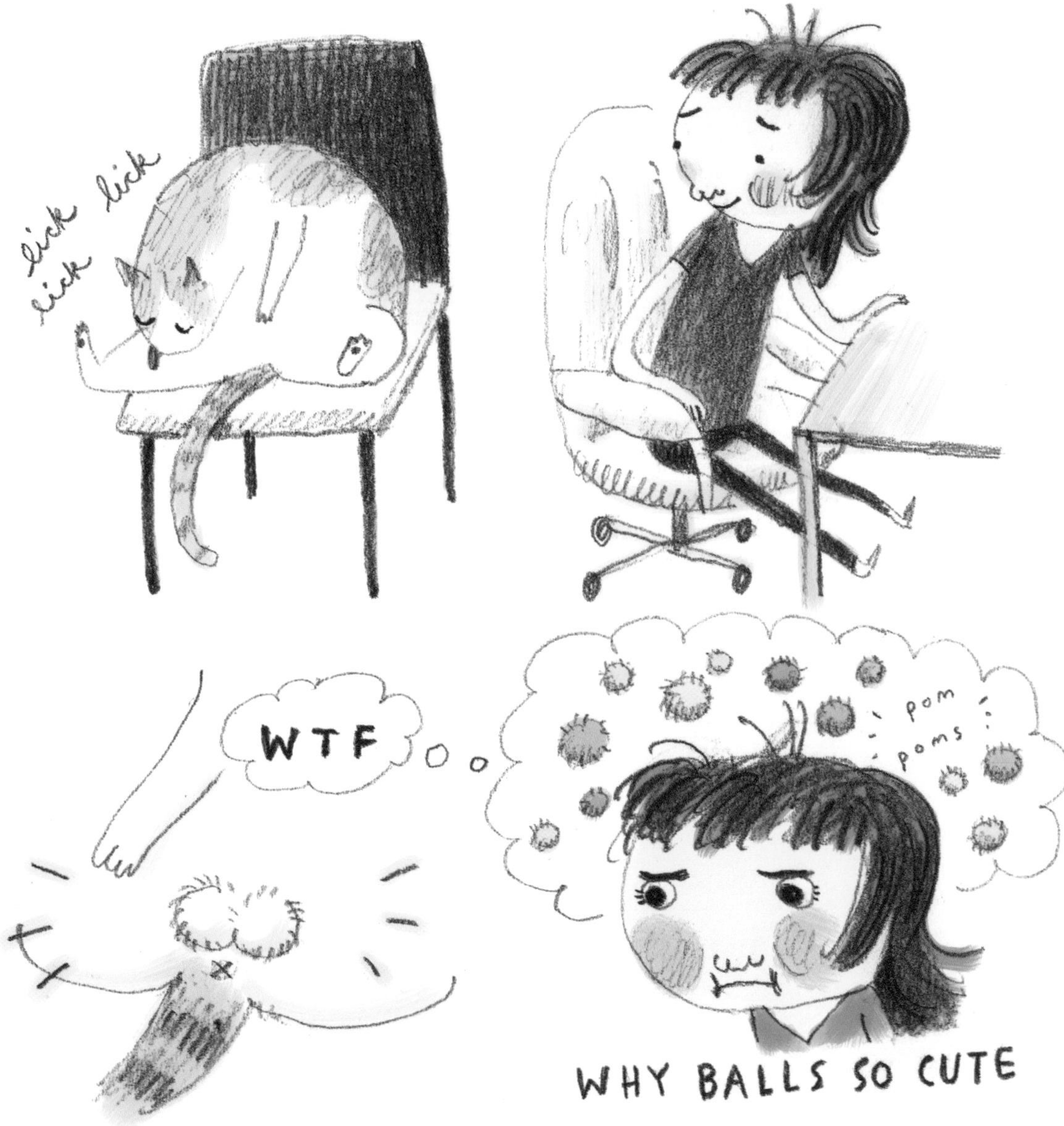
lick lick lick
WTF
pom poms
WHY BALLS SO CUTE
seokim

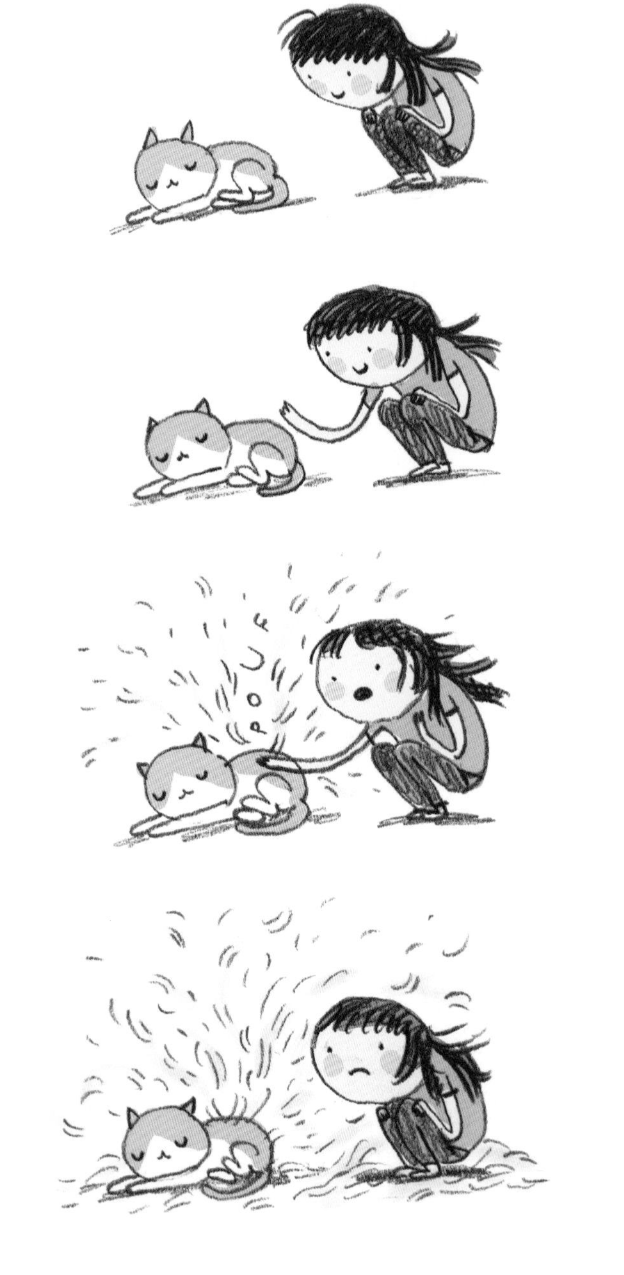
POUF
SEO KIM

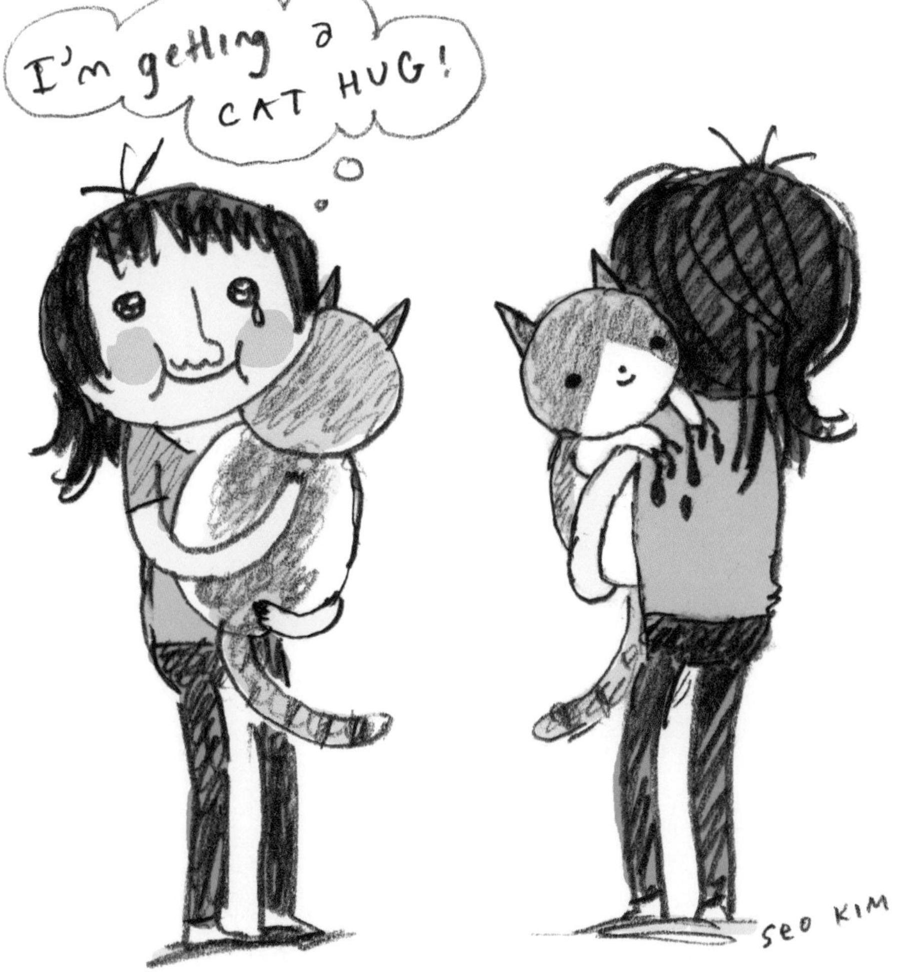
I'm getting a CAT HUG!
SEO KIM

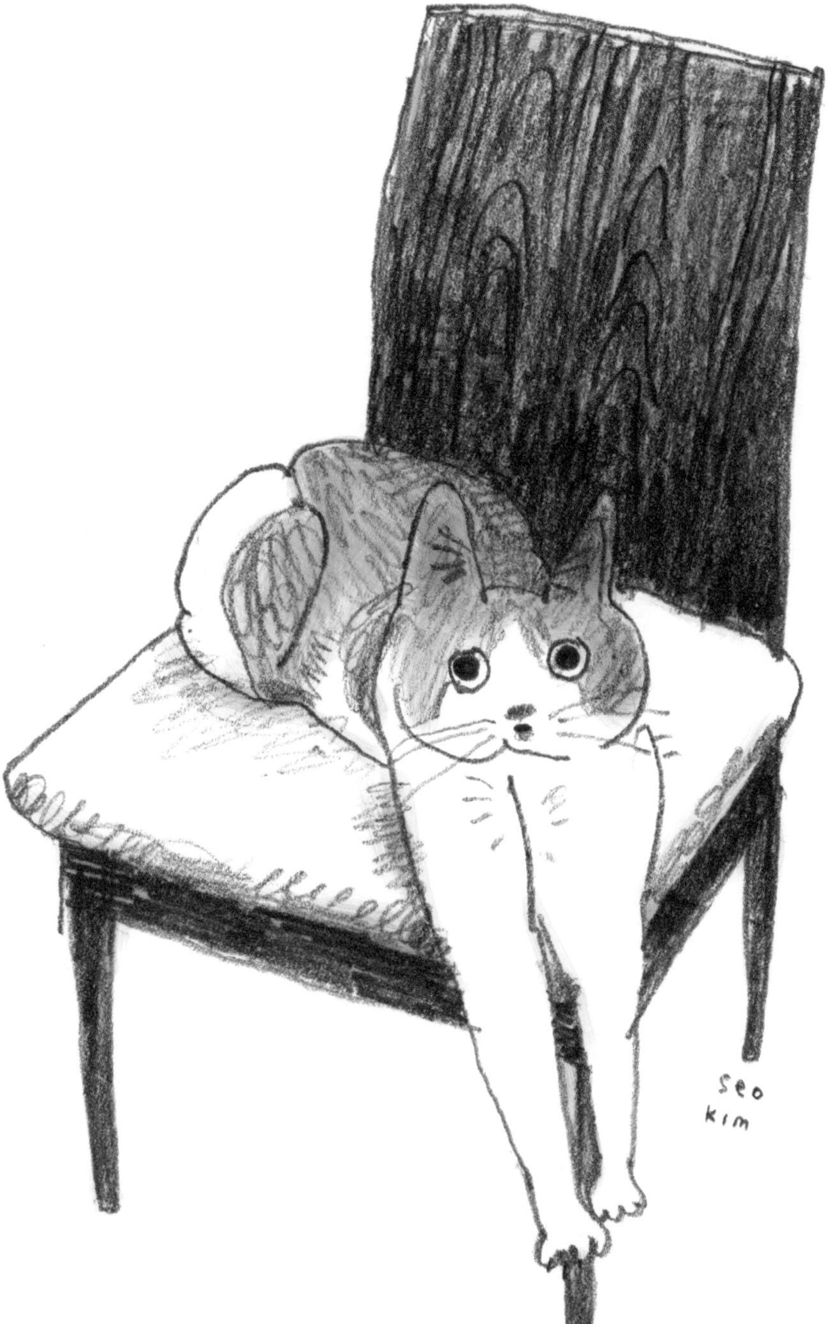
seo
kim

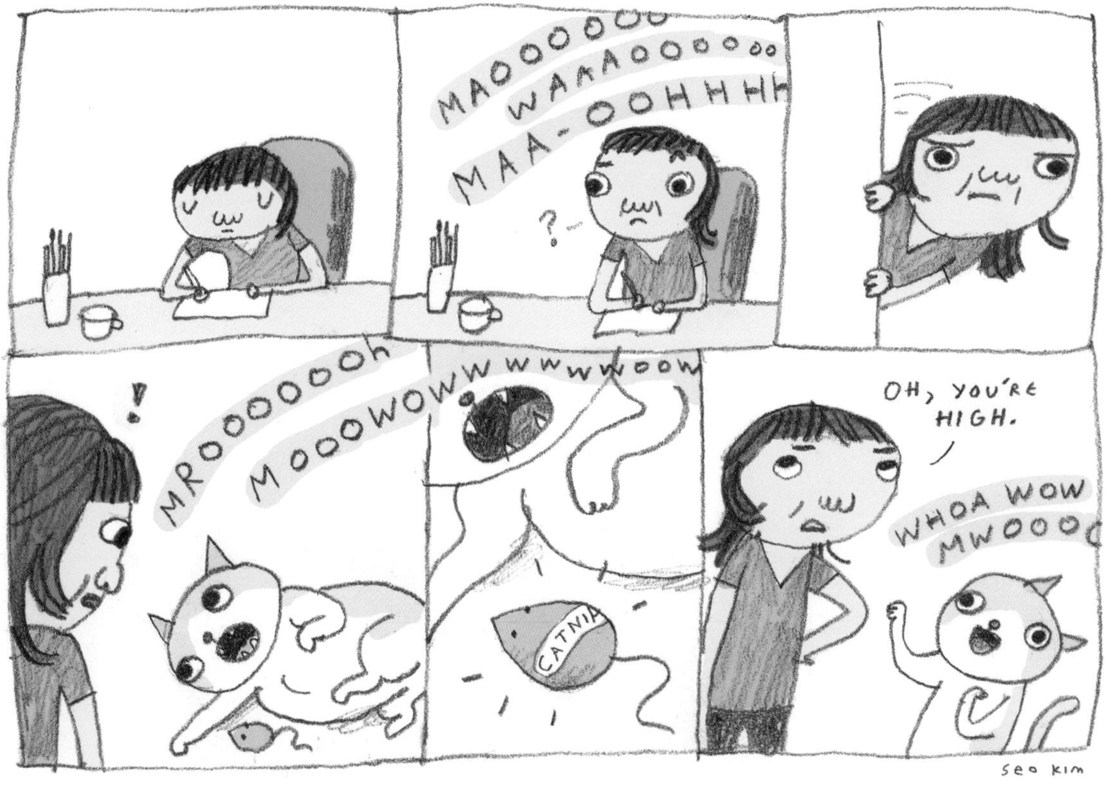

MAOOOOOO
WAAAAOOOOOoo
MAA-OOHHHH
?
!
MROOOOOOOh
MOOOWOWW
WWWWWWOOW
CATNIP
OH, YOU'RE HIGH.
WHOA WOW
MWOOOO
seo kim

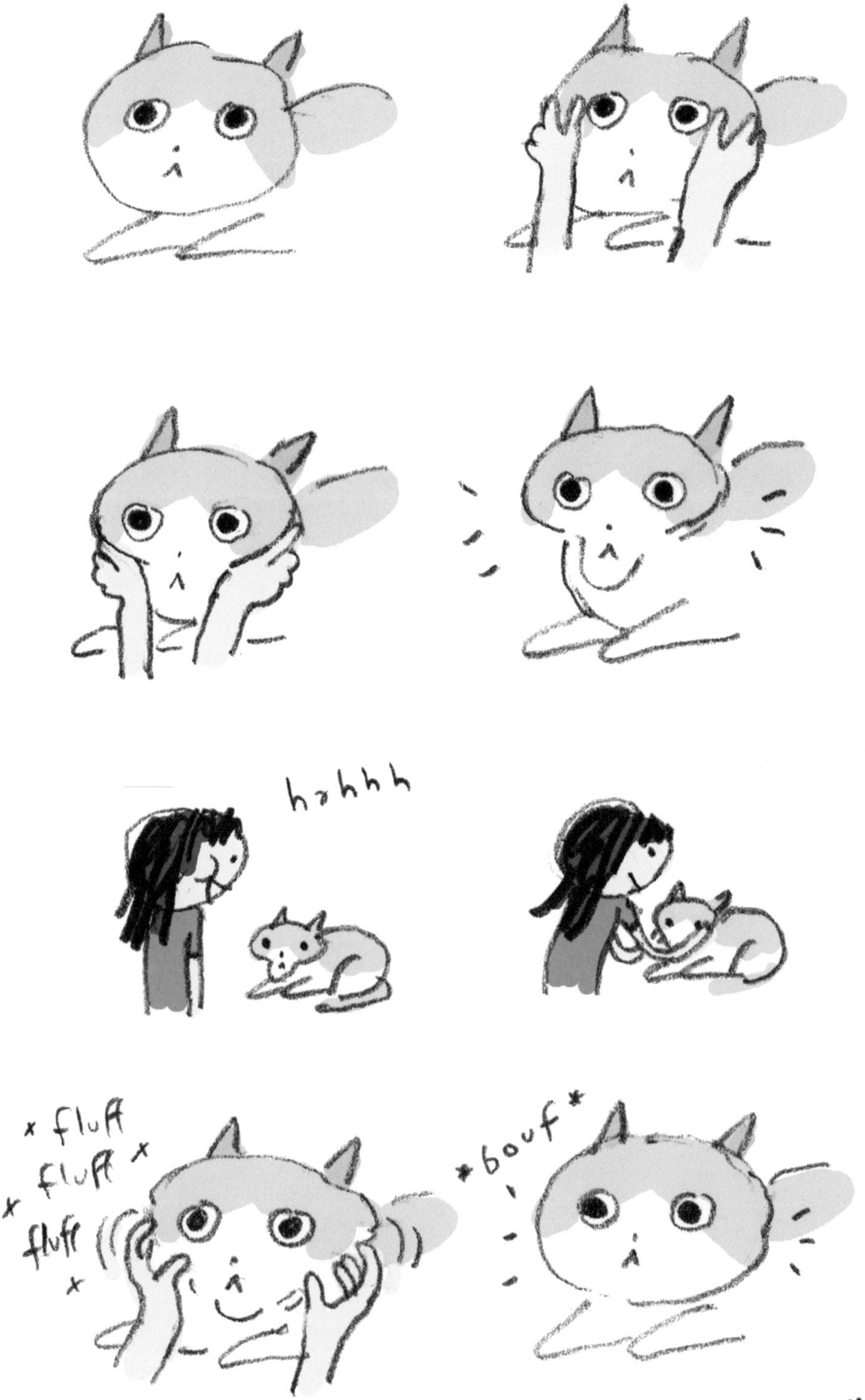
hahhh
*fluff
fluff*
fluff
bouf
seo kim

Seo Kim

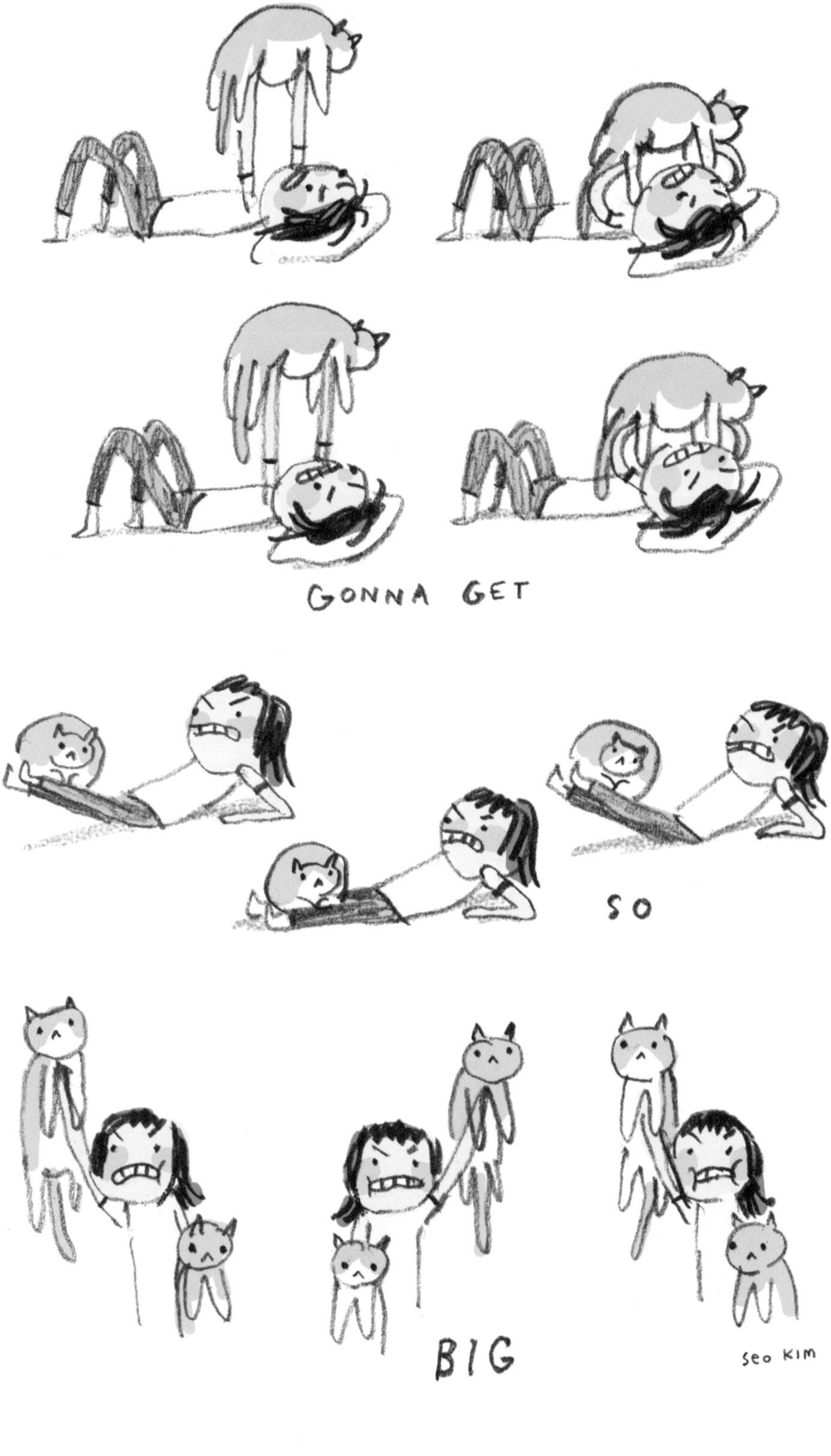
GONNA GET
SO
BIG
seo kim

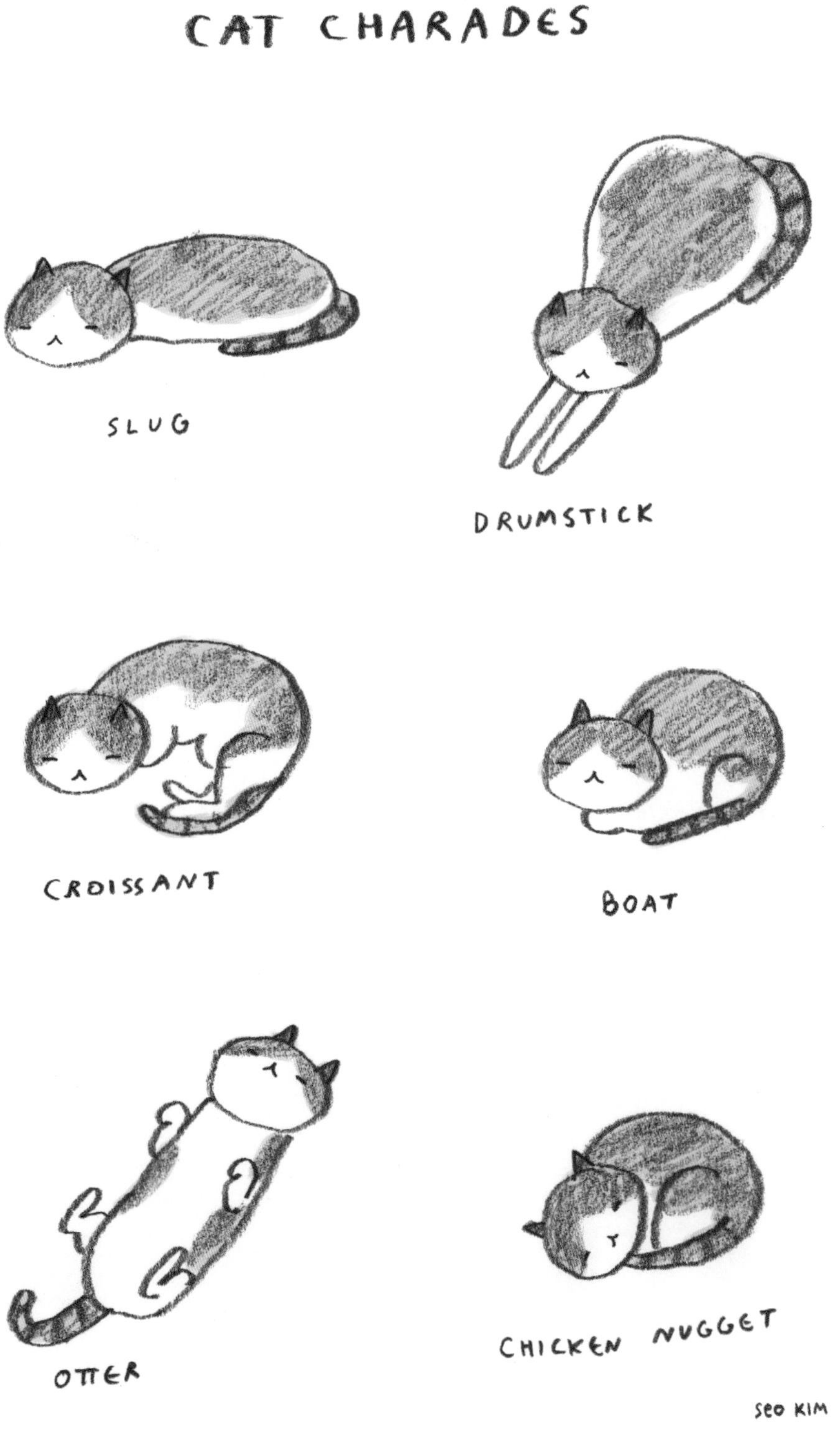
CAT CHARADES
SLUG
DRUMSTICK
CROISSANT
BOAT
OTTER
CHICKEN NUGGET
SEO KIM

Ways to Hug a Cat

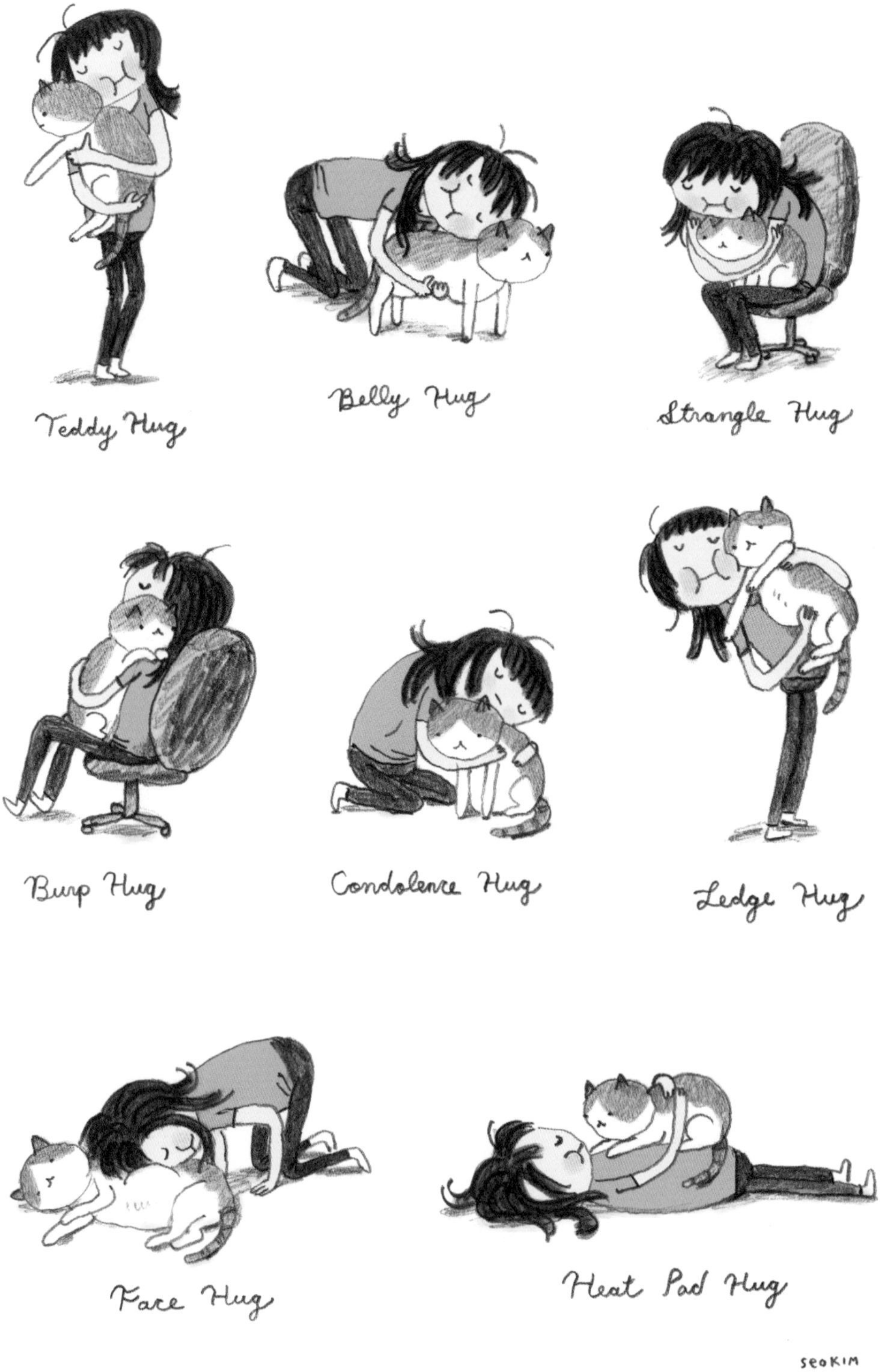
Teddy Hug
Belly Hug
Strangle Hug
Burp Hug
Condolence Hug
Ledge Hug
Face Hug
Heat Pad Hug
SEOKIM

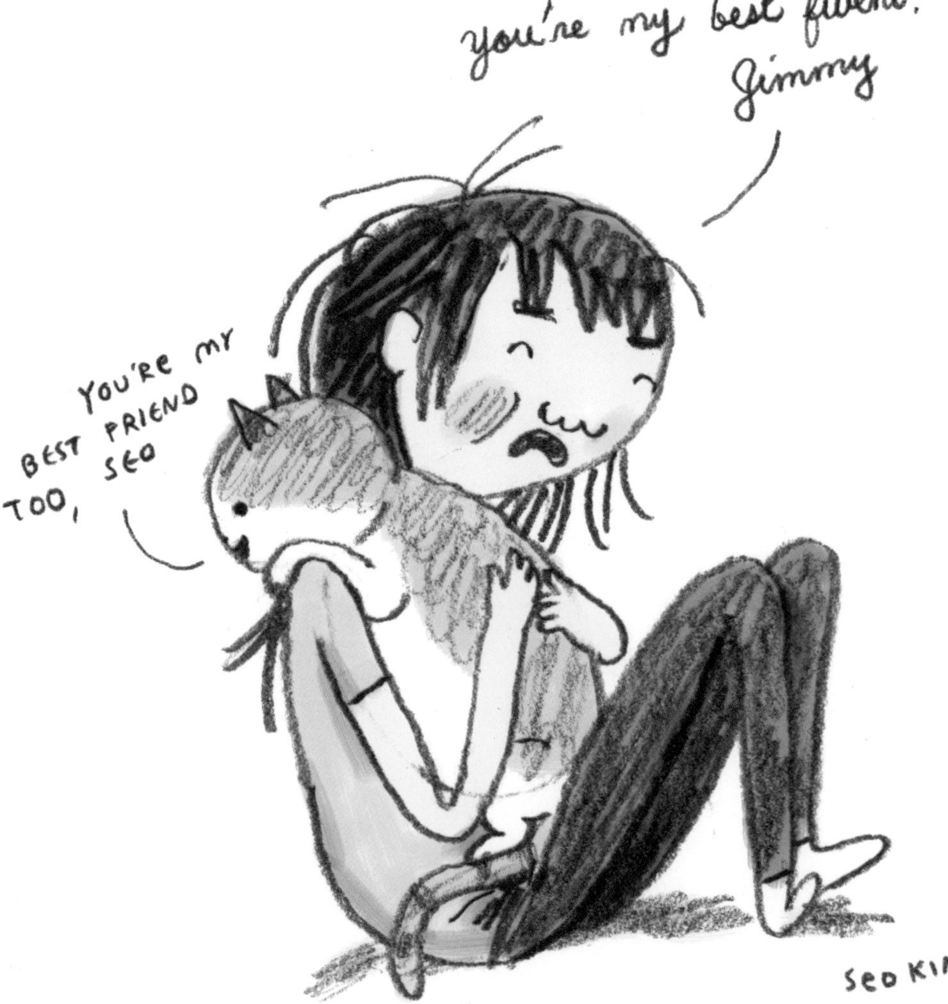
you're my best fwend, Jimmy
YOU'RE MY BEST PRIEND TOO, SEO
SEO KIM

JUST ME

AW MY GOD I FORGOT MY PHONE AT HOME! TODAY OF ALL DAYS! PEOPLE ARE GONNA BE TRYING TO REACH ME. WHY AM I SO STUPID!
THEY'LL THINK I'M A JERK
EVERYONE'S GOING TO HATE ME
CRAP WHAT DO I DO..
AUUGH
LATER THAT NIGHT
NO NEW MSGS
NO MISSED CALLS
seo kim

Wasabi Peas

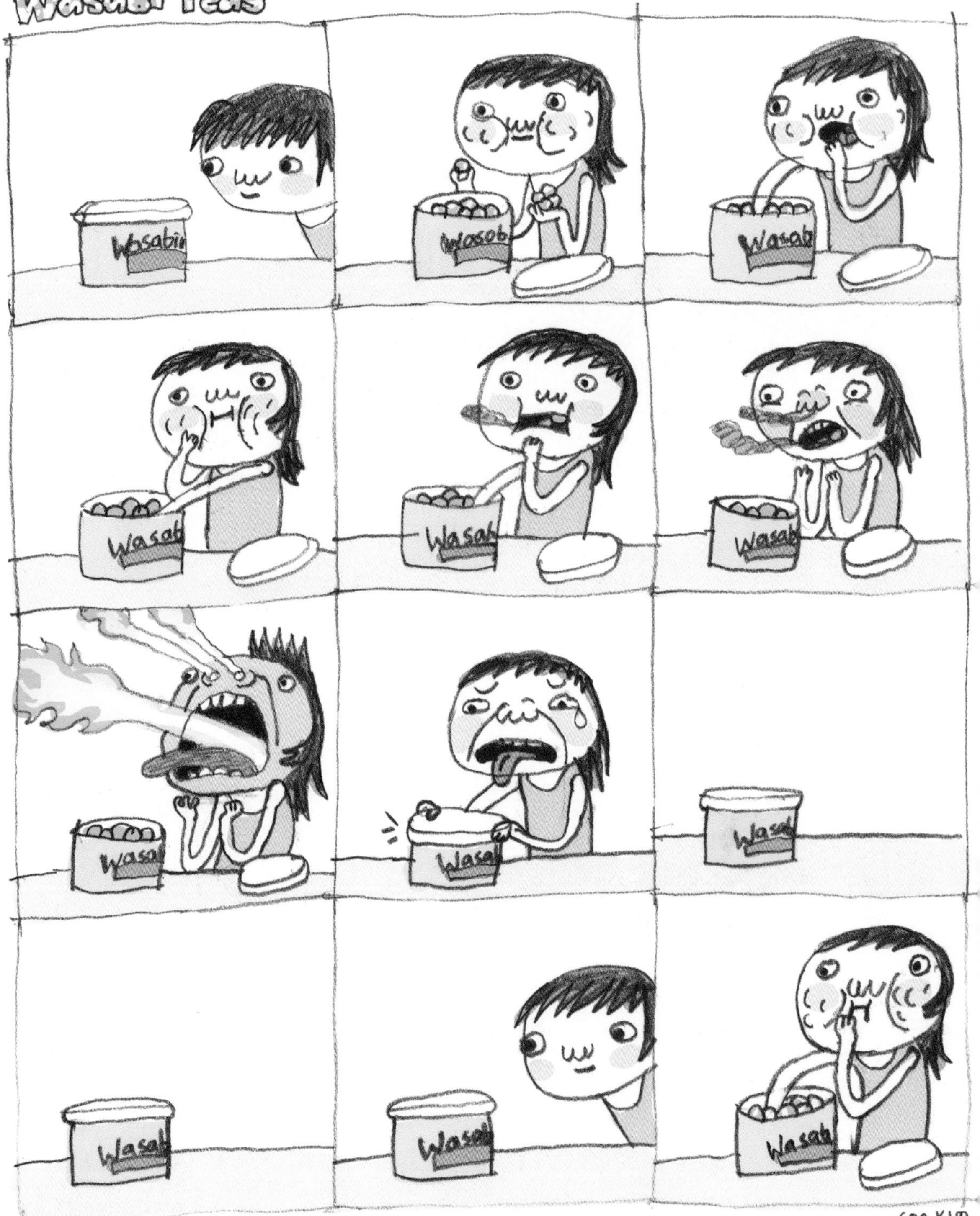

seo kim

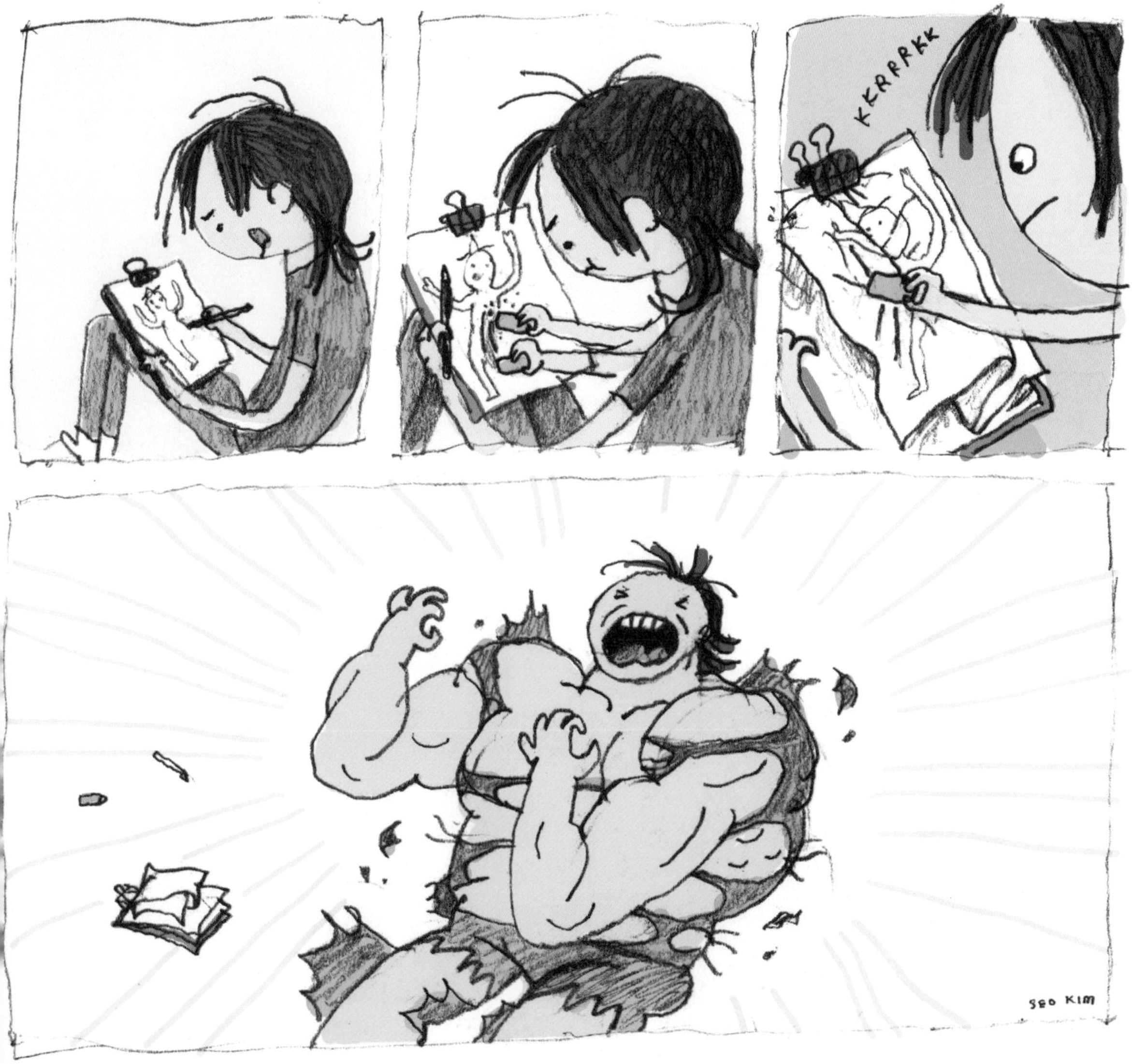

KKRRRKK
SEO KIM

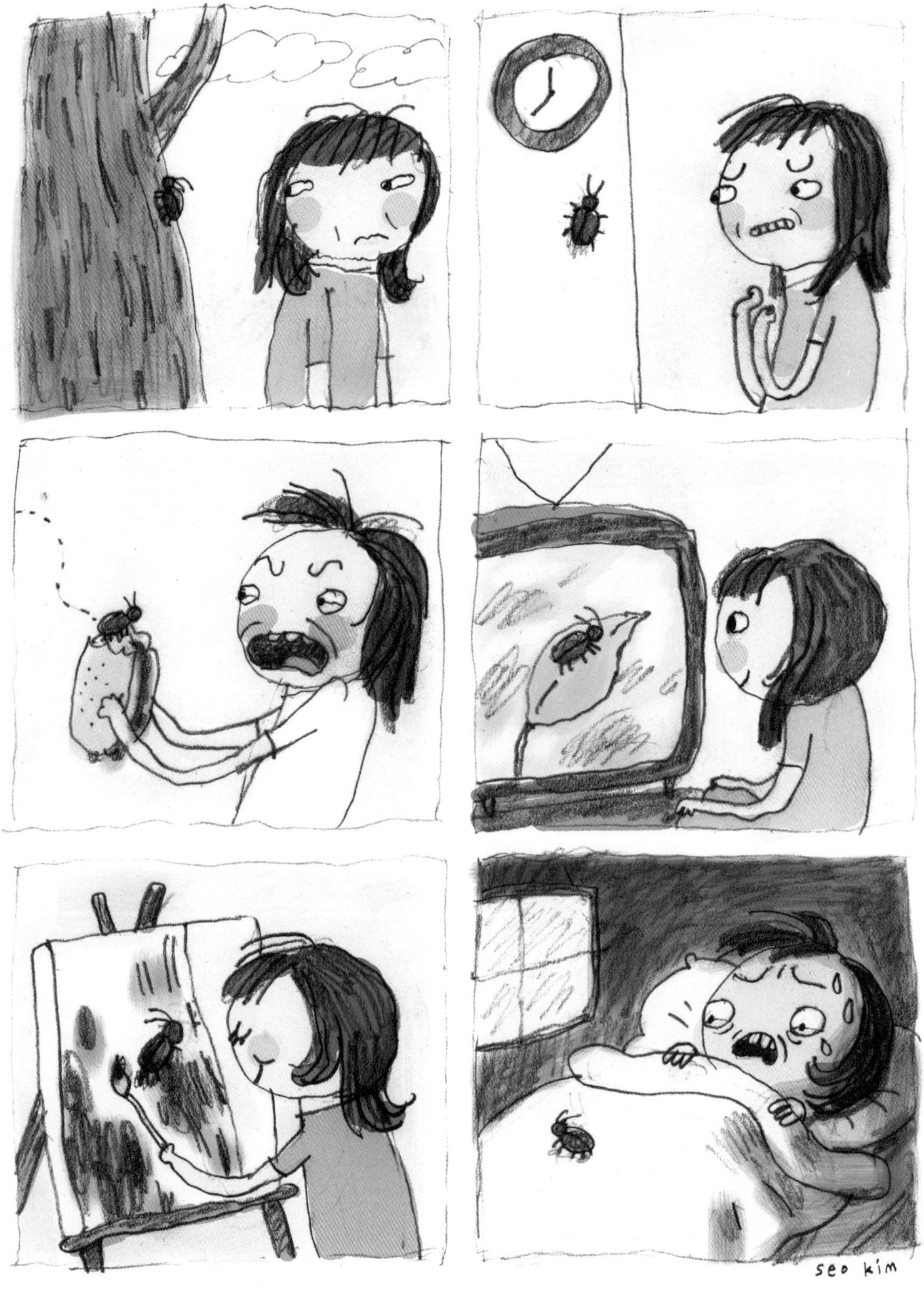
seo kim

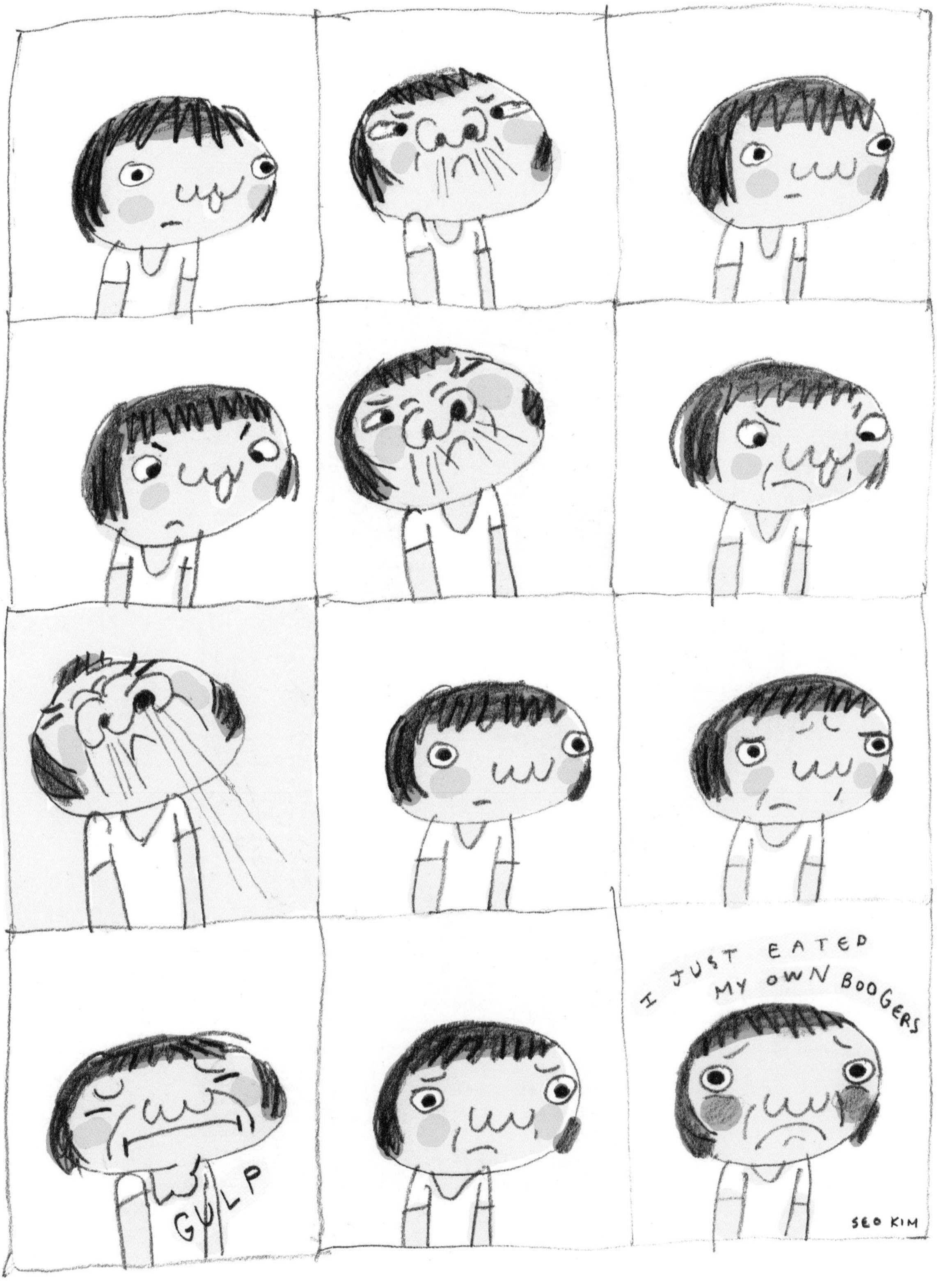
GULP
I JUST EATED MY OWN BOOGERS
SEO KIM

Recipes for the Absent-Minded: How to prepare a cup of Tea

by Seo Kim

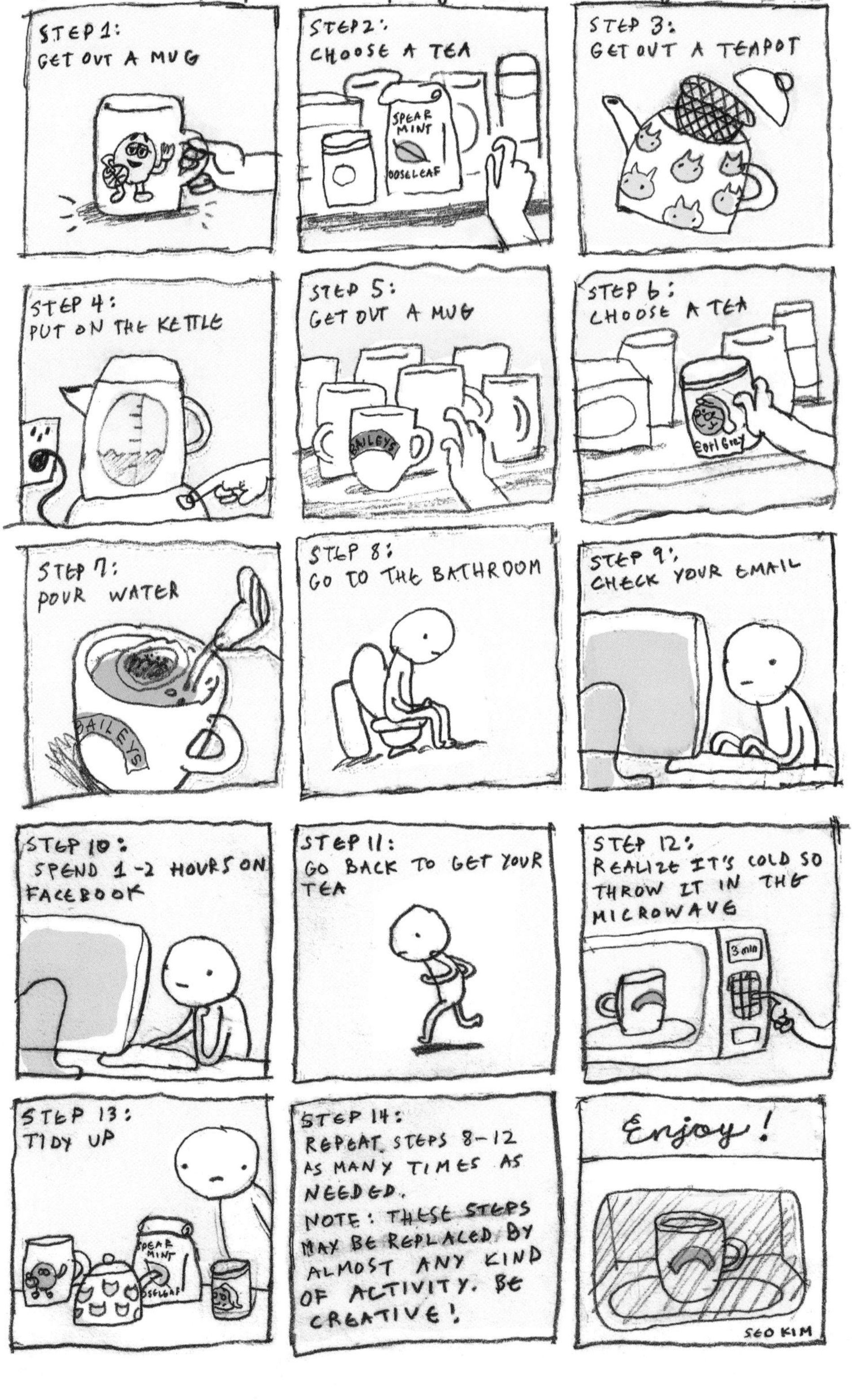

STEP 1: GET OUT A MUG
STEP 2: CHOOSE A TEA
SPEAR MINT
LOOSELEAF
STEP 3: GET OUT A TEAPOT
STEP 4: PUT ON THE KETTLE
STEP 5: GET OUT A MUG
BAILEYS
STEP 6: CHOOSE A TEA
Earl Grey
STEP 7: POUR WATER
BAILEYS
STEP 8: GO TO THE BATHROOM
STEP 9: CHECK YOUR EMAIL
STEP 10: SPEND 1-2 HOURS ON FACEBOOK
STEP 11: GO BACK TO GET YOUR TEA
STEP 12: REALIZE IT'S COLD SO THROW IT IN THE MICROWAVE
3 min
STEP 13: TIDY UP
SPEAR MINT
STEP 14: REPEAT STEPS 8-12 AS MANY TIMES AS NEEDED.
NOTE: THESE STEPS MAY BE REPLACED BY ALMOST ANY KIND OF ACTIVITY. BE CREATIVE!
Enjoy!
SEO KIM

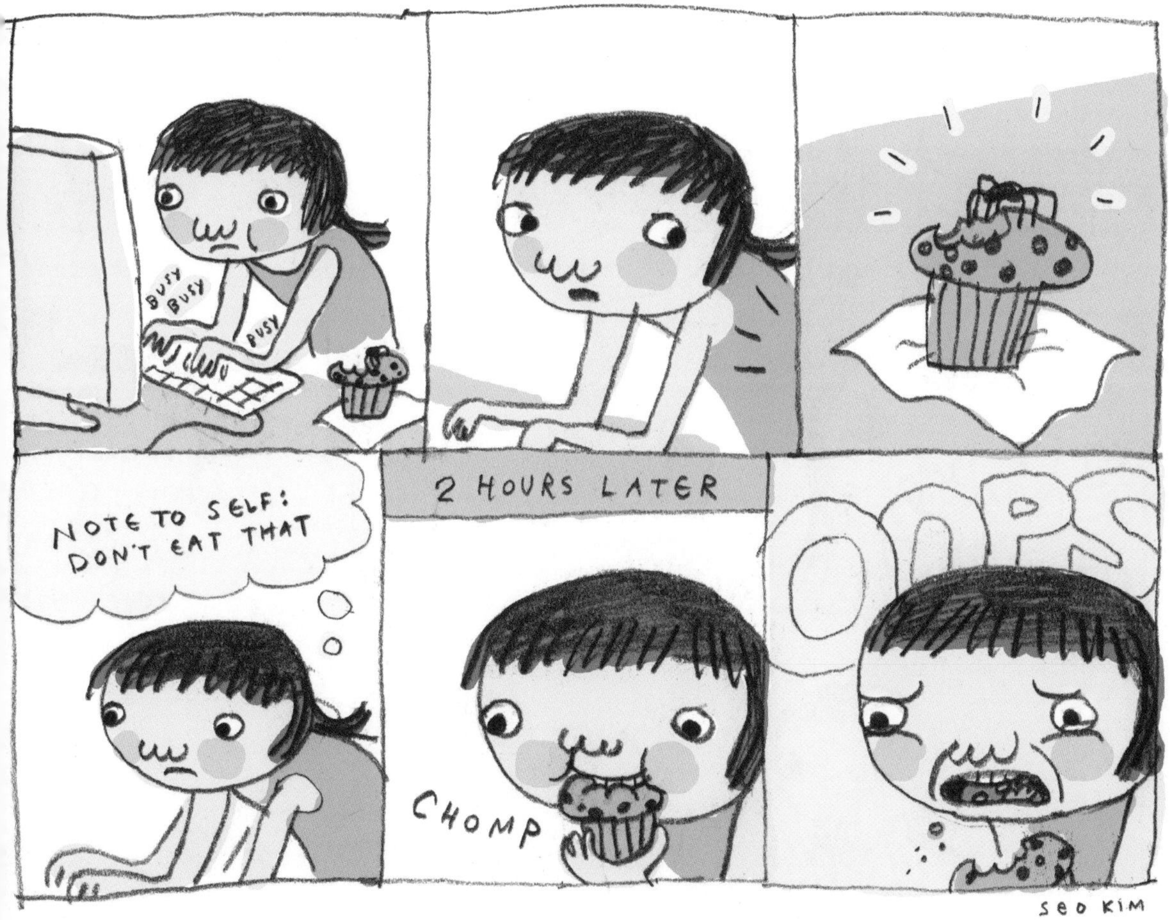
BUSY
BUSY
BUSY
NOTE TO SELF: DON'T EAT THAT
2 HOURS LATER
CHOMP
OOPS
SEO KIM

GUMMY VITES

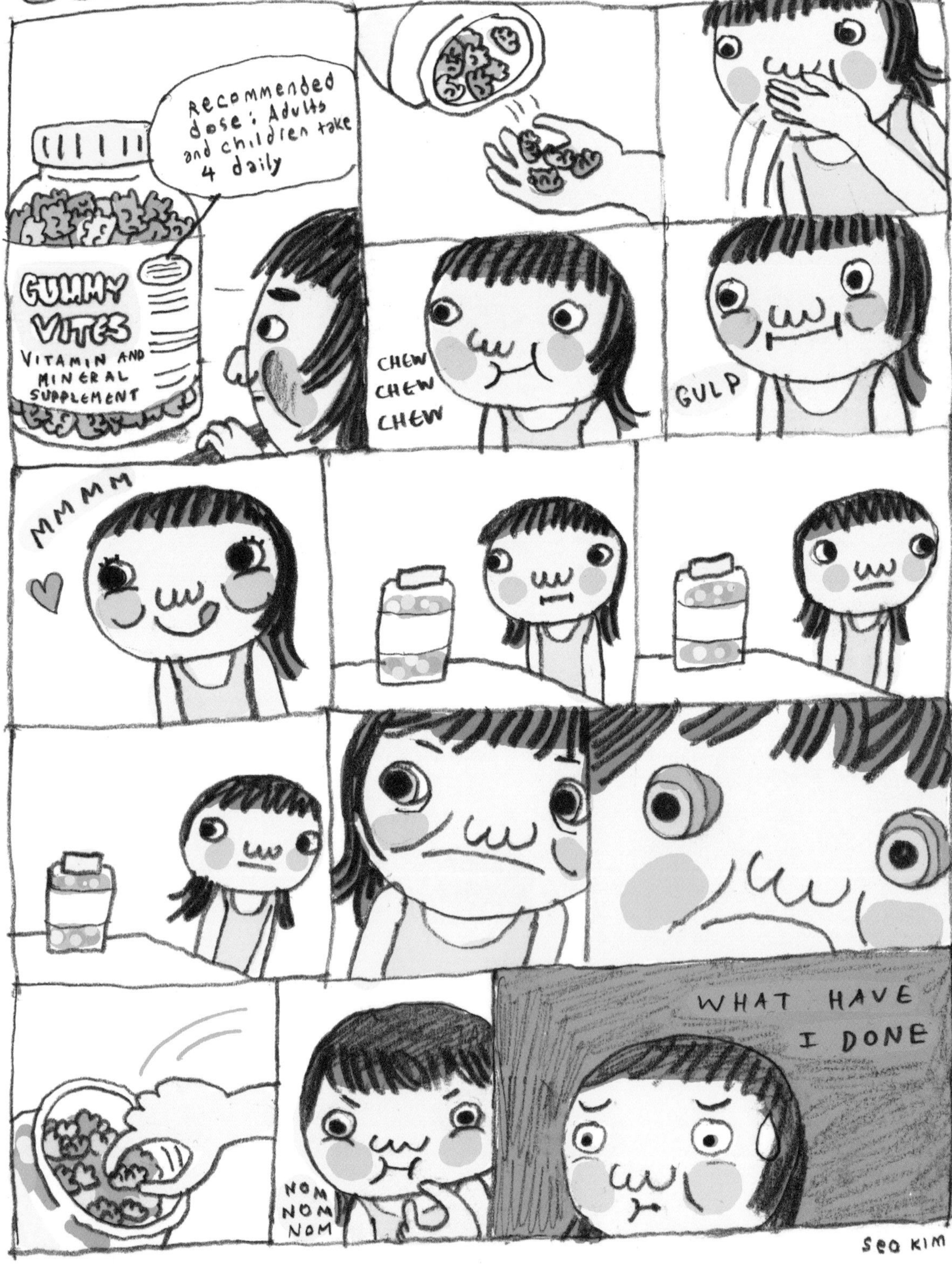

Recommended dose: Adults and children take 4 daily
GUMMY VITES
VITAMIN AND MINERAL SUPPLEMENT
CHEW CHEW CHEW
GULP
MMMM
NOM NOM NOM
WHAT HAVE I DONE

seo kim

morning warm-up

seo KIM

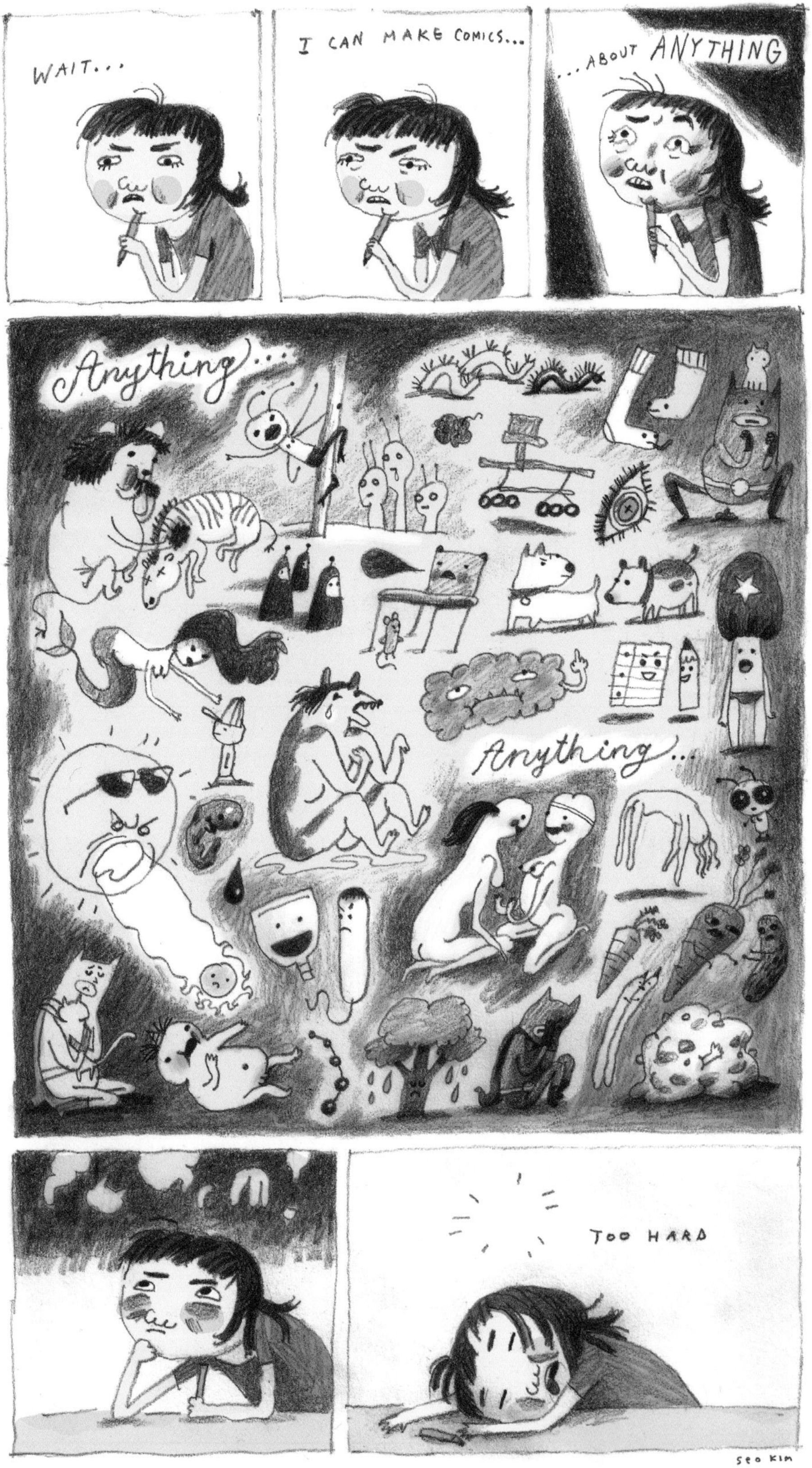
WAIT...
I CAN MAKE COMICS...
...ABOUT ANYTHING
Anything...
Anything...
TOO HARD
SEO KIM

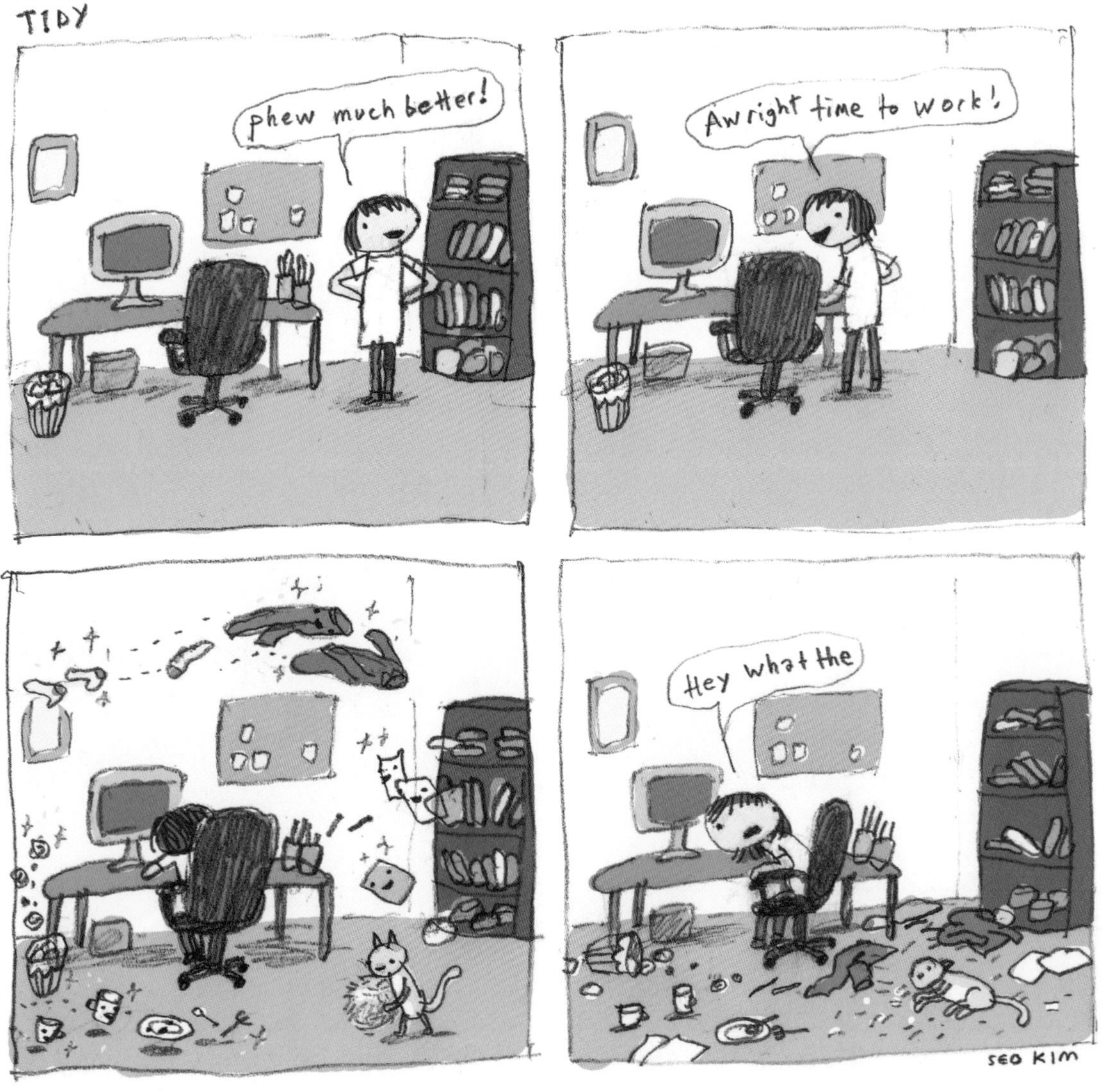
TIDY
phew much better!
Awright time to work!
Hey what the
SEO KIM

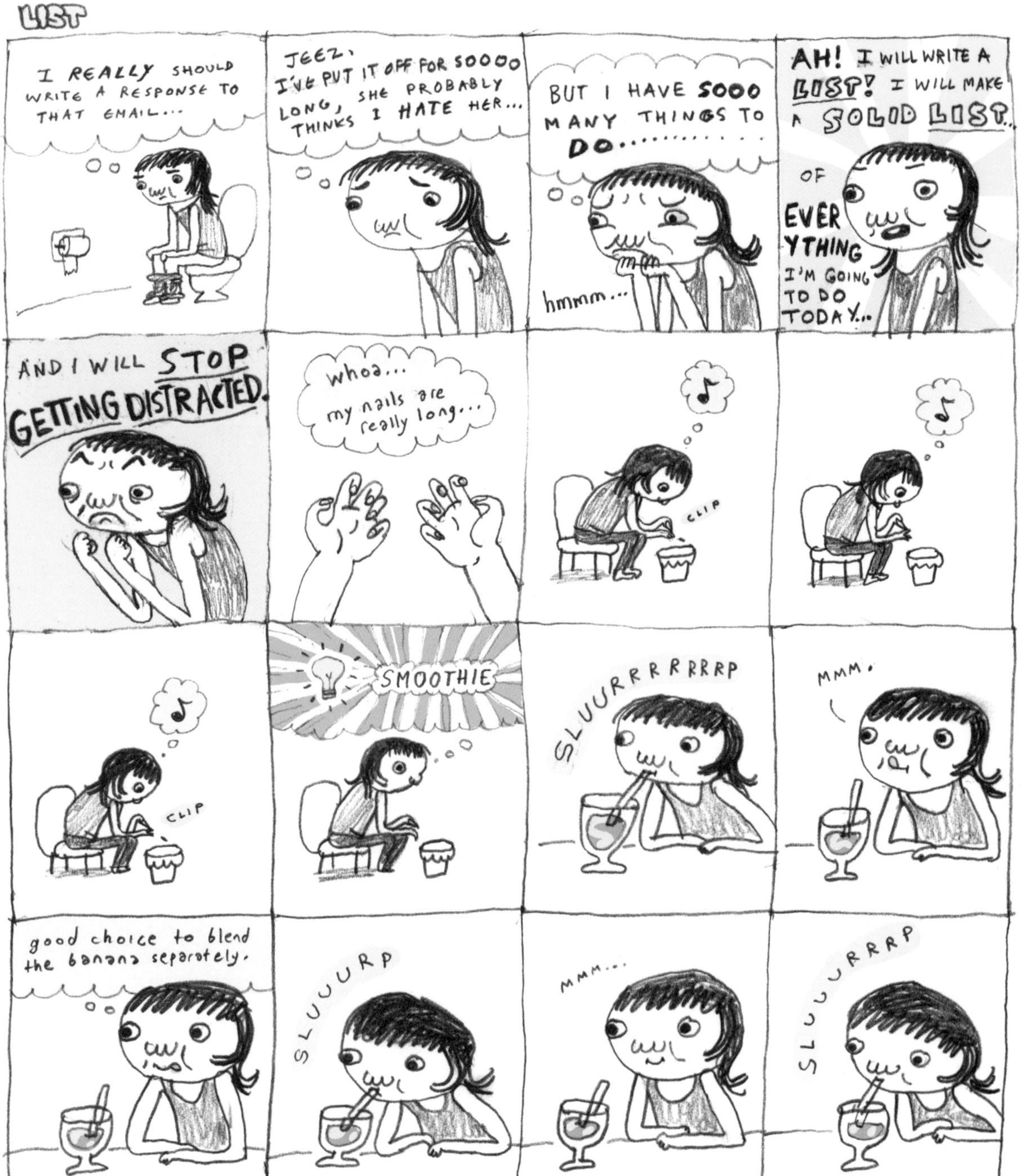
LIST
I REALLY SHOULD WRITE A RESPONSE TO THAT EMAIL...
JEEZ. I'VE PUT IT OFF FOR SOOOO LONG, SHE PROBABLY THINKS I HATE HER...
BUT I HAVE SOOO MANY THINGS TO DO............
hmmm...
AH! I WILL WRITE A LIST! I WILL MAKE A SOLID LIST...
OF EVERYTHING I'M GOING TO DO TODAY...
AND I WILL STOP GETTING DISTRACTED.
whoa... my nails are really long...
CLIP
CLIP
SMOOTHIE
SLUURRRRRRRP
MMM.
good choice to blend the banana separately.
SLUUURP
MMM...
SLUUURRRP
Seo kim

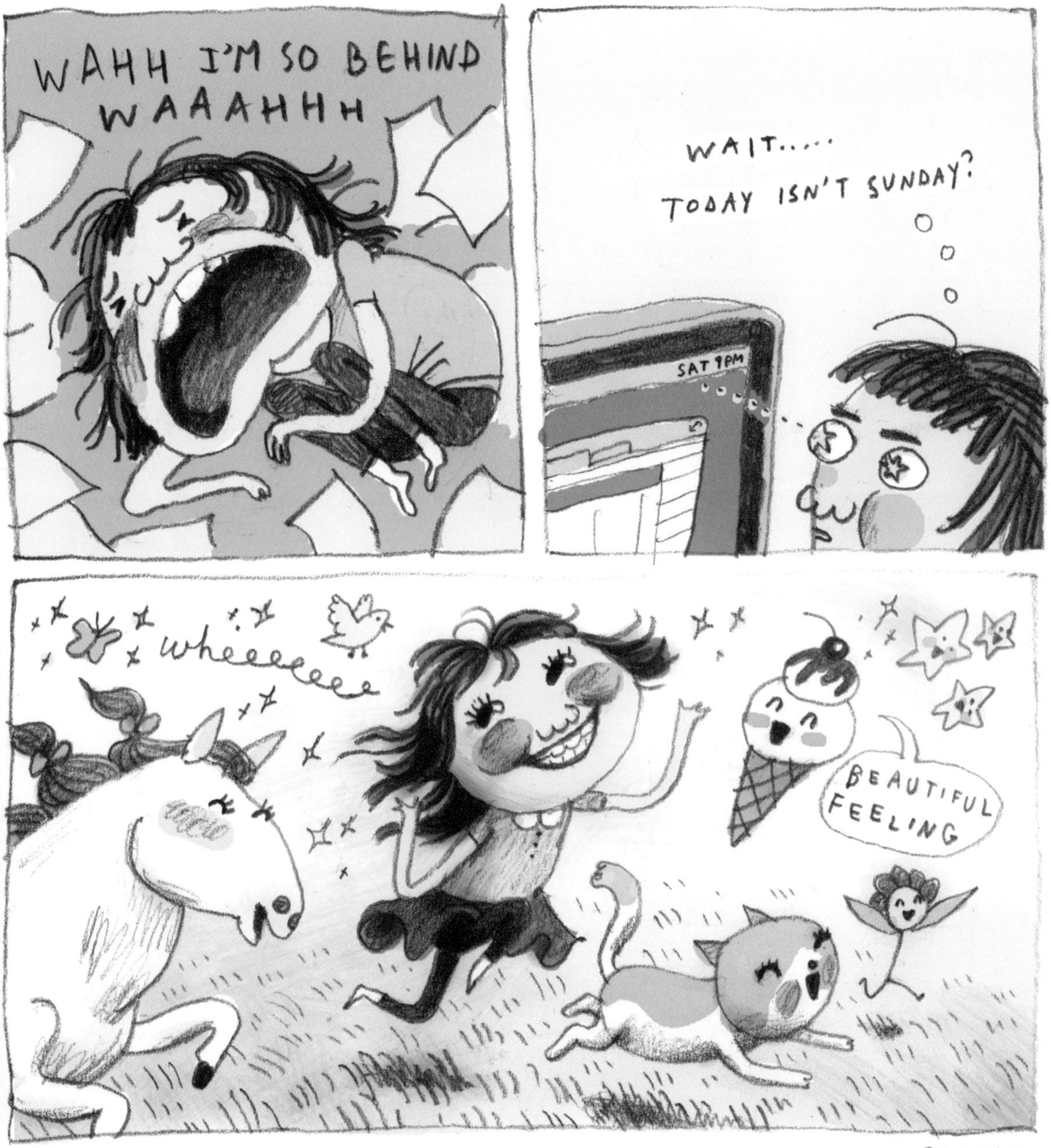
WAHH I'M SO BEHIND WAAAHHH
WAIT.....
TODAY ISN'T SUNDAY?
SAT 9PM
wheeeeeeee
BEAUTIFUL FEELING
SEO KIM

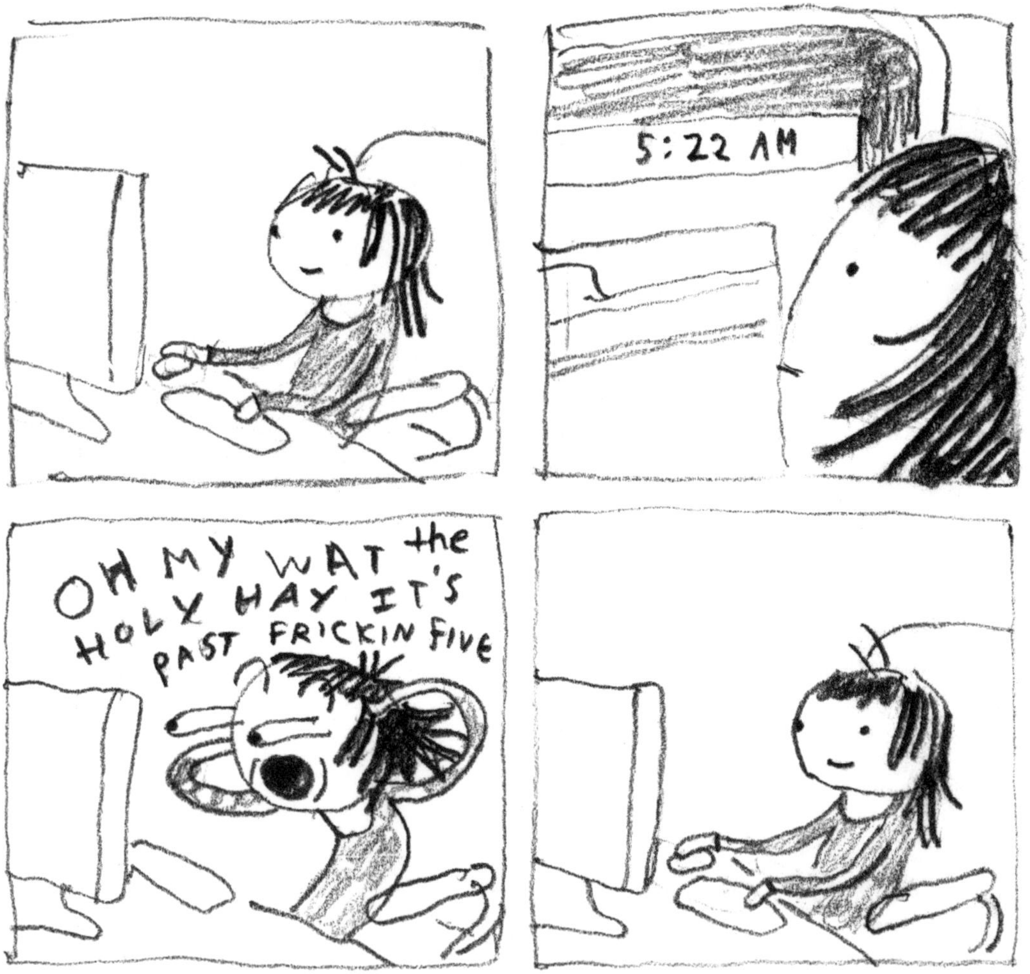
5:22 AM
OH MY WAT the HOLY HAY IT'S PAST FRICKIN FIVE
SEO KIM

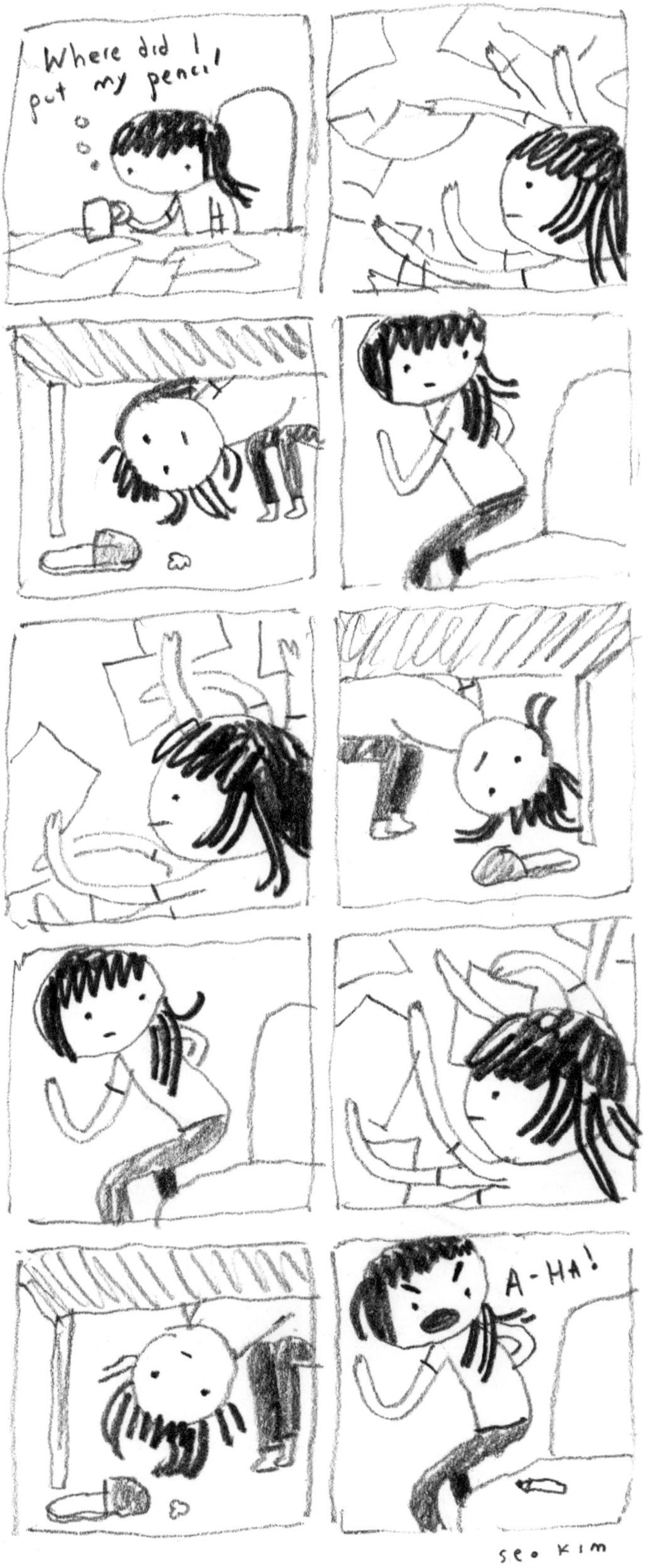
Where did I put my pencil
A-HA!

seo kim

FACEBOOK

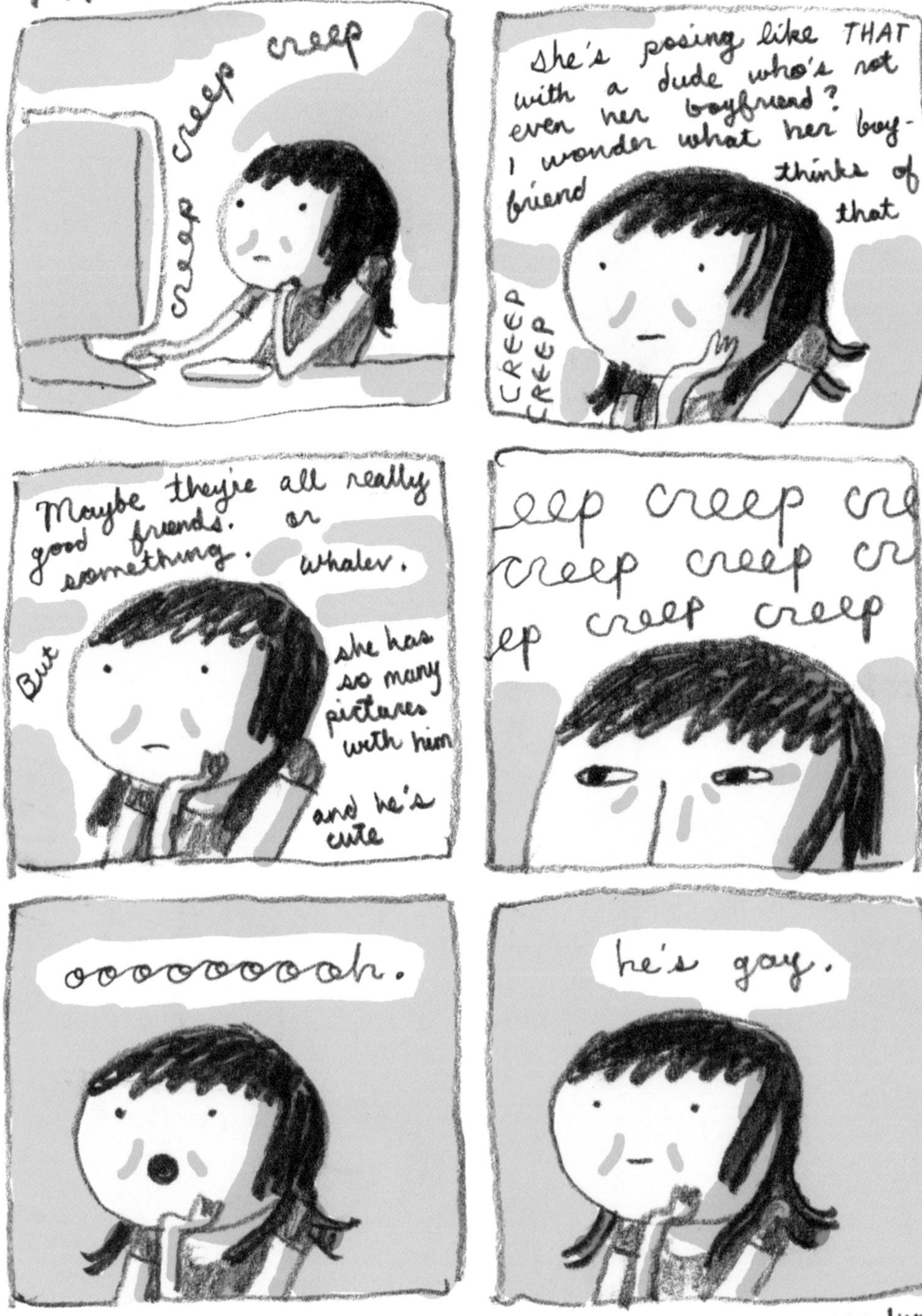

seo kim

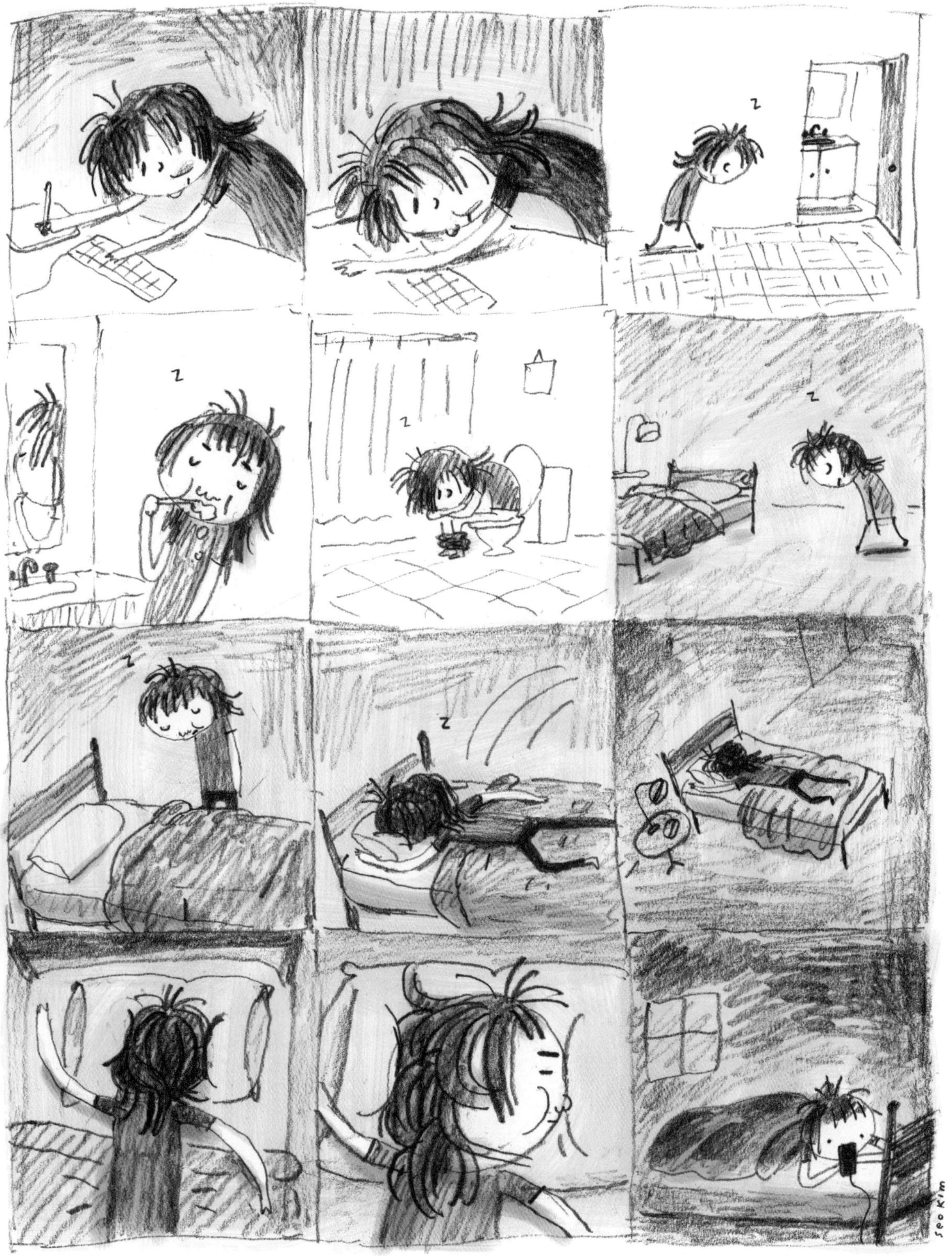
z
z
z
z
z
z
Seo Kim

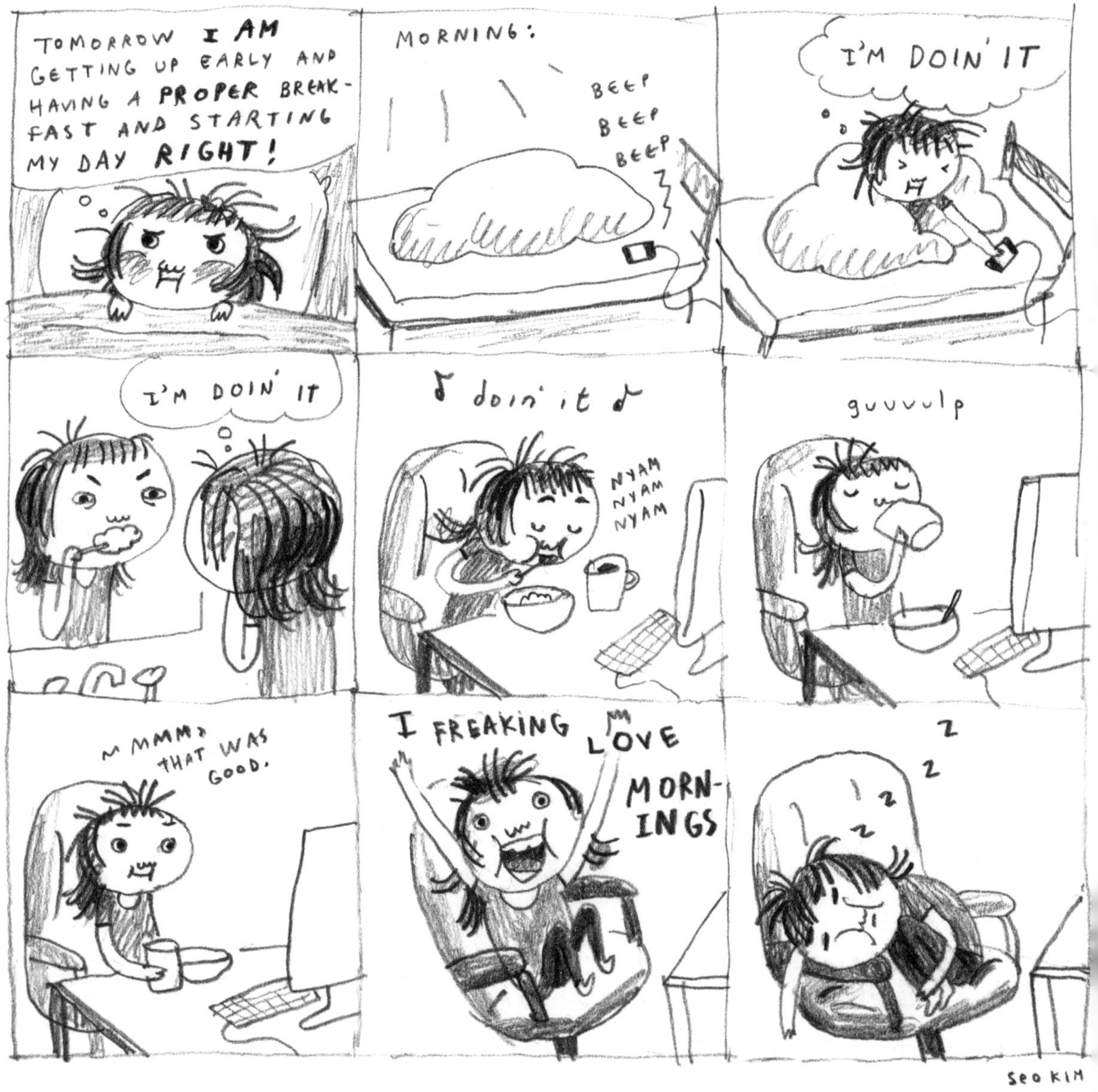
TOMORROW I AM GETTING UP EARLY AND HAVING A PROPER BREAK-FAST AND STARTING MY DAY RIGHT!
MORNING:
BEEP
BEEP
BEEP
I'M DOIN' IT
I'M DOIN' IT
doin' it
NYAM
NYAM
NYAM
guuuulp
MMMM, THAT WAS GOOD.
I FREAKING LOVE MORN-INGS
Z
Z
Z
Z
SEO KIM

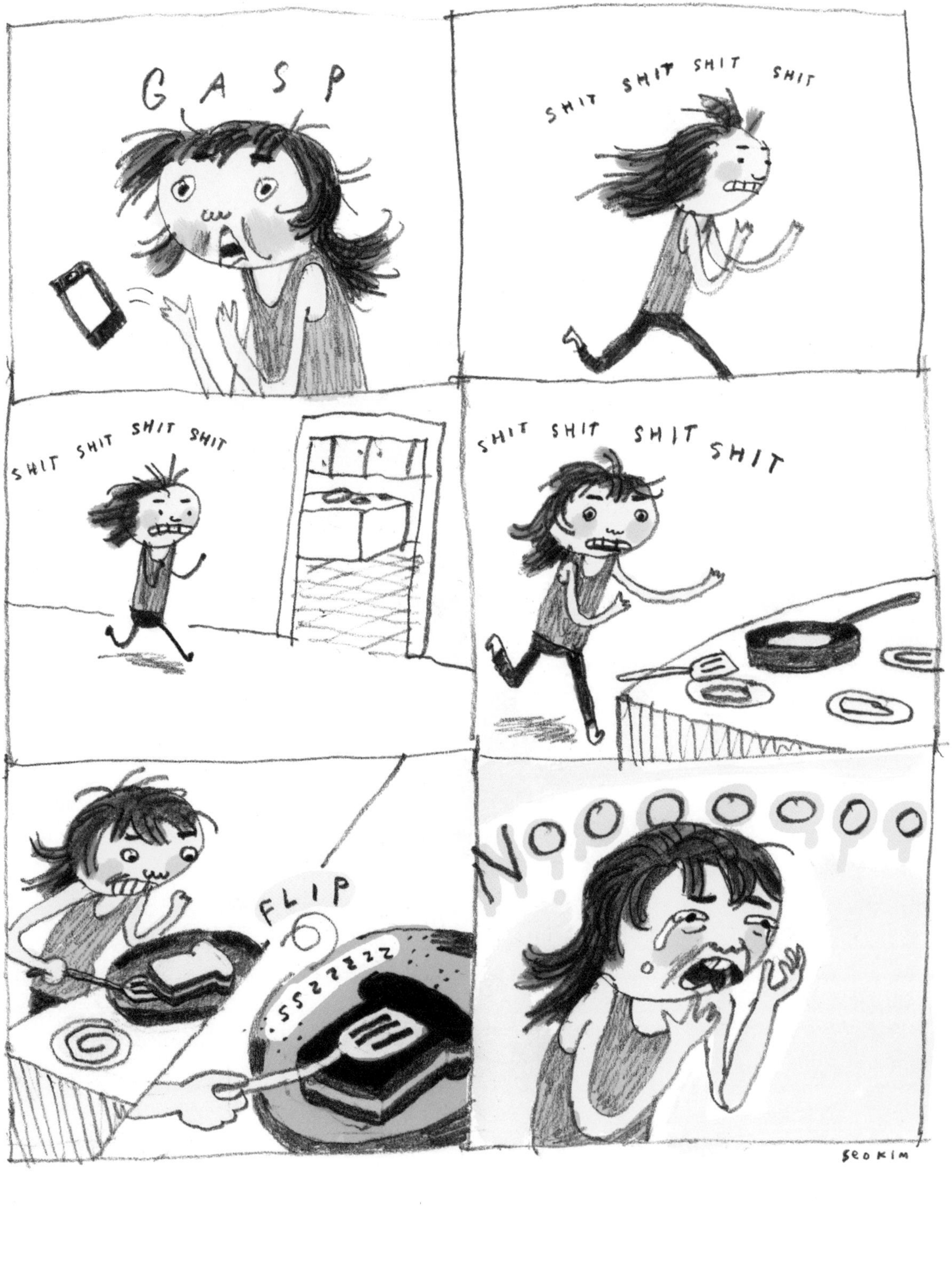
GASP
SHIT SHIT SHIT SHIT
SHIT SHIT SHIT SHIT
SHIT SHIT SHIT SHIT
FLIP
SSZZZZZ
NOOOOOOOO
SEO KIM

CHEESECAKE TIME

frozen

Seo Kim

CHEESECAKE TIME

- PART 2 -

Seo Kim

ONE TRIP

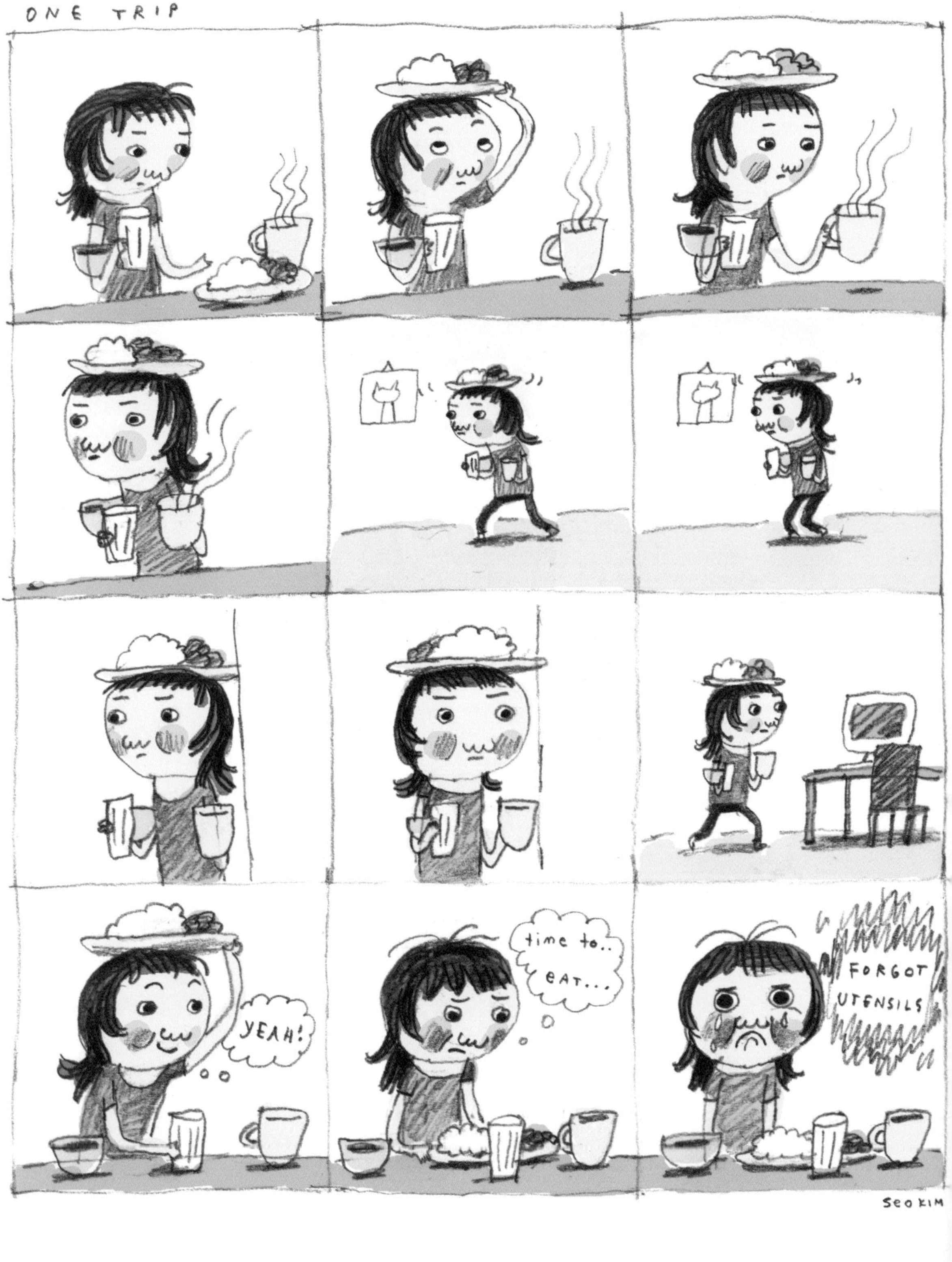

YEAH!
time to..
eat...
FORGOT UTENSILS

SEO KIM

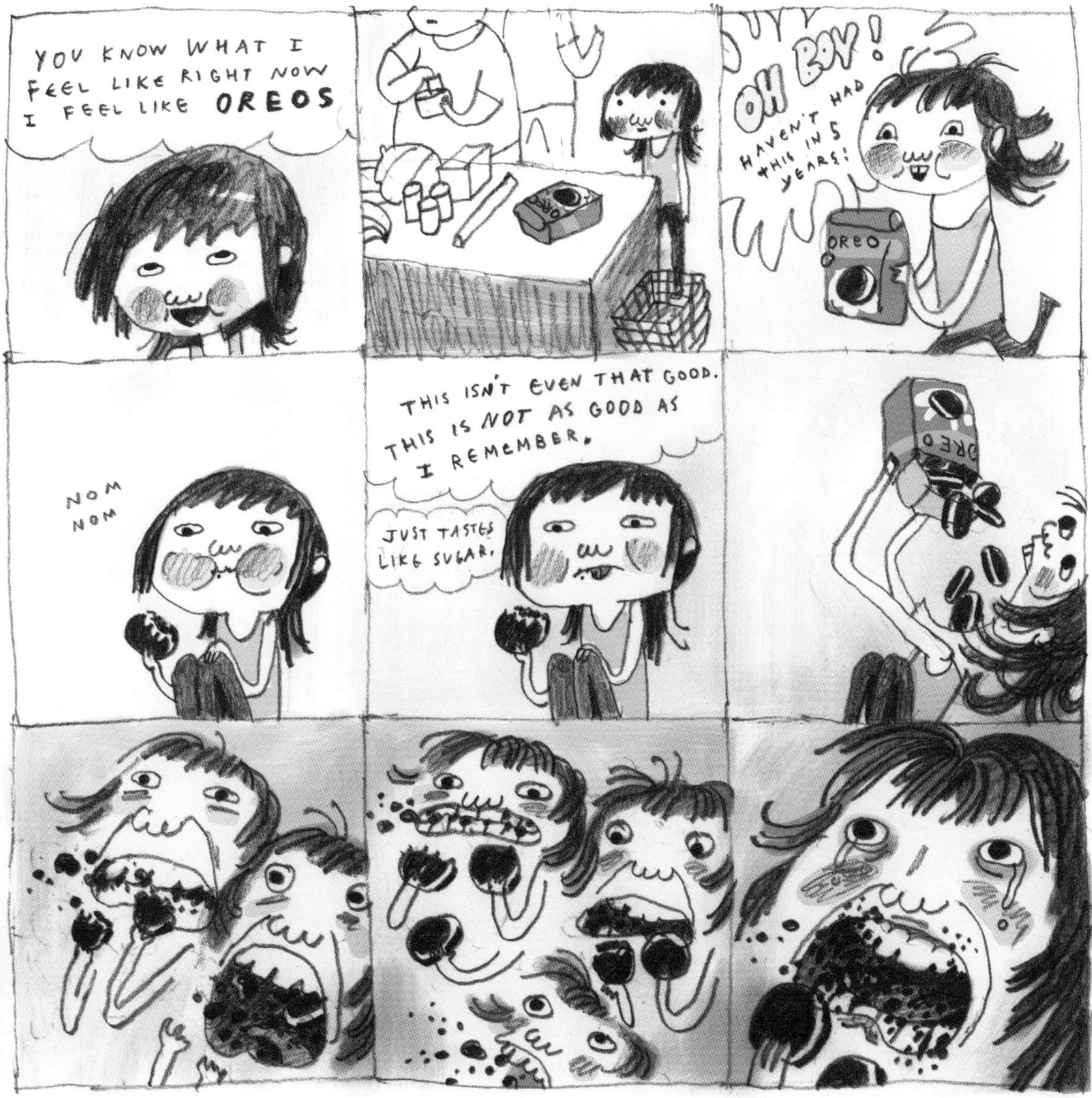
YOU KNOW WHAT I FEEL LIKE RIGHT NOW I FEEL LIKE OREOS
OREO
OH BOY!
HAVEN'T HAD THIS IN 5 YEARS!
OREO
NOM NOM
THIS ISN'T EVEN THAT GOOD. THIS IS NOT AS GOOD AS I REMEMBER.
JUST TASTES LIKE SUGAR.
OREO

SEO KIM

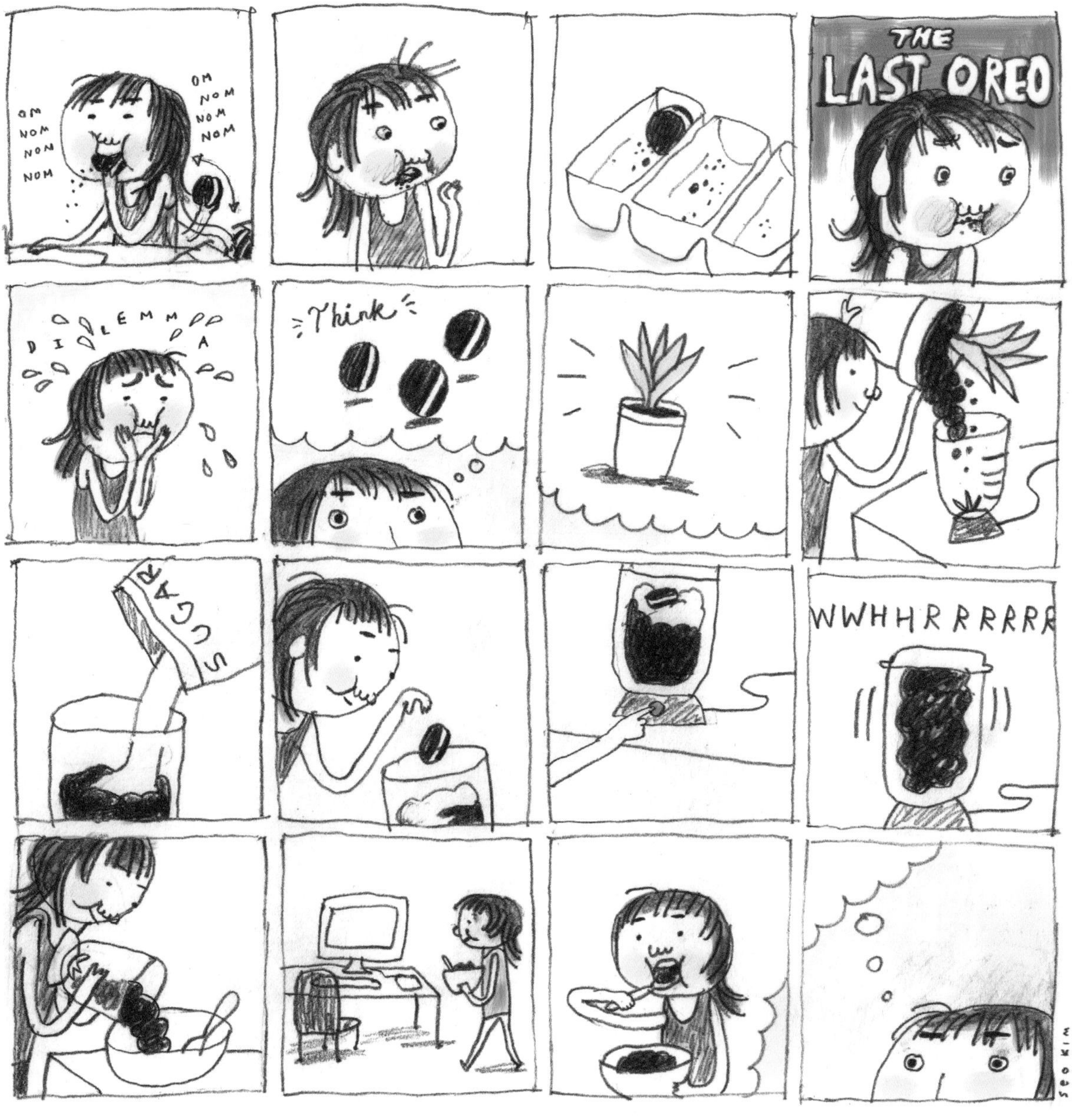
OM
NOM
NON
NOM
OM
NOM
NOM
NOM
THE
LAST OREO
D I L E M M A
Think
SUGAR
WWHHRRRRRR
SEO KIM

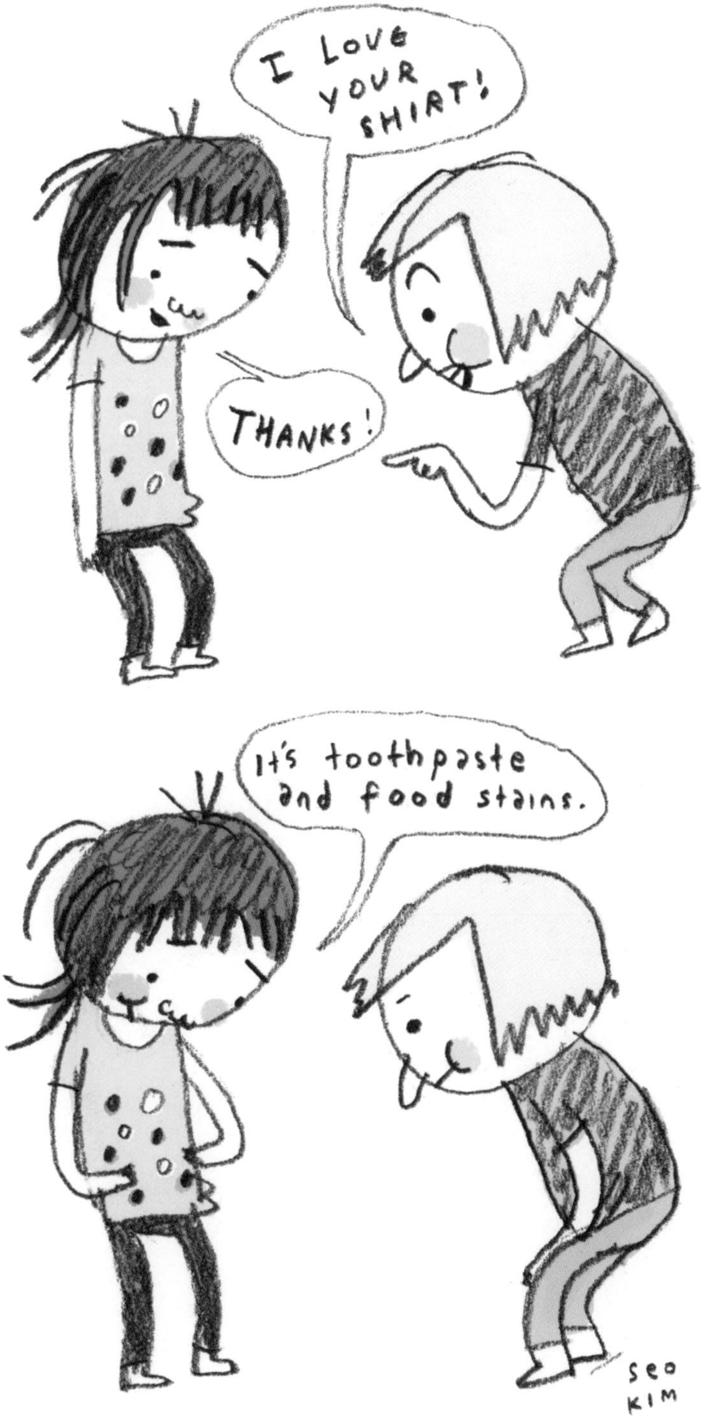
I LOVE YOUR SHIRT!
THANKS!
It's toothpaste and food stains.
SEO KIM

The meaning of Oreos

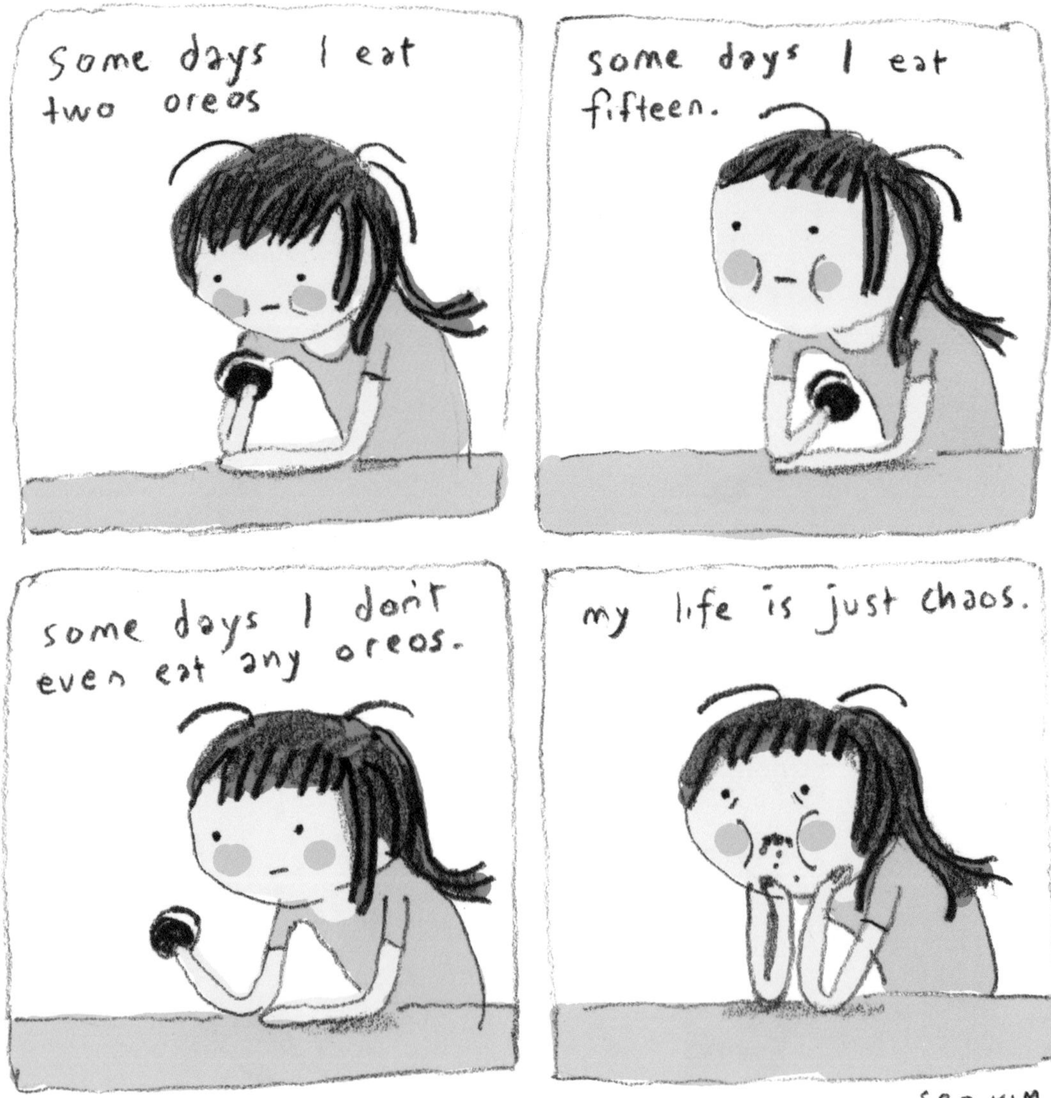
some days I eat two oreos
some days I eat fifteen.
some days I don't even eat any oreos.
my life is just chaos.
SEO KIM

Saturday

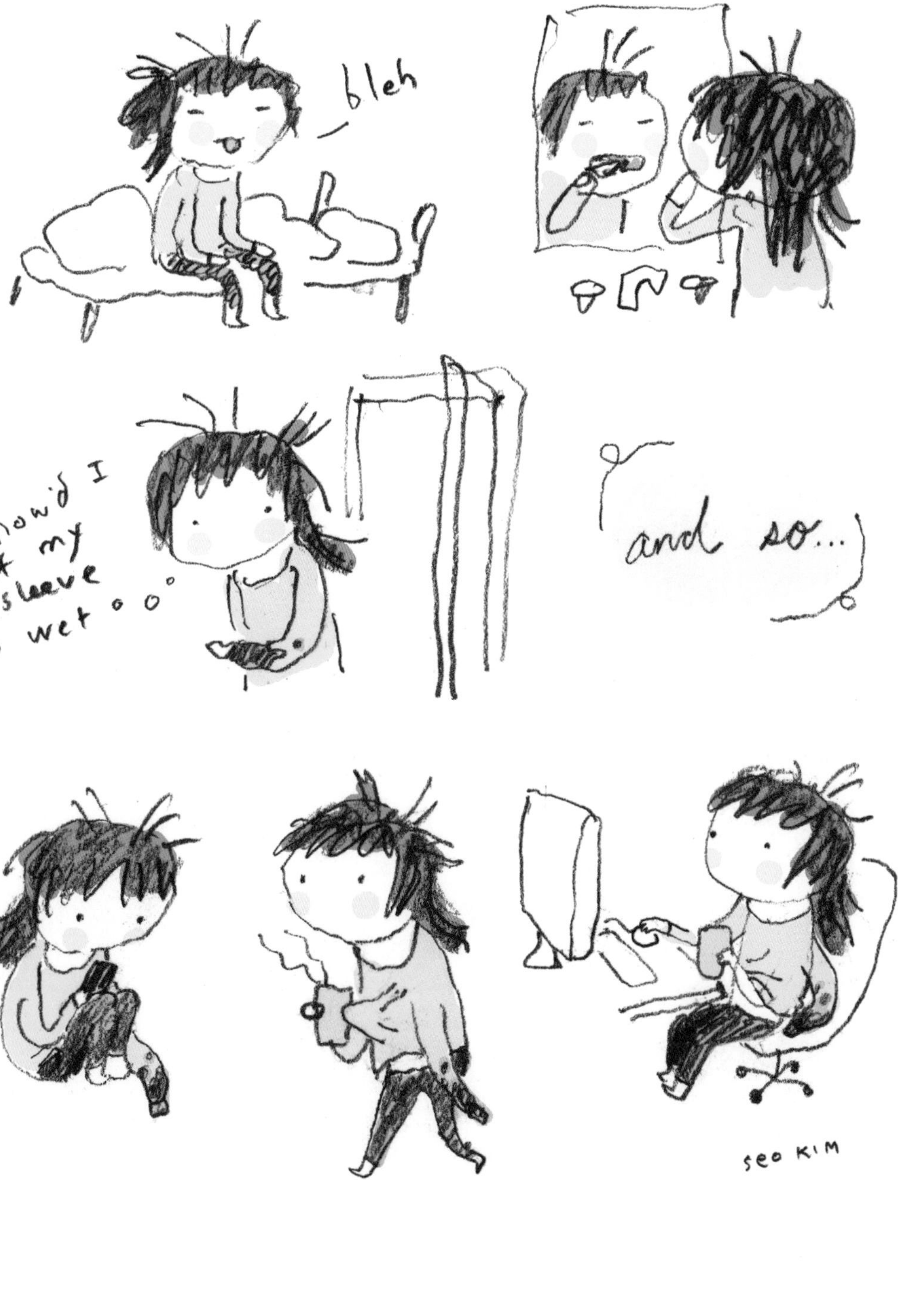
bleh
how'd I get my sleeve so wet
and so...
SEO KIM

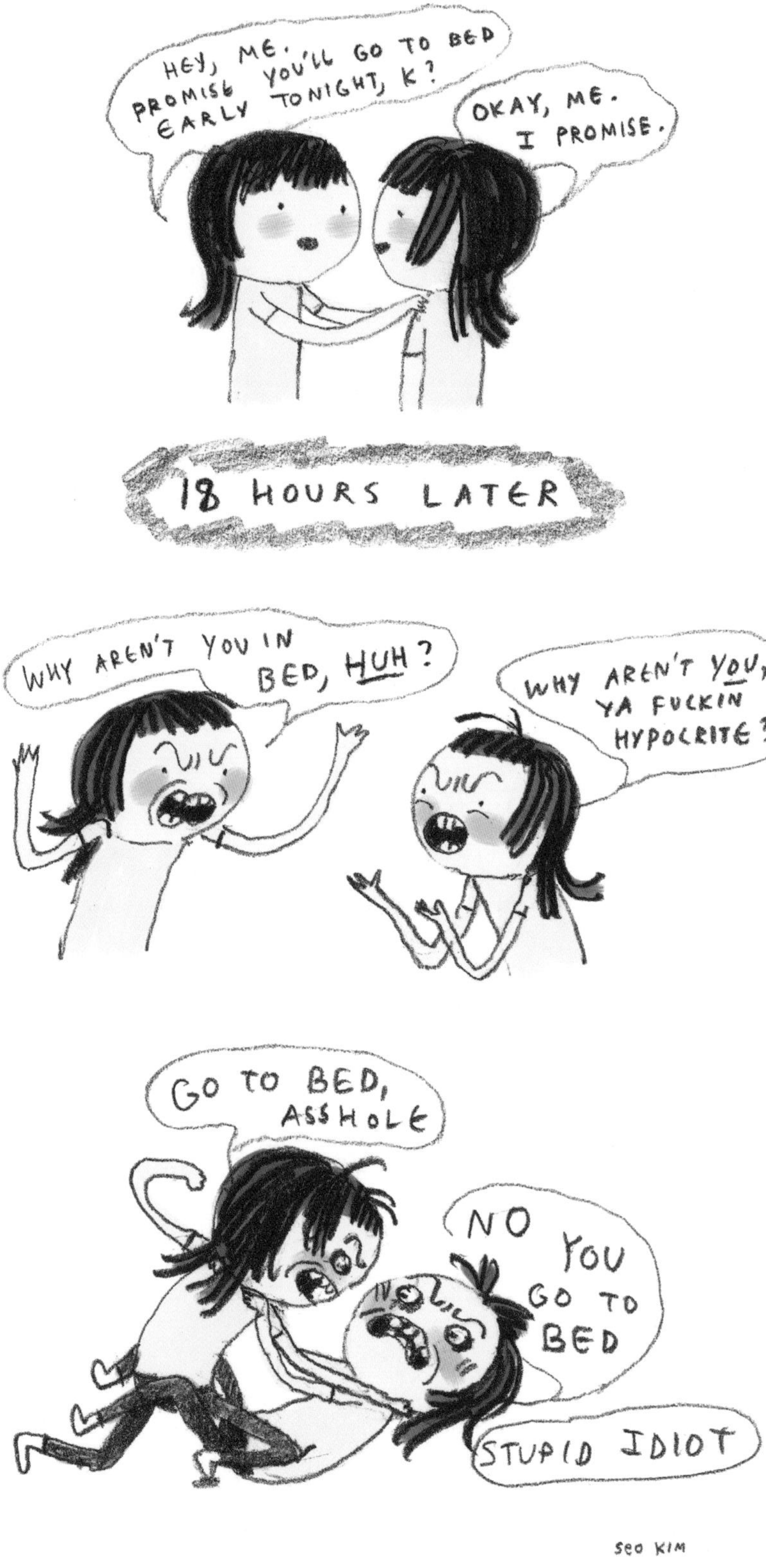
HEY, ME. PROMISE YOU'LL GO TO BED EARLY TONIGHT, K?
OKAY, ME. I PROMISE.
18 HOURS LATER
WHY AREN'T YOU IN BED, HUH?
WHY AREN'T YOU, YA FUCKIN HYPOCRITE?
GO TO BED, ASSHOLE
NO YOU GO TO BED
STUPID IDIOT
SEO KIM

Actually Happened:

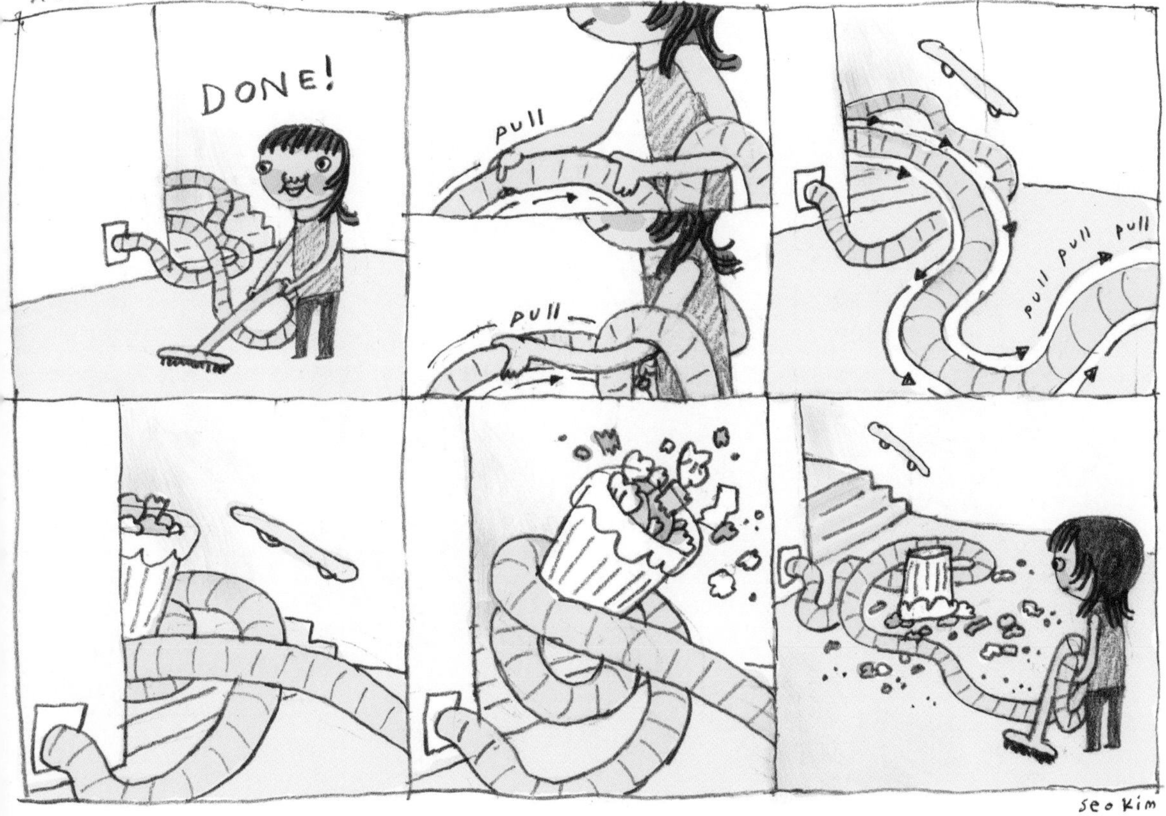
DONE!
pull
pull
pull pull pull

seo kim

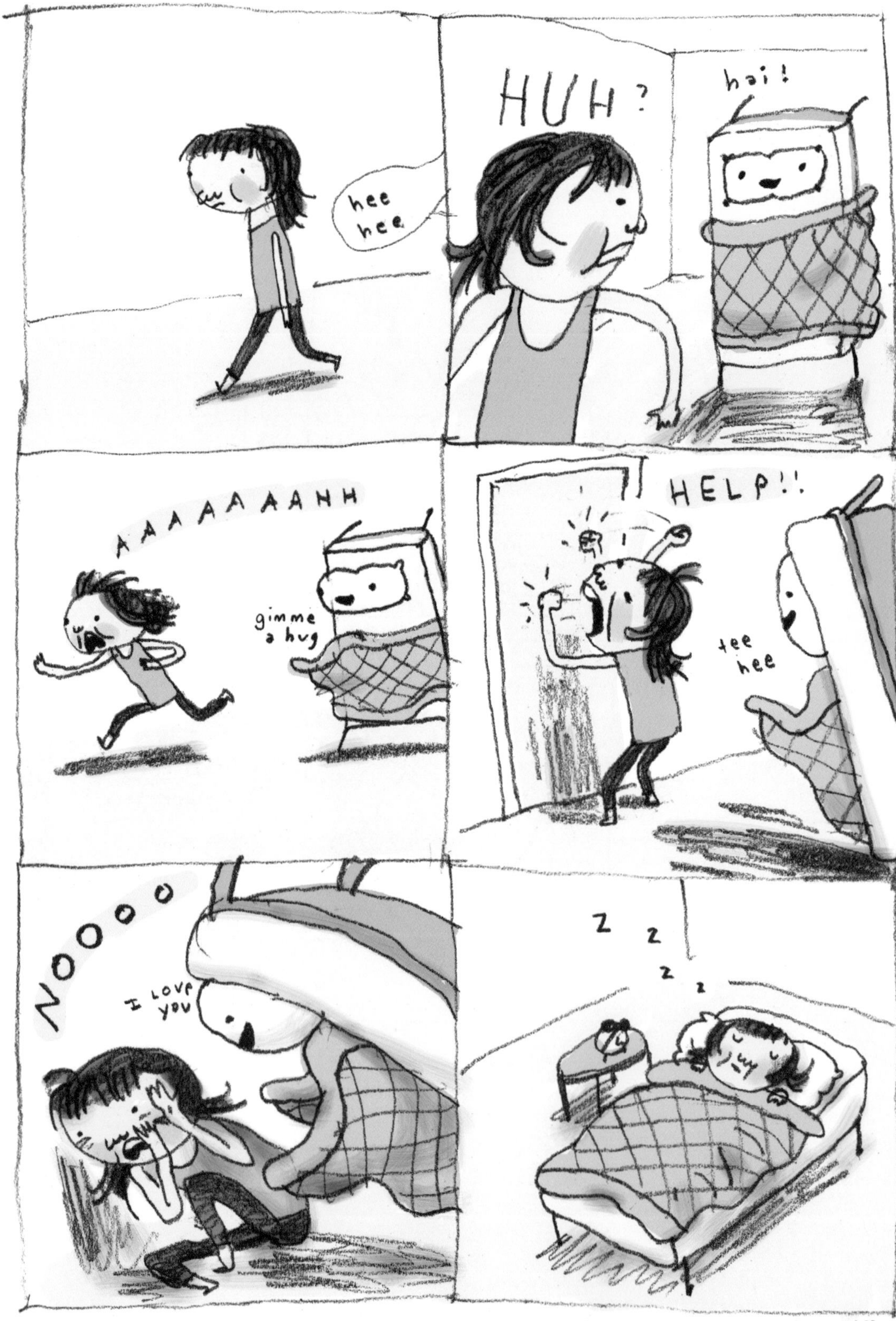
hee hee
HUH?
hai!
AAAAAAAHH
gimme a hug
HELP!!
tee hee
NOOOO
I LOVE YOU
Z Z Z Z

seo kim

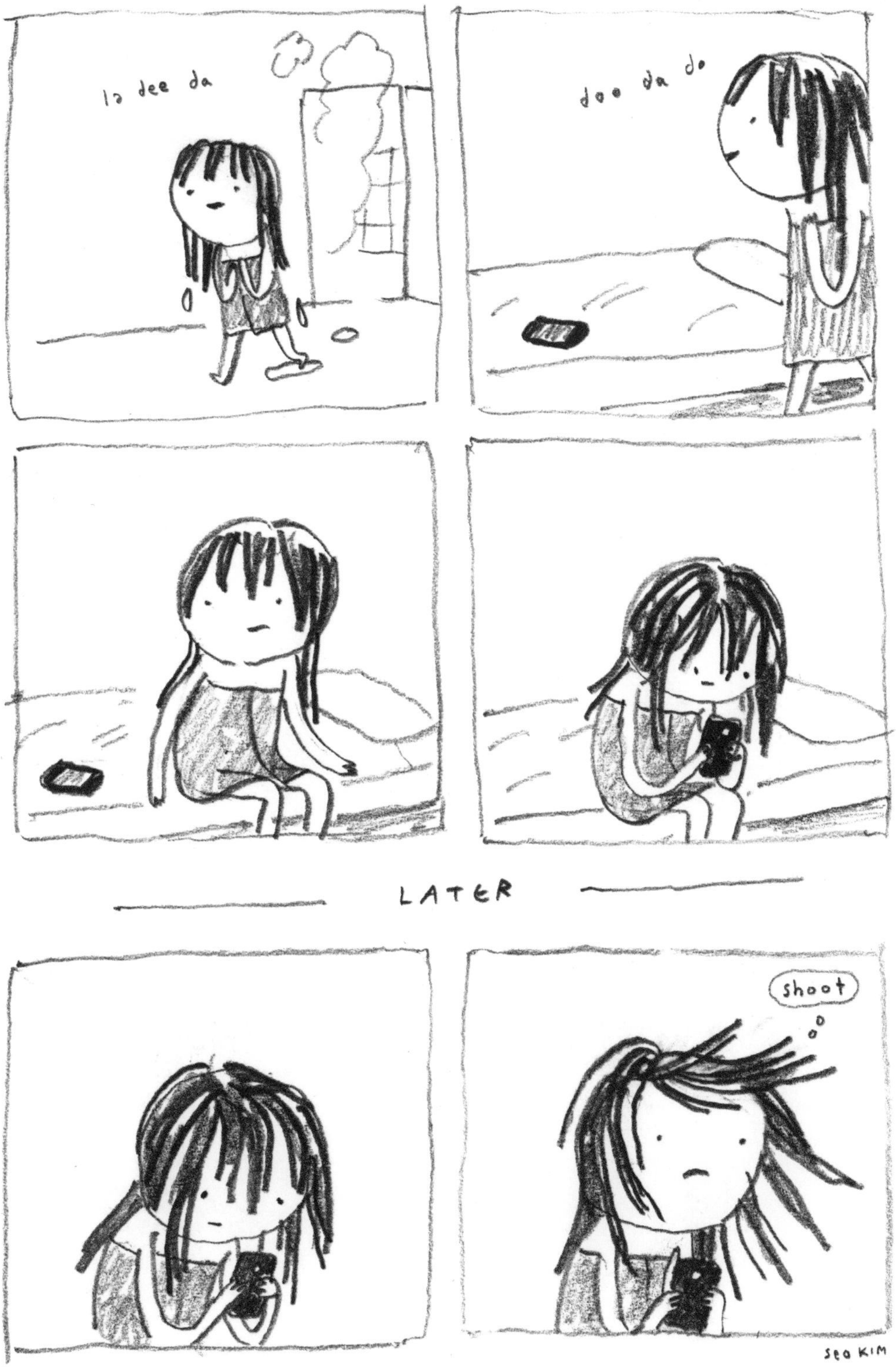
la dee da
doo da do
LATER
shoot
SEO KIM

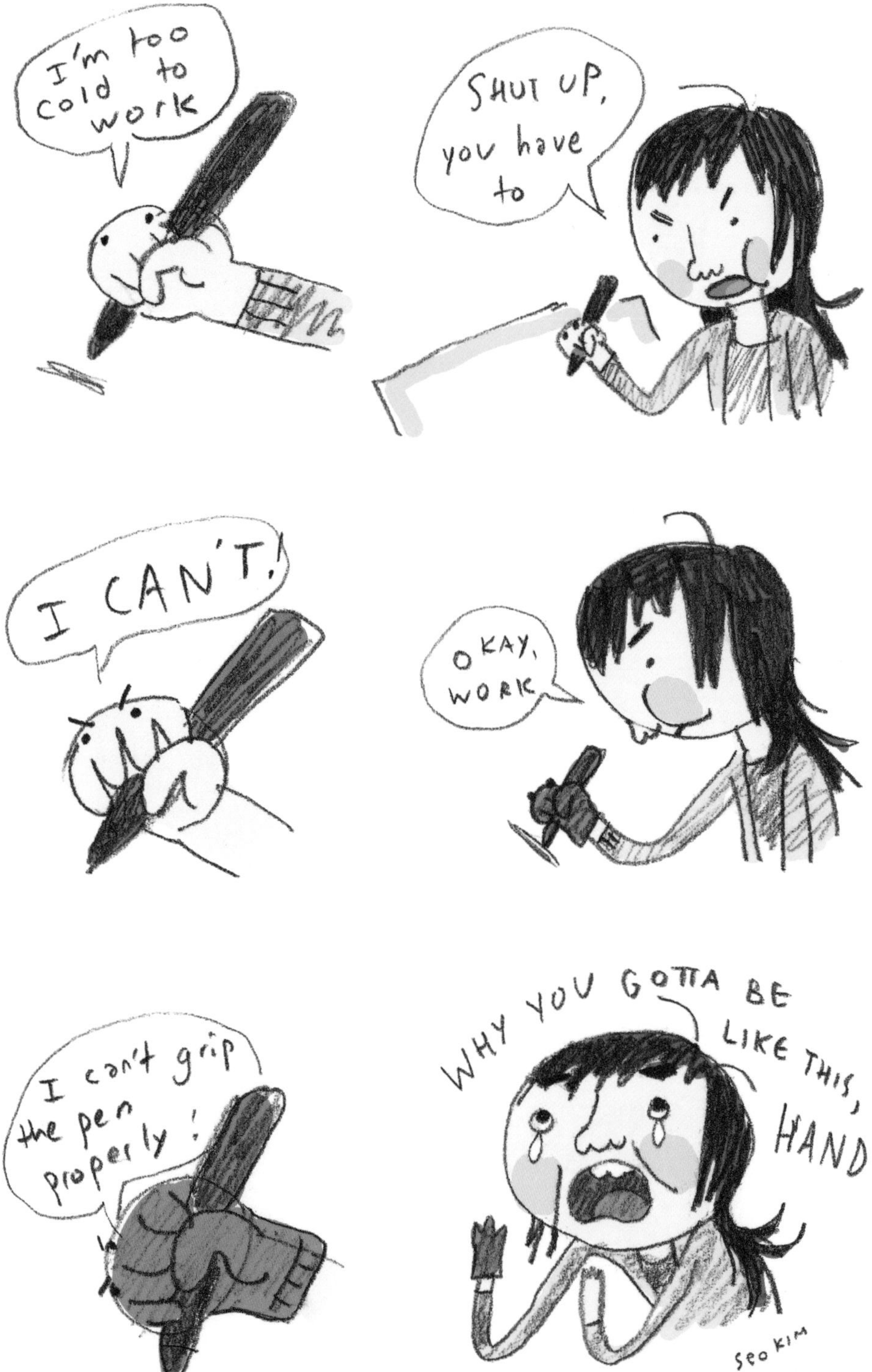
I'm too cold to work
SHUT UP, you have to
I CAN'T!
OKAY, WORK
I can't grip the pen properly!
WHY YOU GOTTA BE LIKE THIS, HAND
SEO KIM

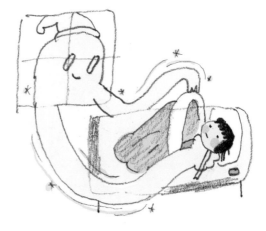

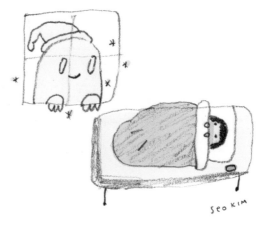
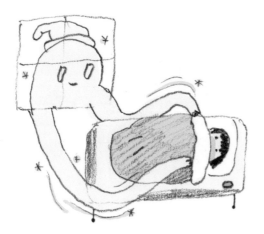

seo kim

POOPADVENTURES!

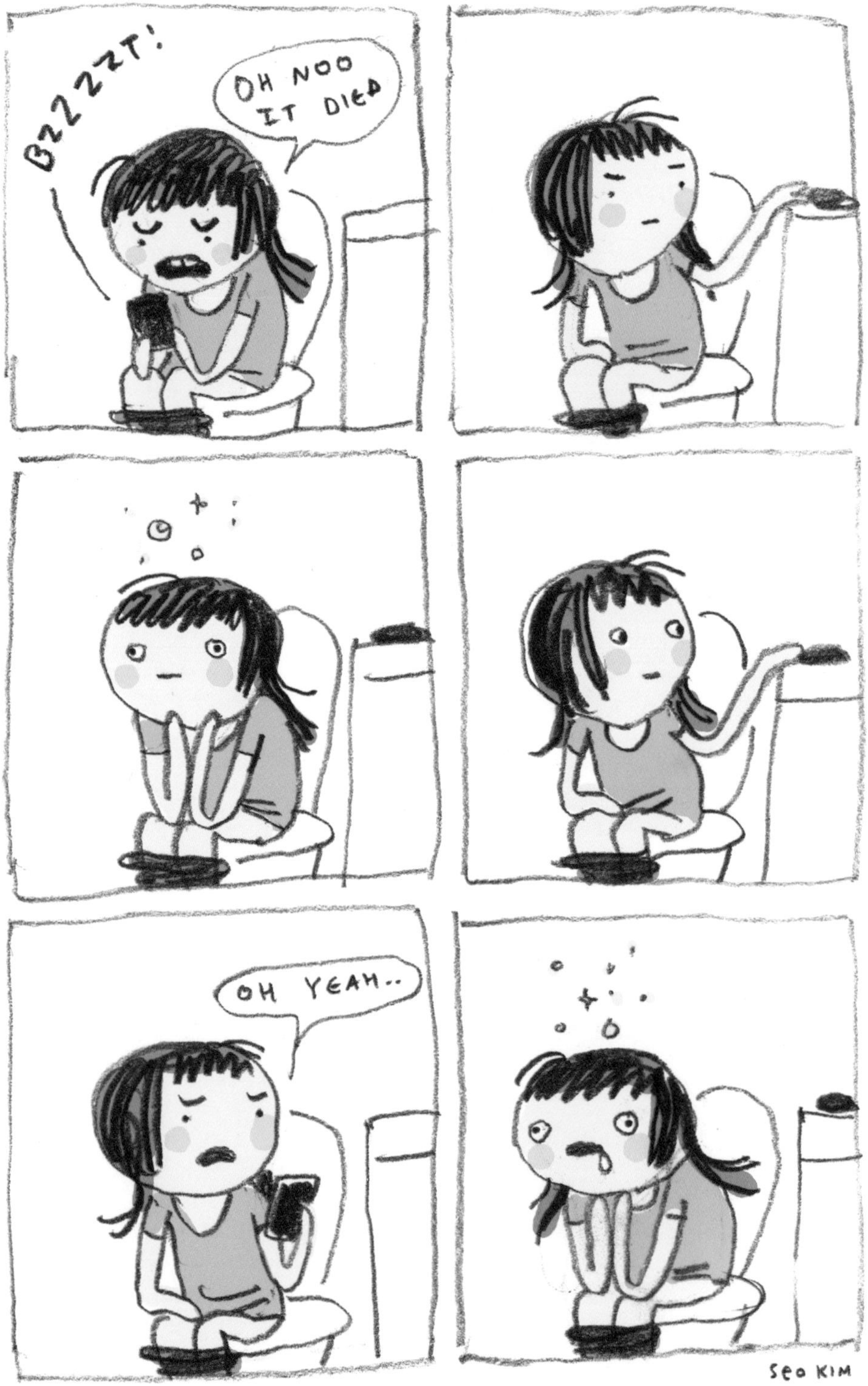
BZZZZT!
OH NOO IT DIED
OH YEAH..

SEO KIM

ugh
my body
is
so boring

there

seo kim

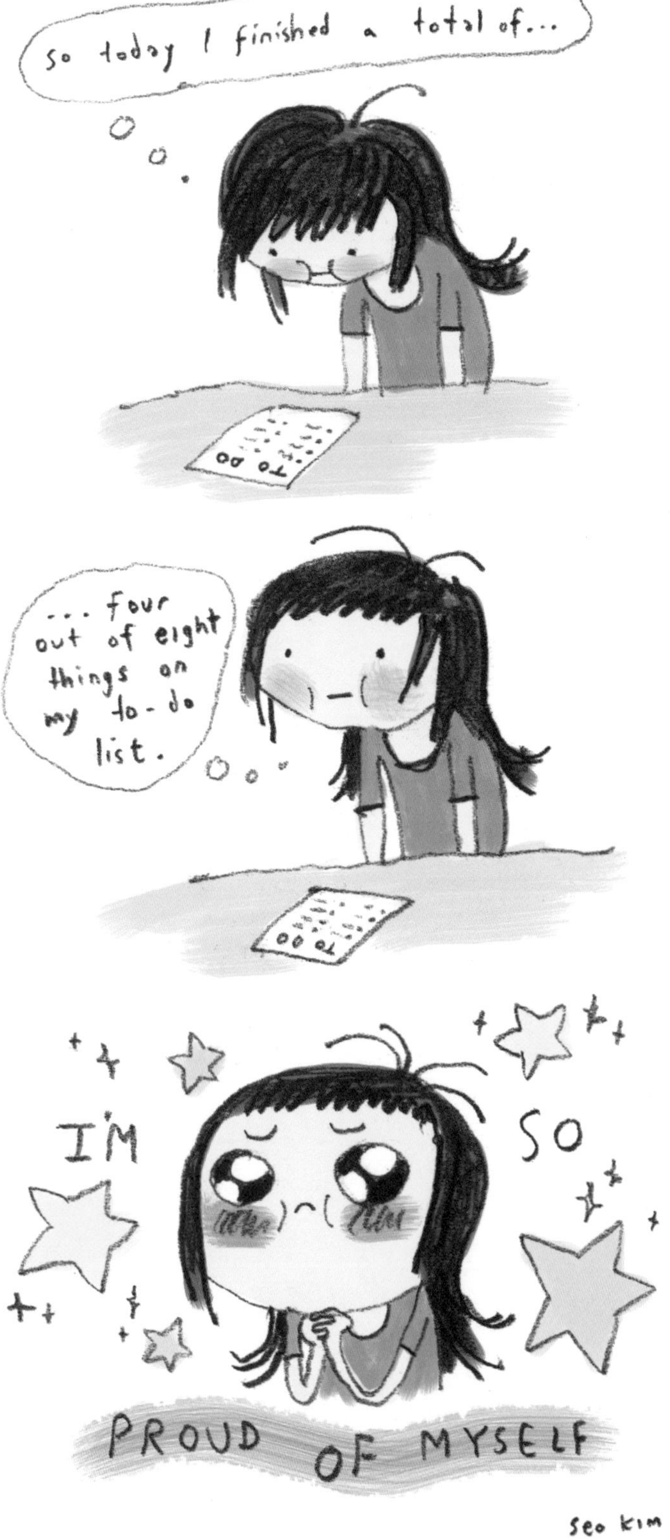
so today I finished a total of...
TO DO
...four out of eight things on my to-do list.
TO DO
I'M SO PROUD OF MYSELF
seo kim

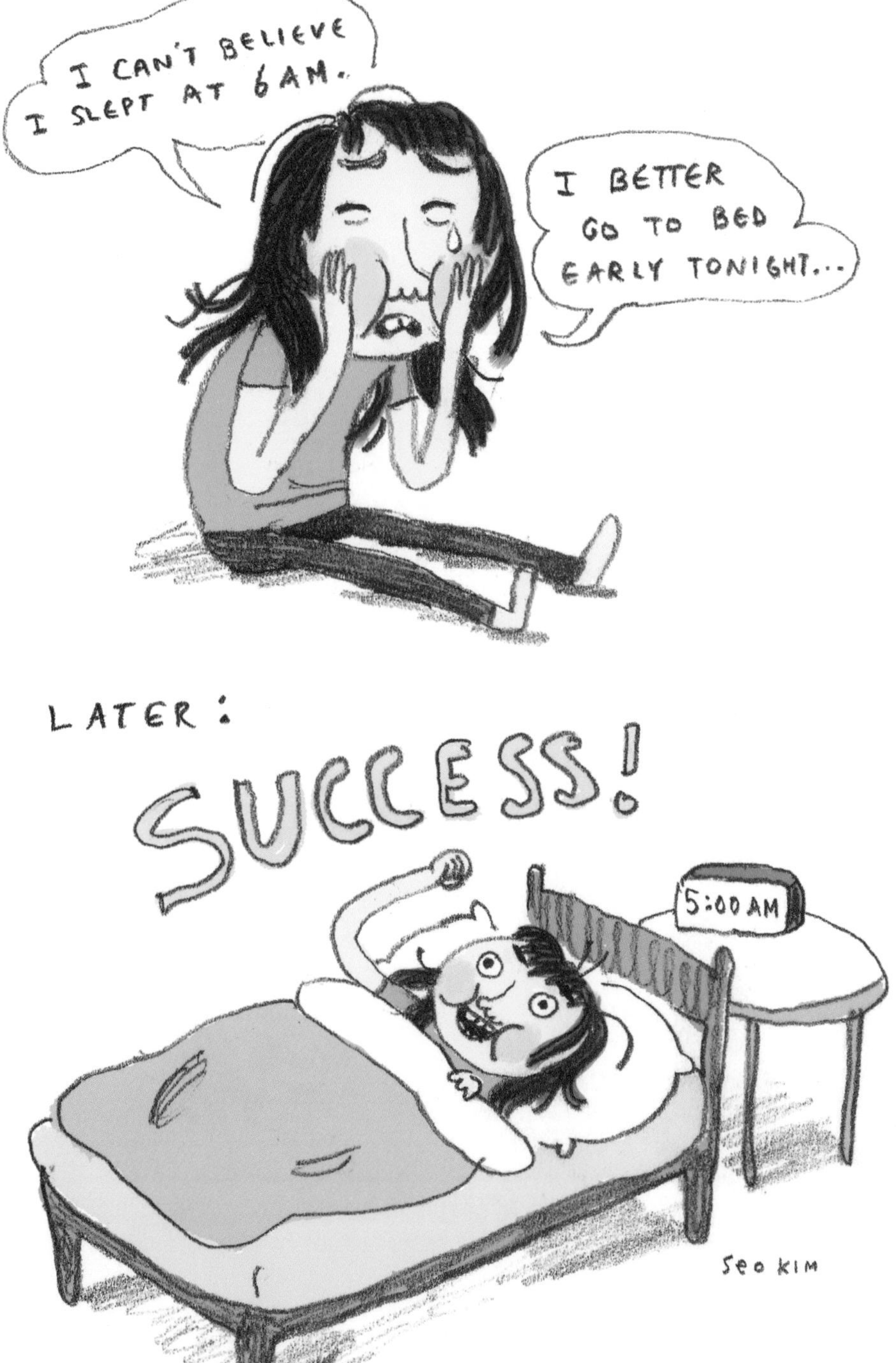
I CAN'T BELIEVE I SLEPT AT 6AM.
I BETTER GO TO BED EARLY TONIGHT...
LATER:
SUCCESS!
5:00AM
SEO KIM

IT'S NORMAL TO HAVE FEELINGS, EVEN NEGATIVE ONES

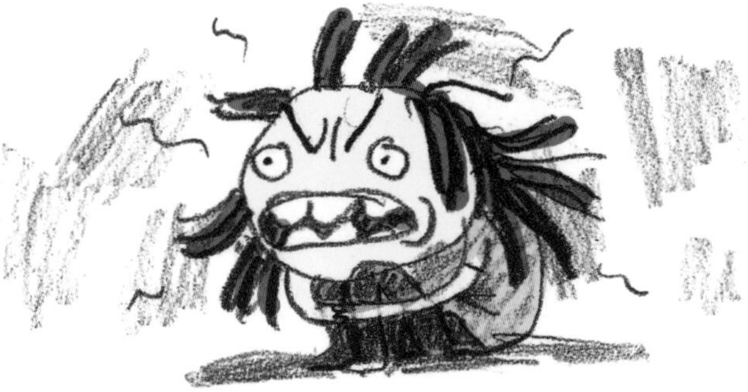

AND IT DOESN'T HELP TO GET MAD AT YOURSELF FOR HAVING THEM.

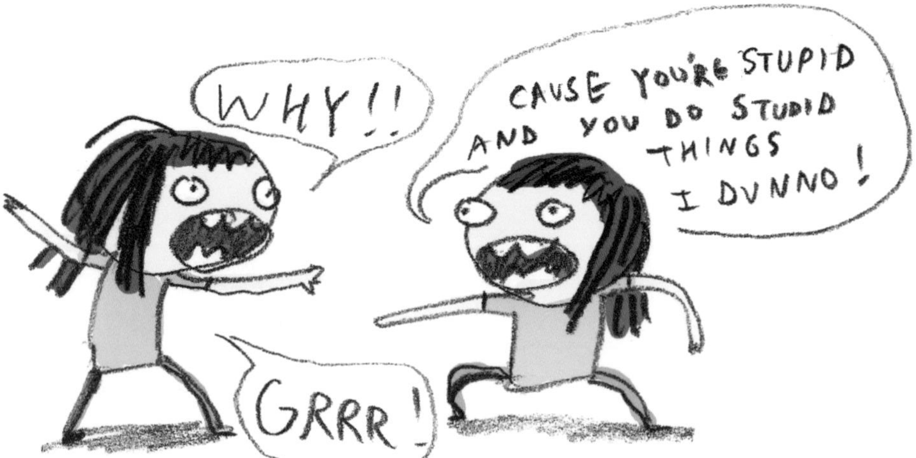
WHY!!
CAUSE YOU'RE STUPID AND YOU DO STUPID THINGS I DUNNO!
GRRR!

YOU CAN, HOWEVER, GET MAD AT YOUR FEELINGS, SINCE YOUR FEELINGS DON'T HAVE FEELINGS.

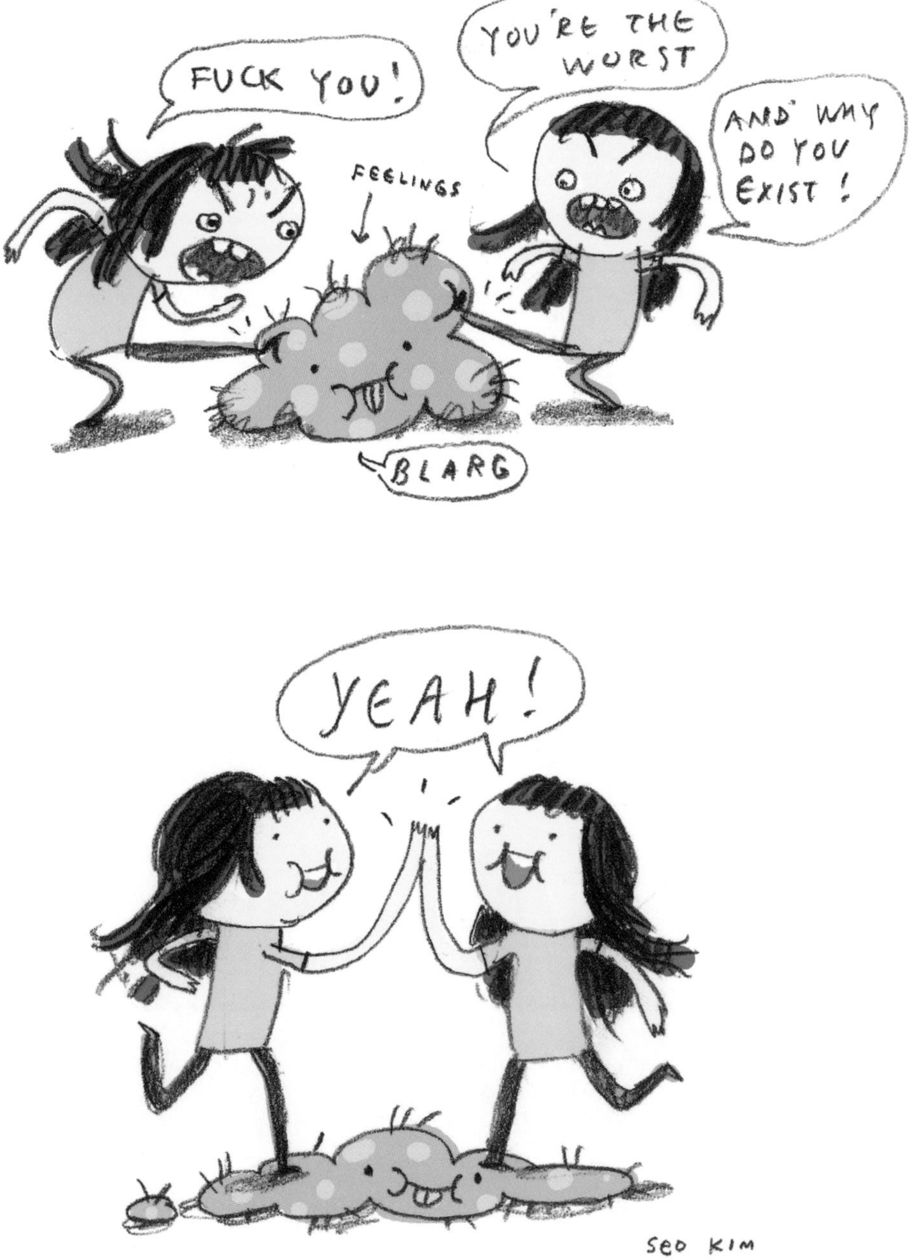
FUCK YOU!
YOU'RE THE WORST
AND WHY DO YOU EXIST!
FEELINGS
BLARG
YEAH!
SEO KIM

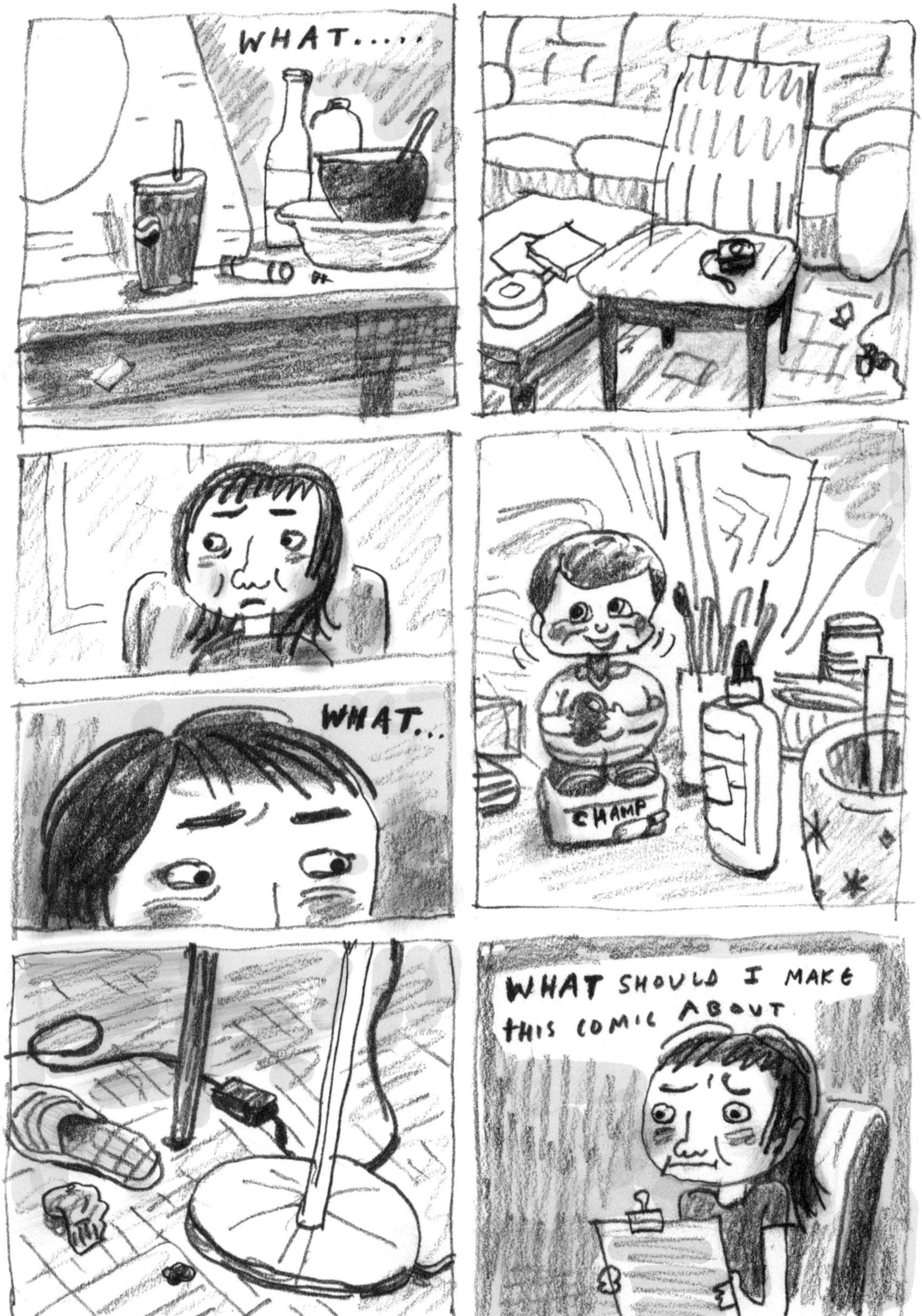
WHAT.....
CHAMP
WHAT...
WHAT SHOULD I MAKE THIS COMIC ABOUT

SEO KIM

EPIPHANY

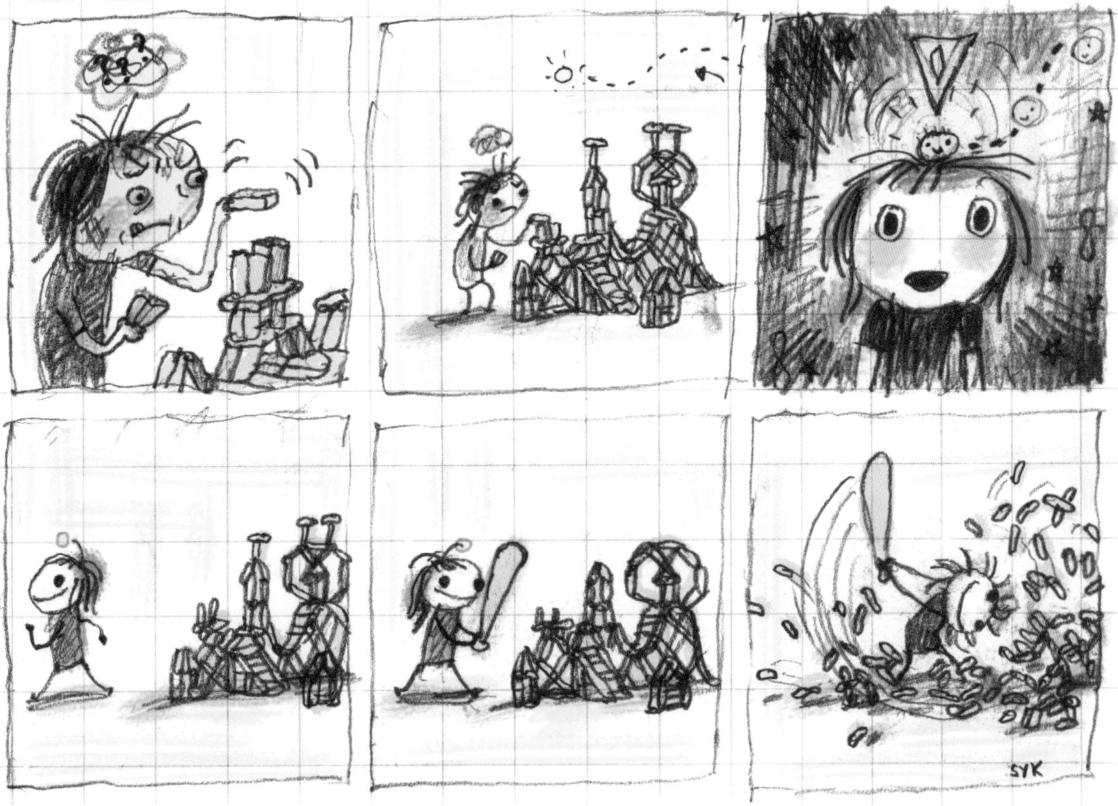
SYK

JUST ME II

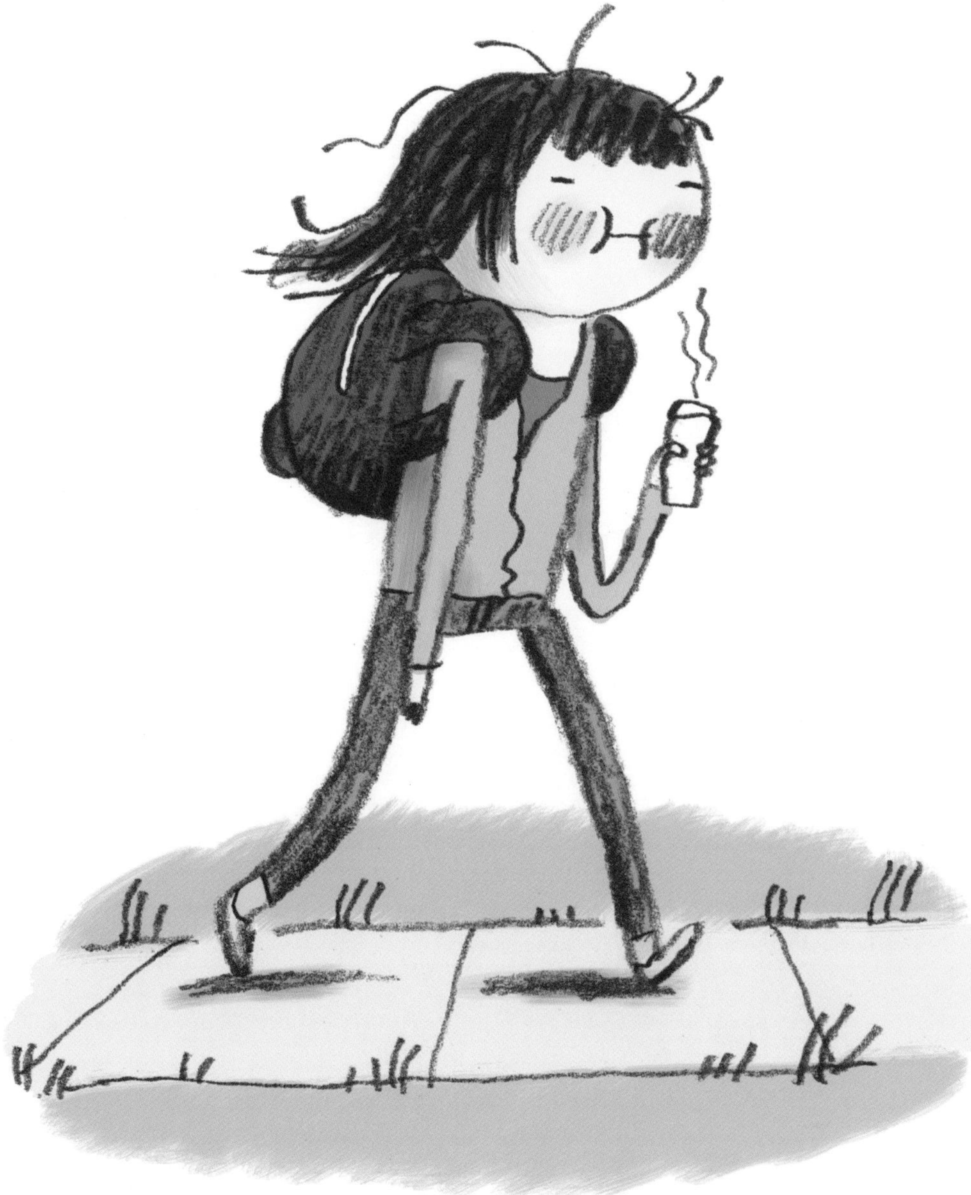

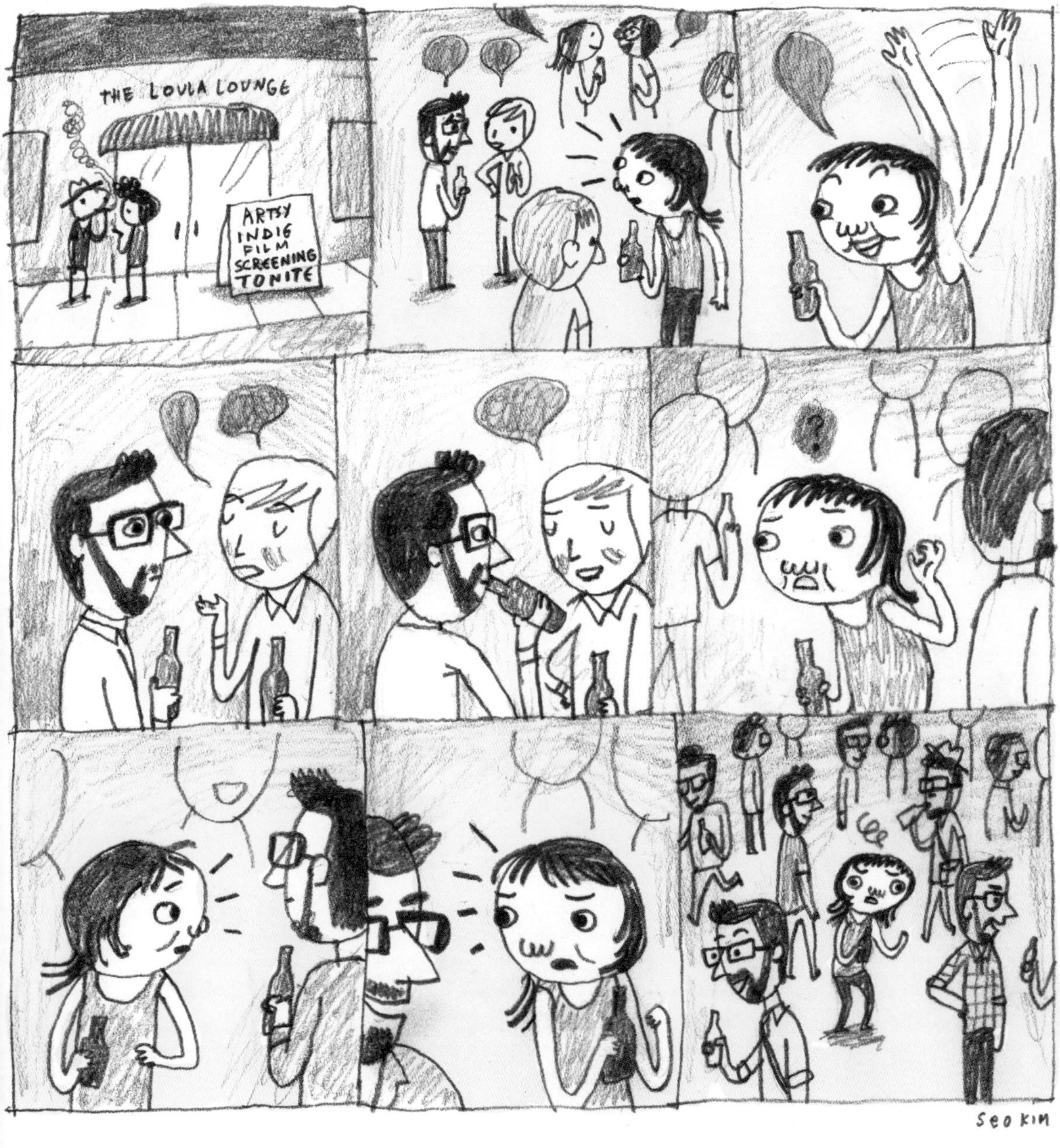
THE LOULA LOUNGE
ARTSY INDIE FILM SCREENING TONITE
?
SEO KIM

SUBWAY ADVENTURES

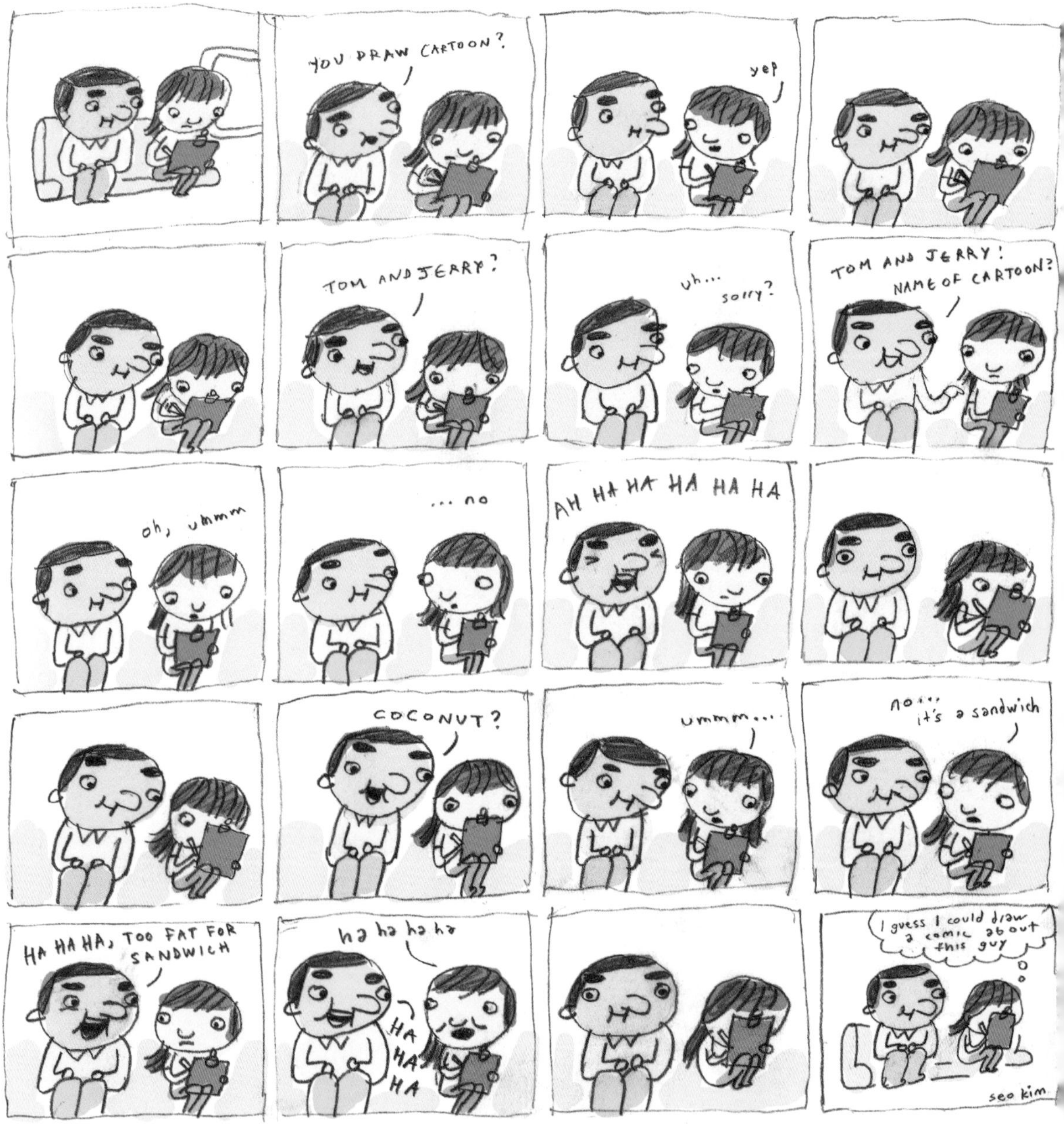
YOU DRAW CARTOON?
yep
TOM AND JERRY?
uh... sorry?
TOM AND JERRY! NAME OF CARTOON?
oh, ummm
... no
AH HA HA HA HA HA
COCONUT?
ummm...
no... it's a sandwich
HA HA HA, TOO FAT FOR SANDWICH
ha ha ha ha
HA HA HA
I guess I could draw a comic about this guy
seo kim

coffee habit

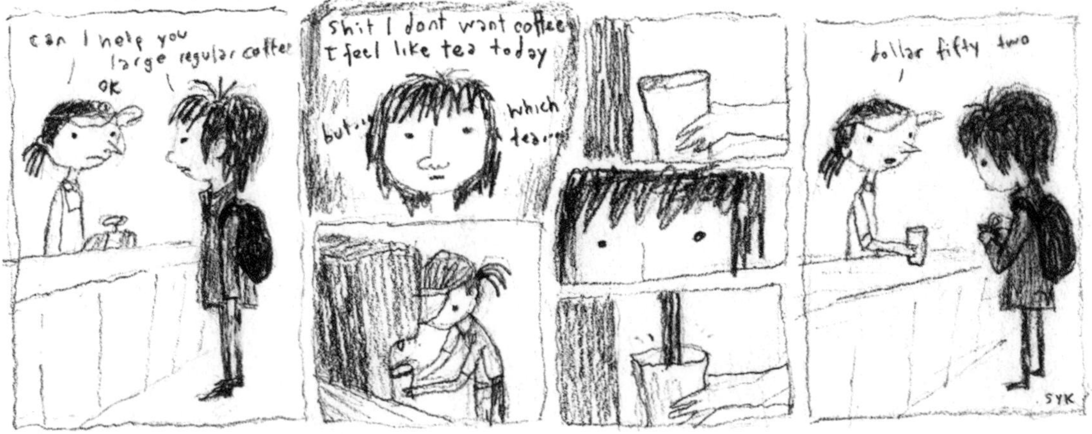

can I help you
large regular coffee
ok
Shit I dont want coffee
I feel like tea today
but...
which tea...
dollar fifty two
SYK

CONCERT

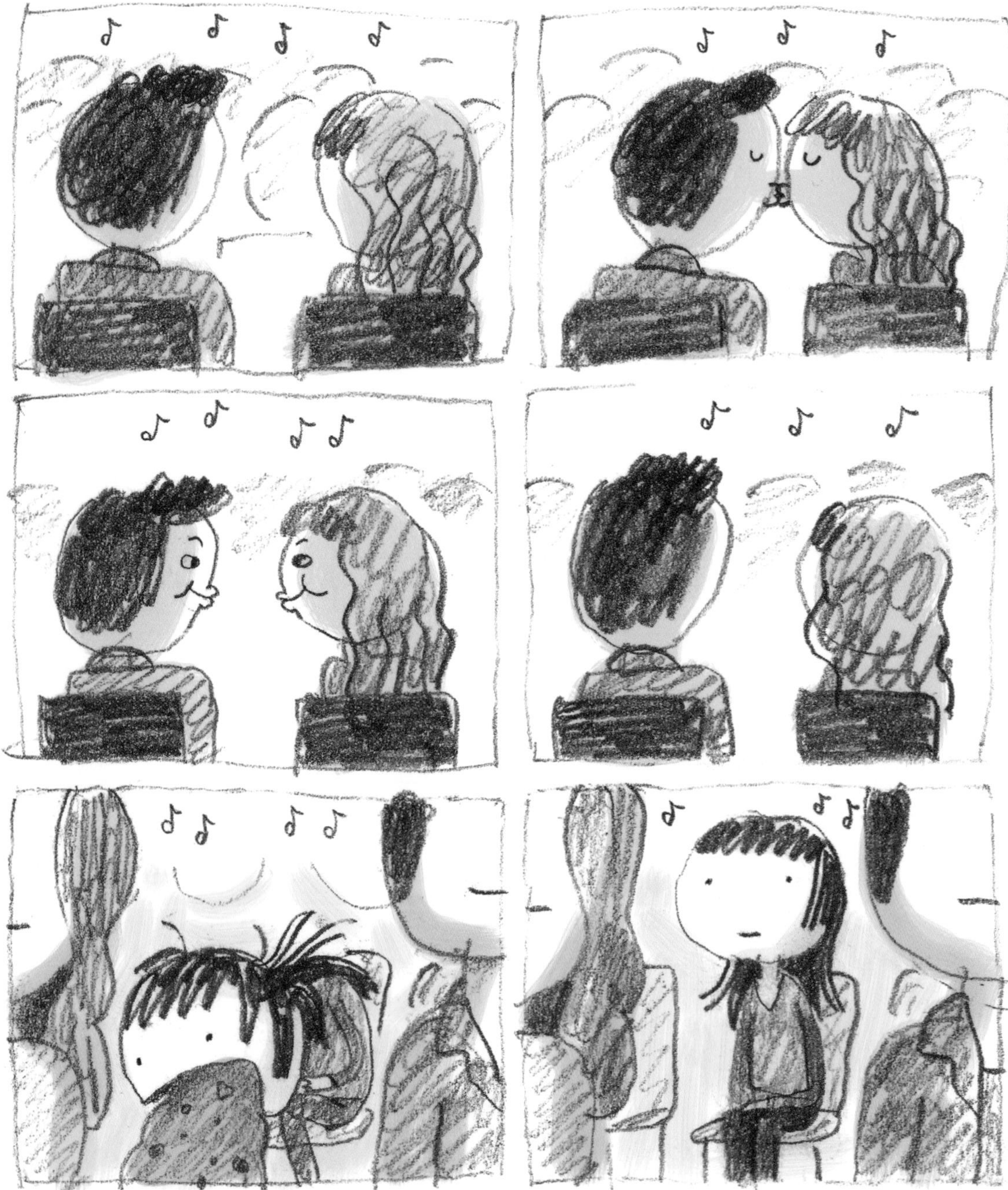

SEO KIM

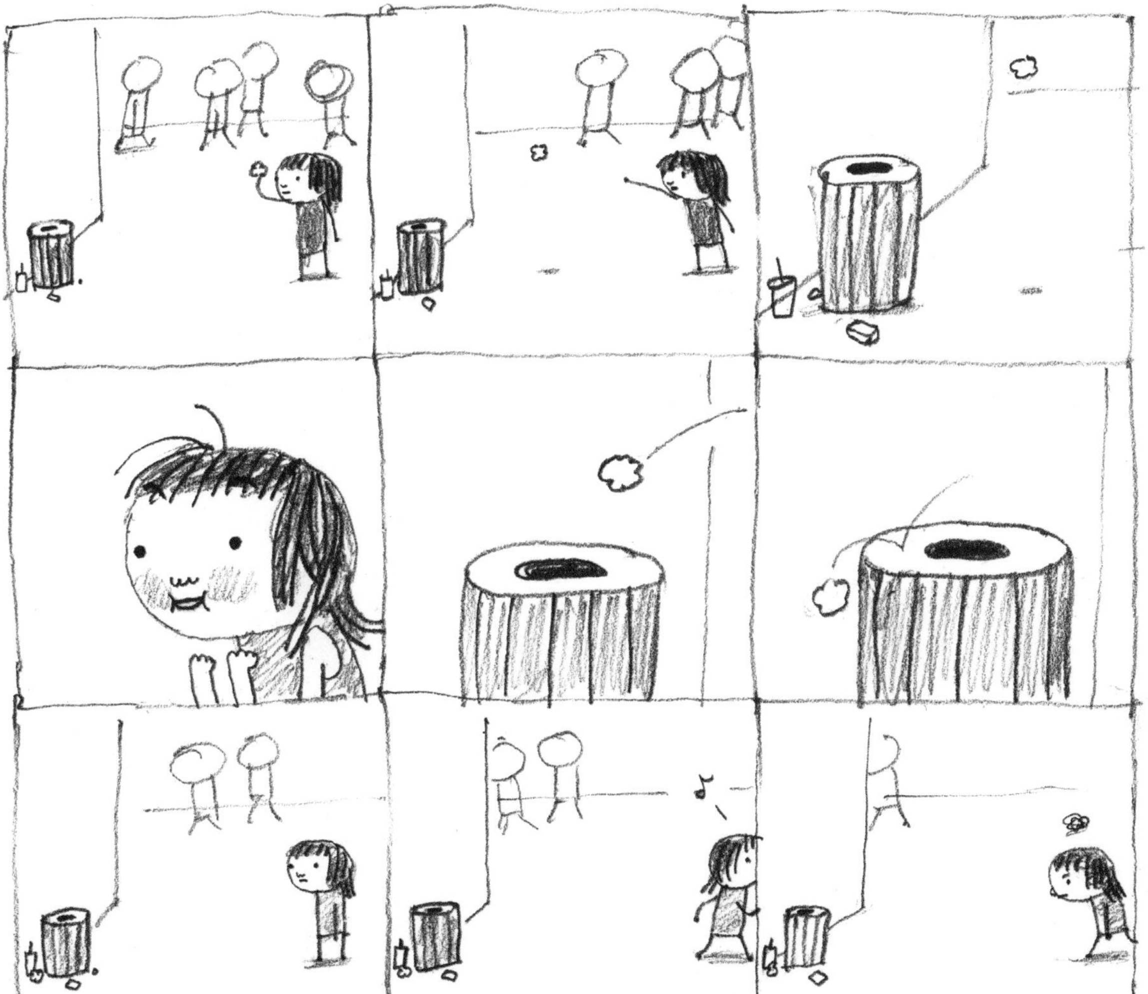

seo kim

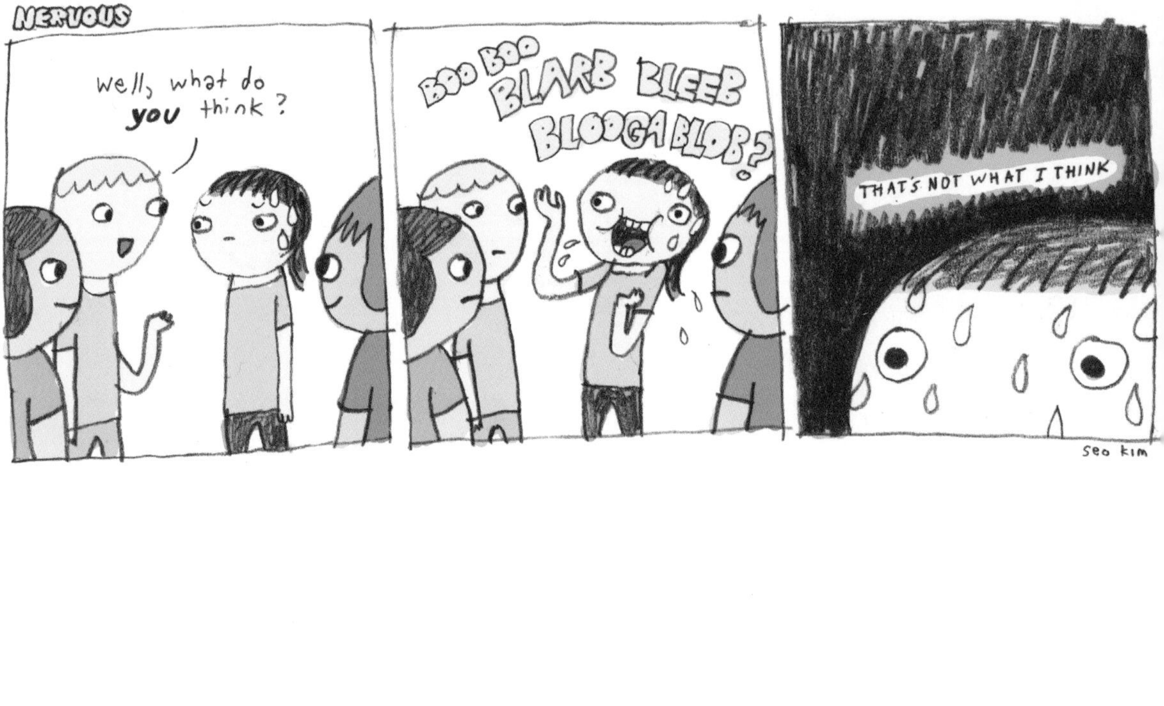
NERVOUS
Well, what do **you** think?
BOO BOO BLARB BLEEB BLOOGA BLOB?
THAT'S NOT WHAT I THINK
seo kim

"ASIAN GLOW"

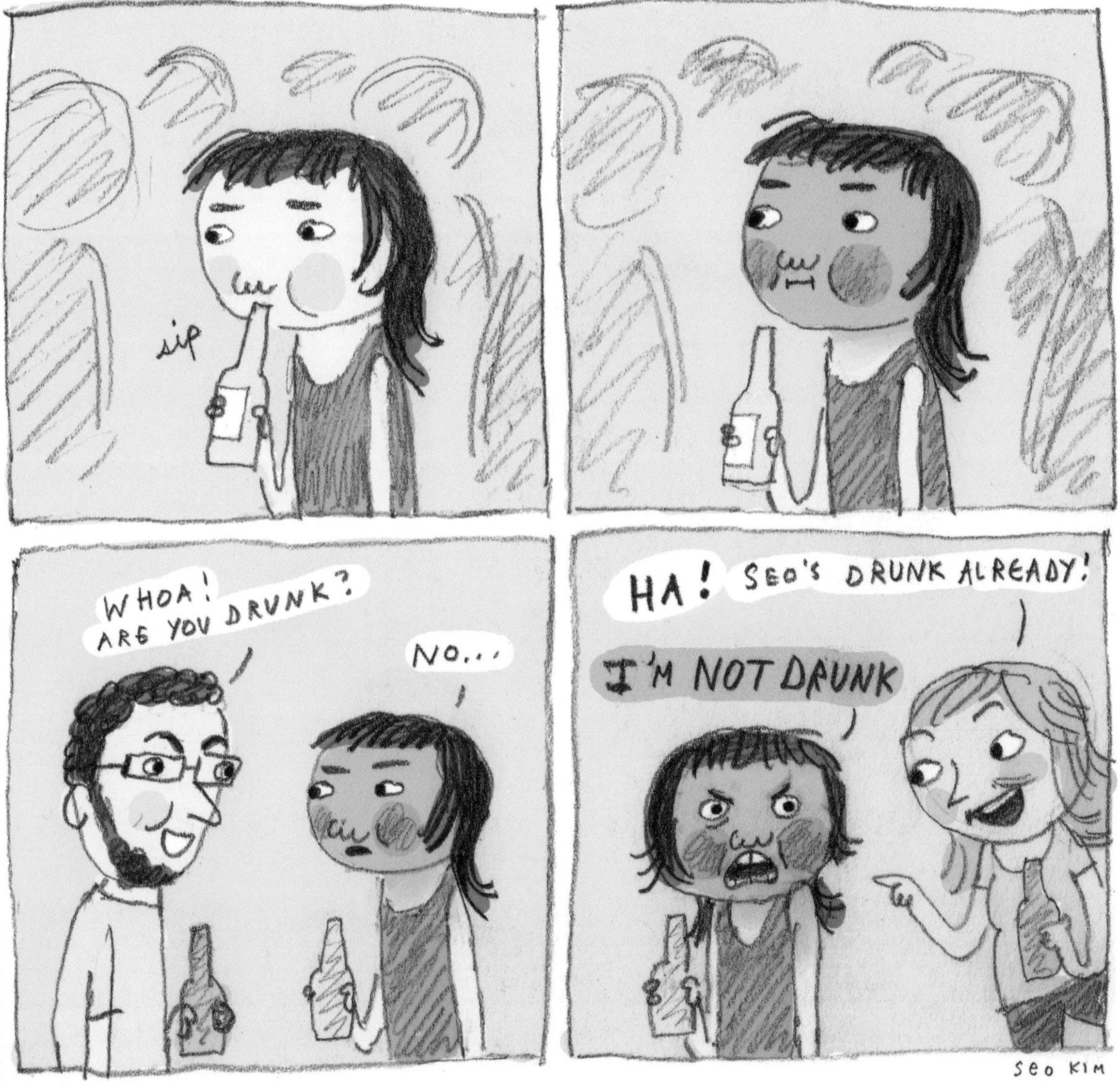
sip
WHOA! ARE YOU DRUNK?
NO...
HA! SEO'S DRUNK ALREADY!
I'M NOT DRUNK

SEO KIM

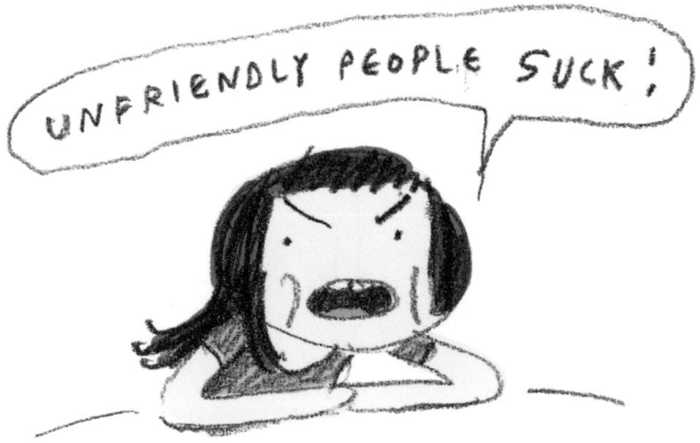
UNFRIENDLY PEOPLE SUCK!

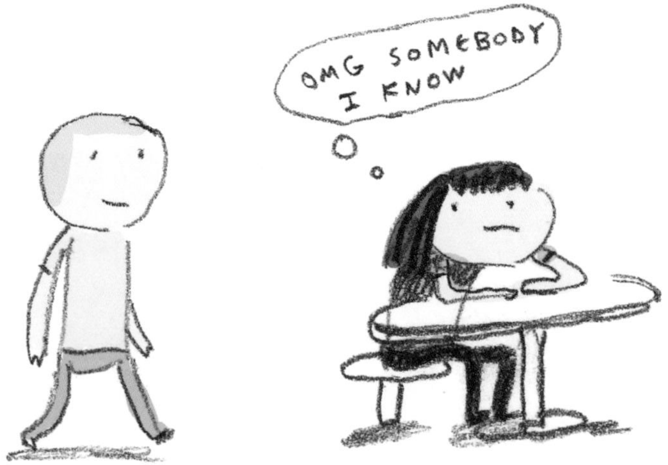
OMG SOMEBODY I KNOW

I'M NOT UNFRIENDLY I'M JUST SHY!
SEO KIM

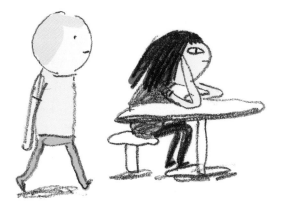

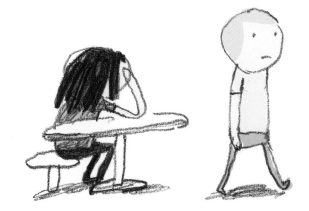

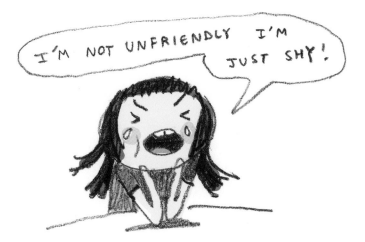

yogurt

POP

BOOSH

WTF

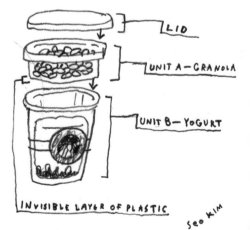
LID

UNIT A — GRANOLA

UNIT B — YOGURT

INVISIBLE LAYER OF PLASTIC

Seo Kim

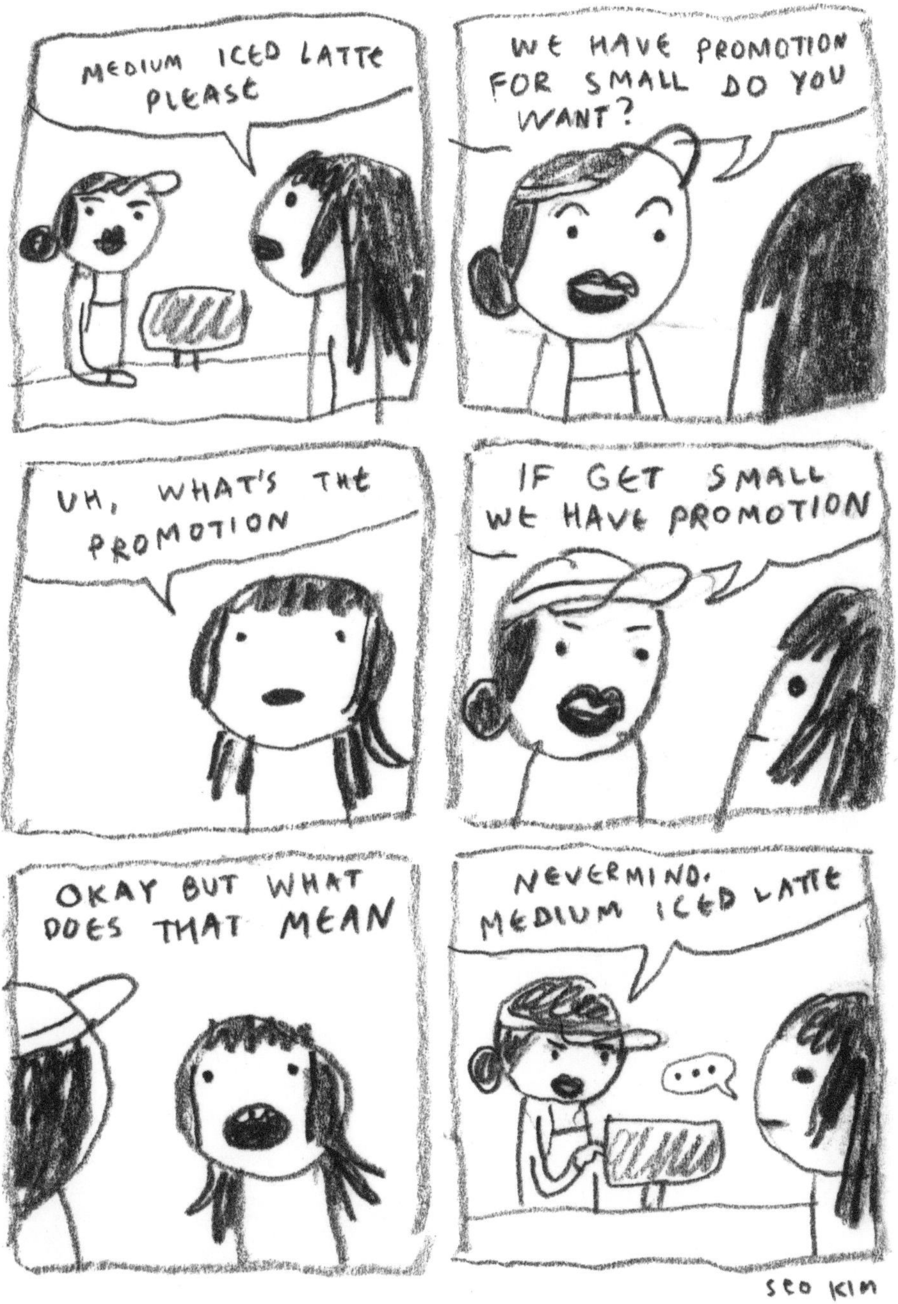
MEDIUM ICED LATTE PLEASE
WE HAVE PROMOTION FOR SMALL DO YOU WANT?
UH, WHAT'S THE PROMOTION
IF GET SMALL WE HAVE PROMOTION
OKAY BUT WHAT DOES THAT MEAN
NEVERMIND. MEDIUM ICED LATTE
...
SEO KIM

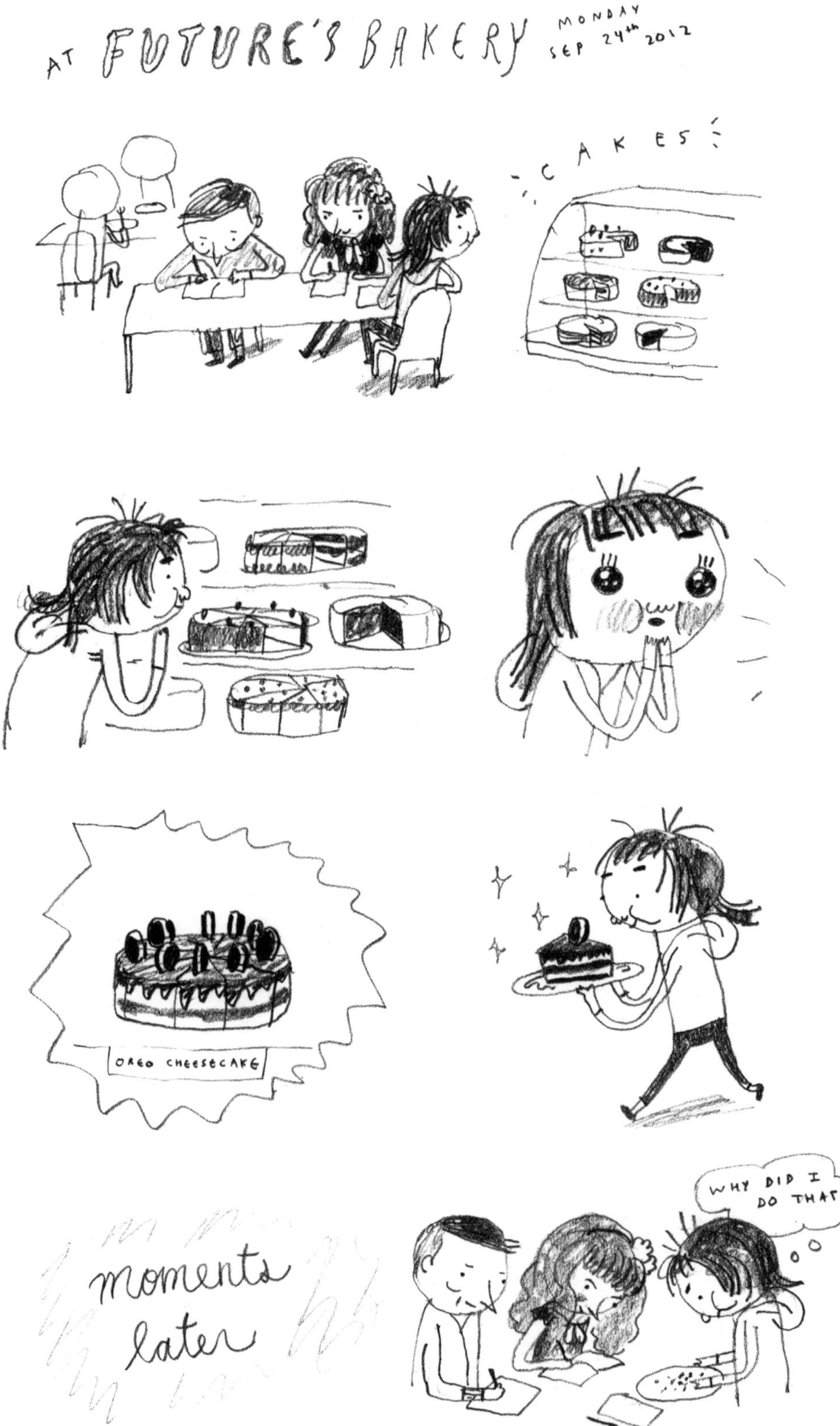
AT FUTURE'S BAKERY
MONDAY SEP 24th 2012
CAKES
OREO CHEESECAKE
moments later
WHY DID I DO THAT
SEO KIM

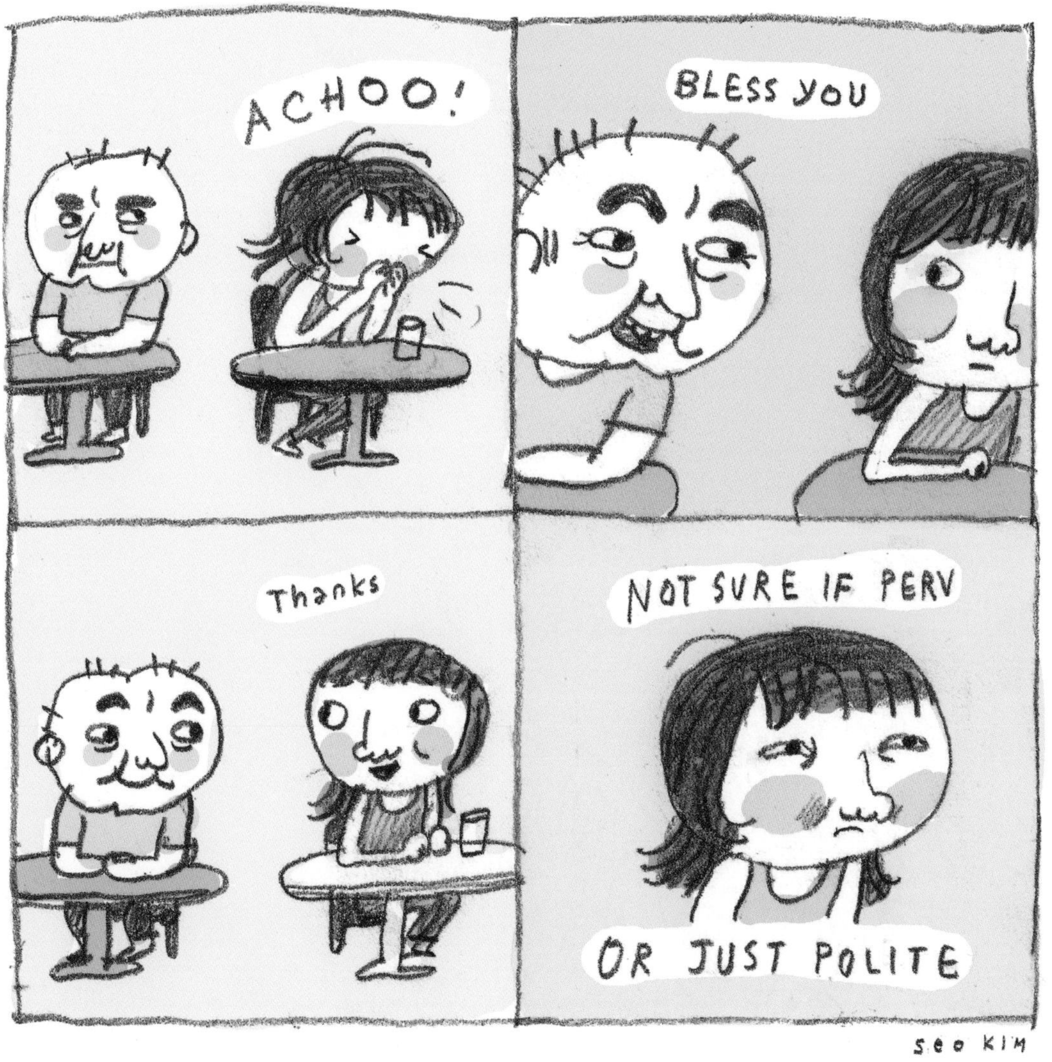
ACHOO!
BLESS YOU
Thanks
NOT SURE IF PERV
OR JUST POLITE
SEO KIM

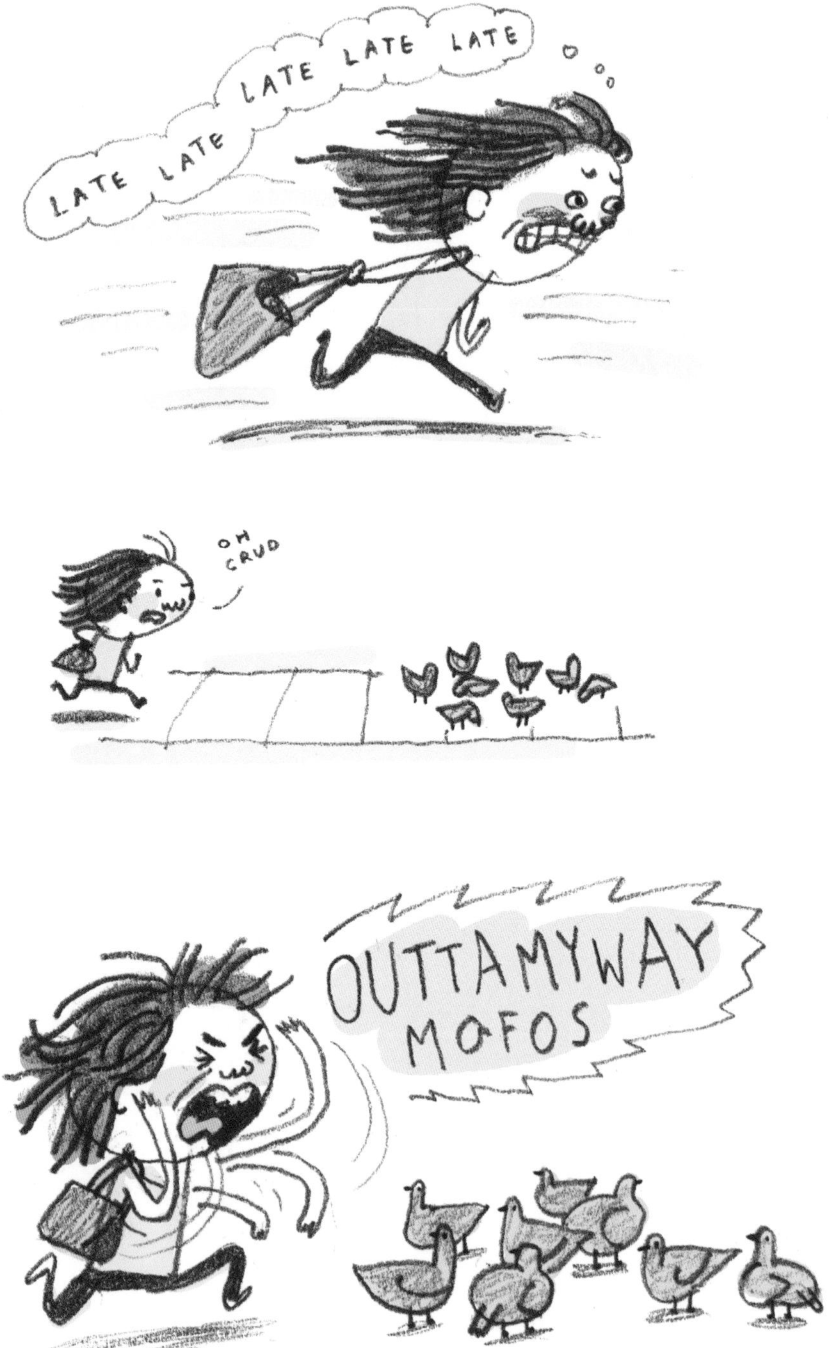
LATE LATE LATE LATE LATE
OH CRUD
OUTTAMYWAY MOFOS

GOD. DAMMIT... STUPID BIRDS!
LADY! CALM YOUR SHIT
YEAH YOU'RE NOT THE ONLY ONE WHO HAS TO BE SOMEWHERE!

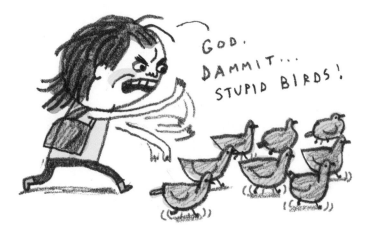

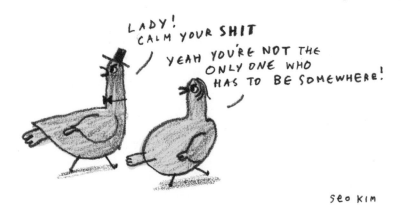

seo kim

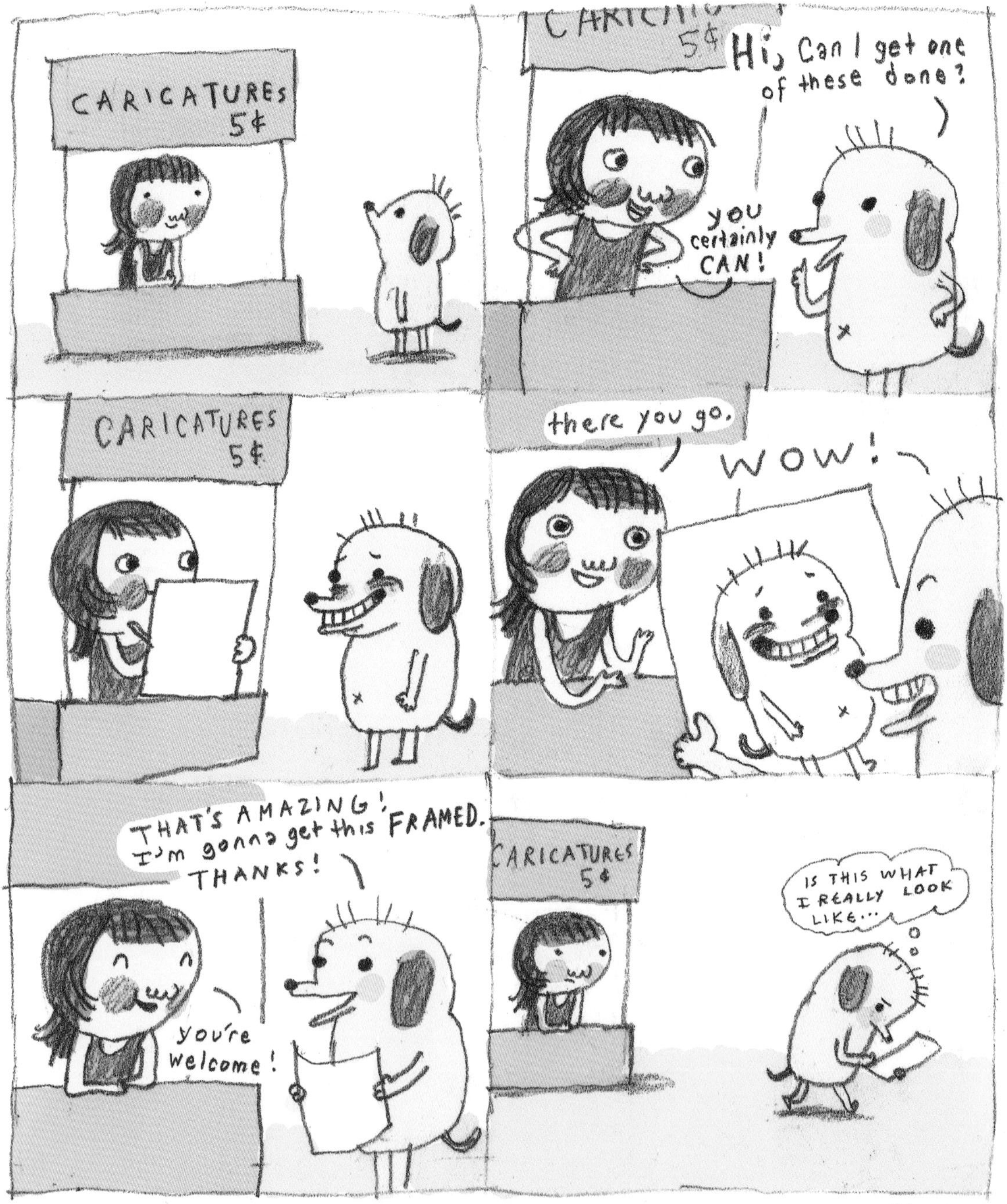
CARICATURES 5¢
Hi, Can I get one of these done?
you certainly CAN!
CARICATURES 5¢
there you go.
WOW!
THAT'S AMAZING! I'm gonna get this FRAMED. THANKS!
you're welcome!
CARICATURES 5¢
IS THIS WHAT I REALLY LOOK LIKE...

SEO KIM

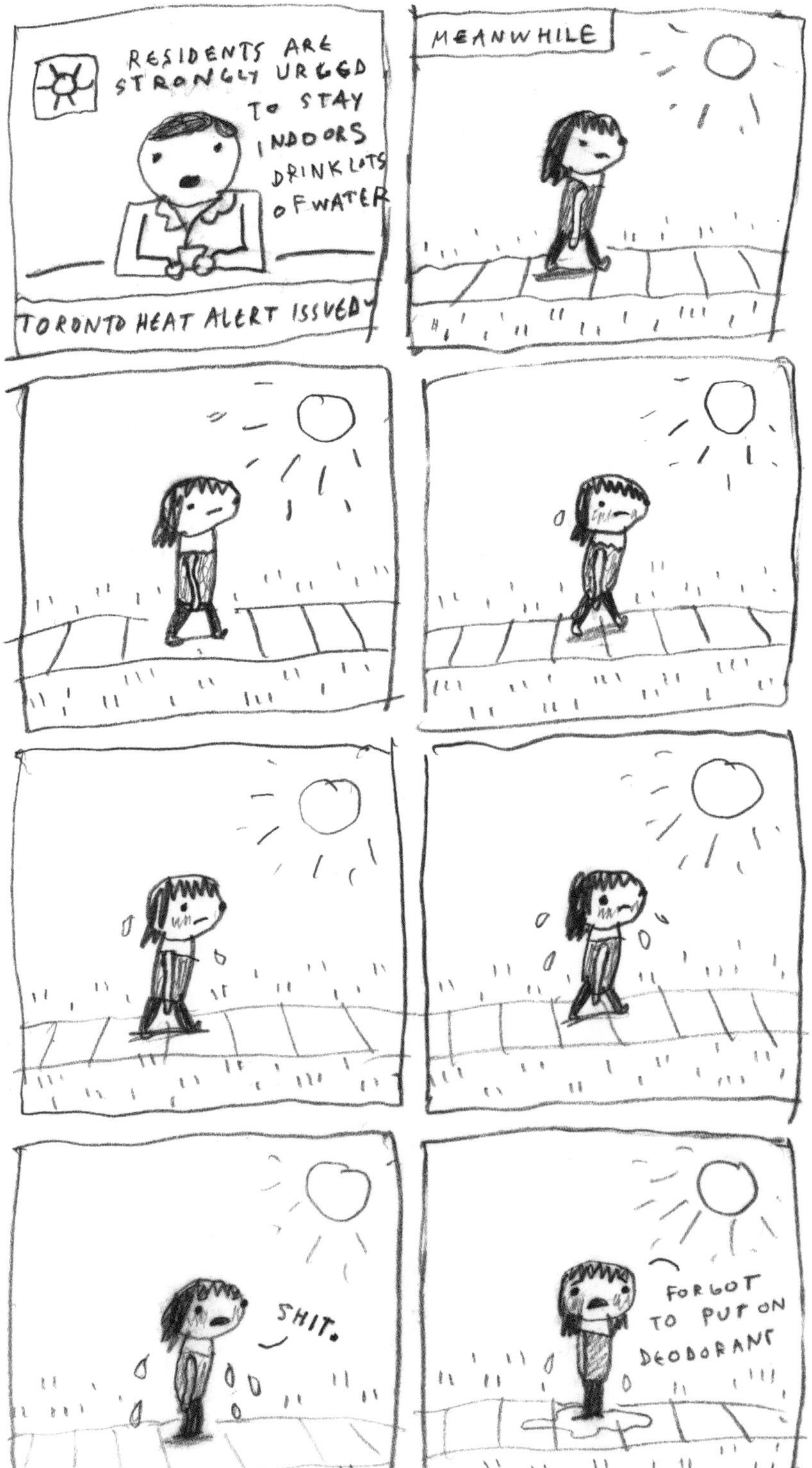
RESIDENTS ARE STRONGLY URGED TO STAY INDOORS DRINK LOTS OF WATER
TORONTO HEAT ALERT ISSUED
MEANWHILE
SHIT.
FORGOT TO PUT ON DEODORANT
SEO KIM

HUMMUS PART 1

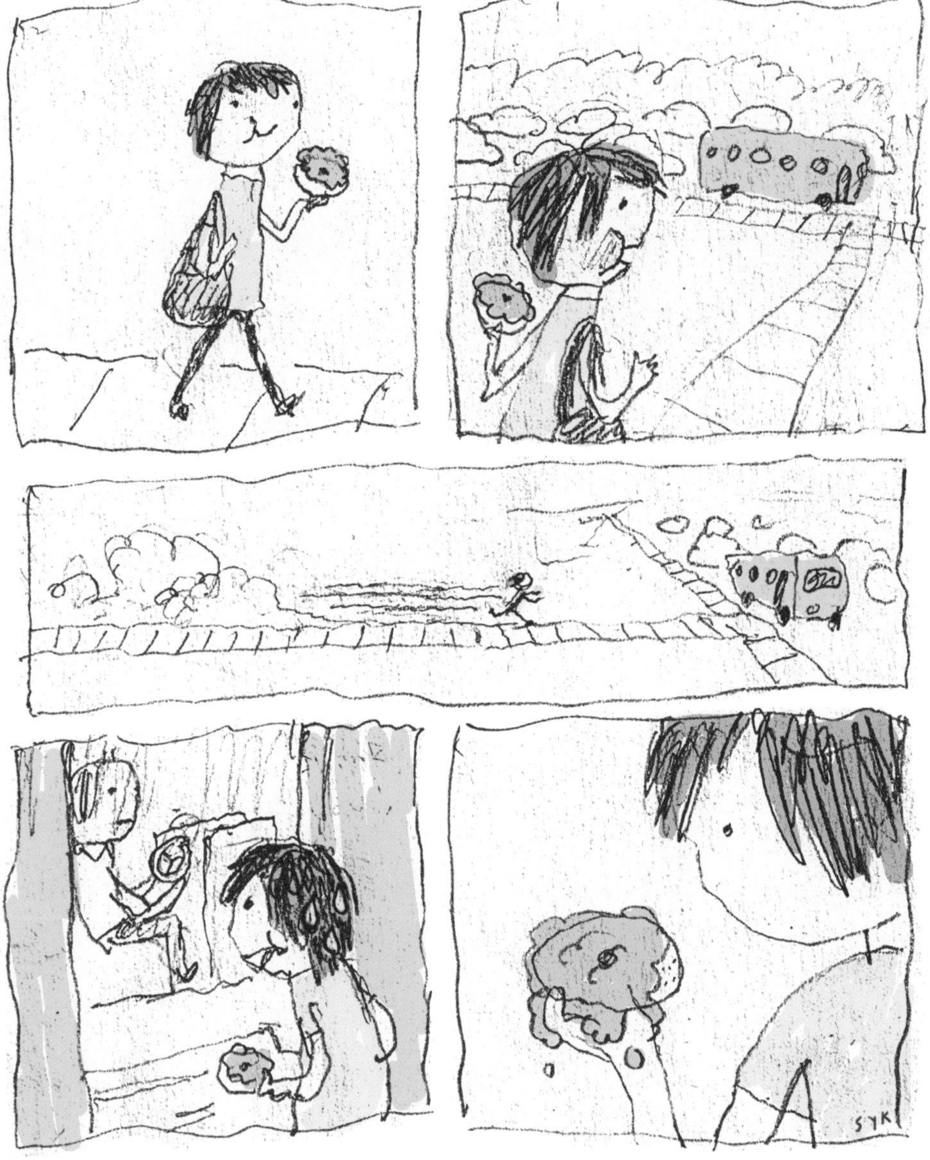
SYK

HUMMUS PART 2

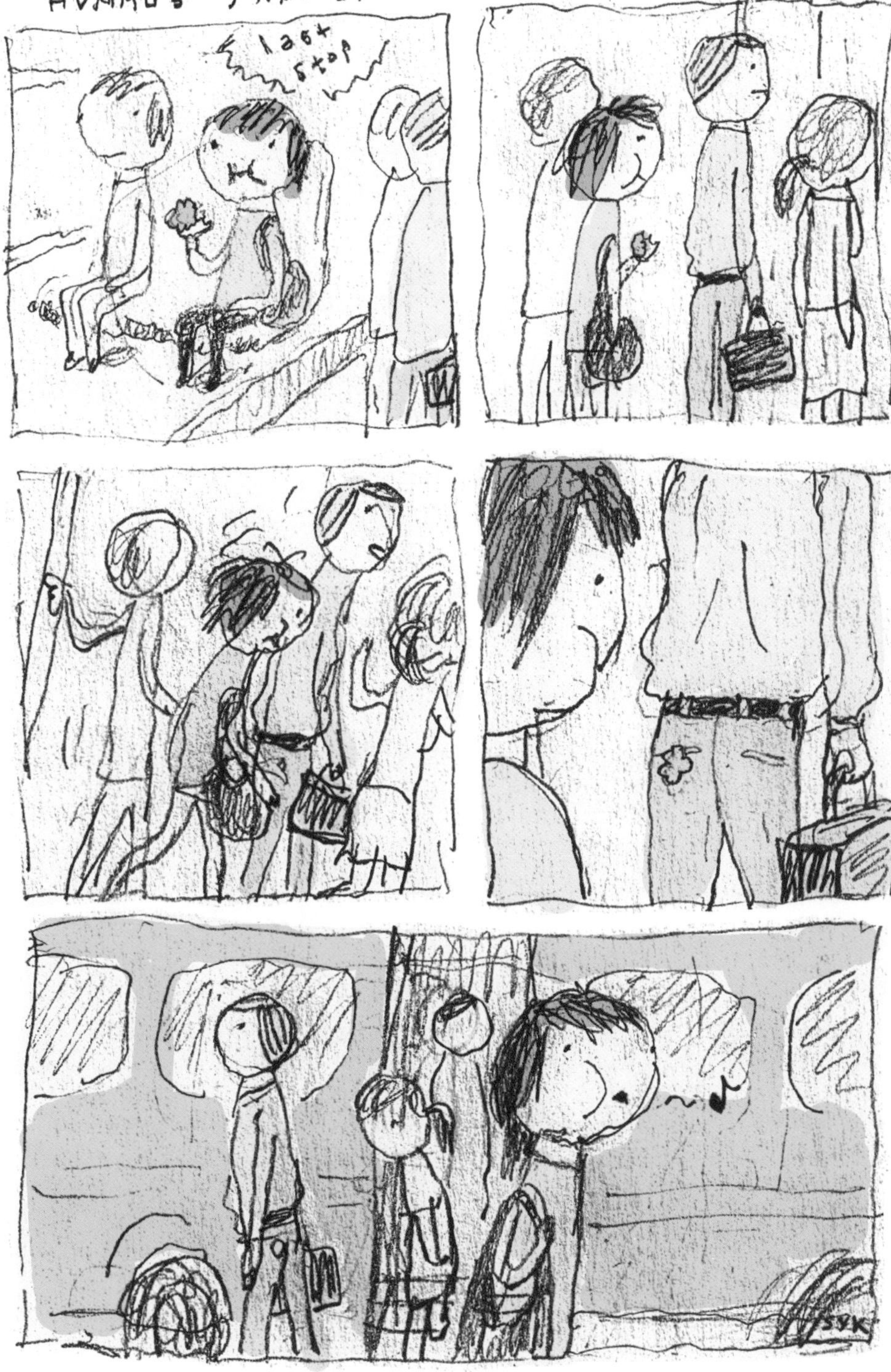

the wrong bus

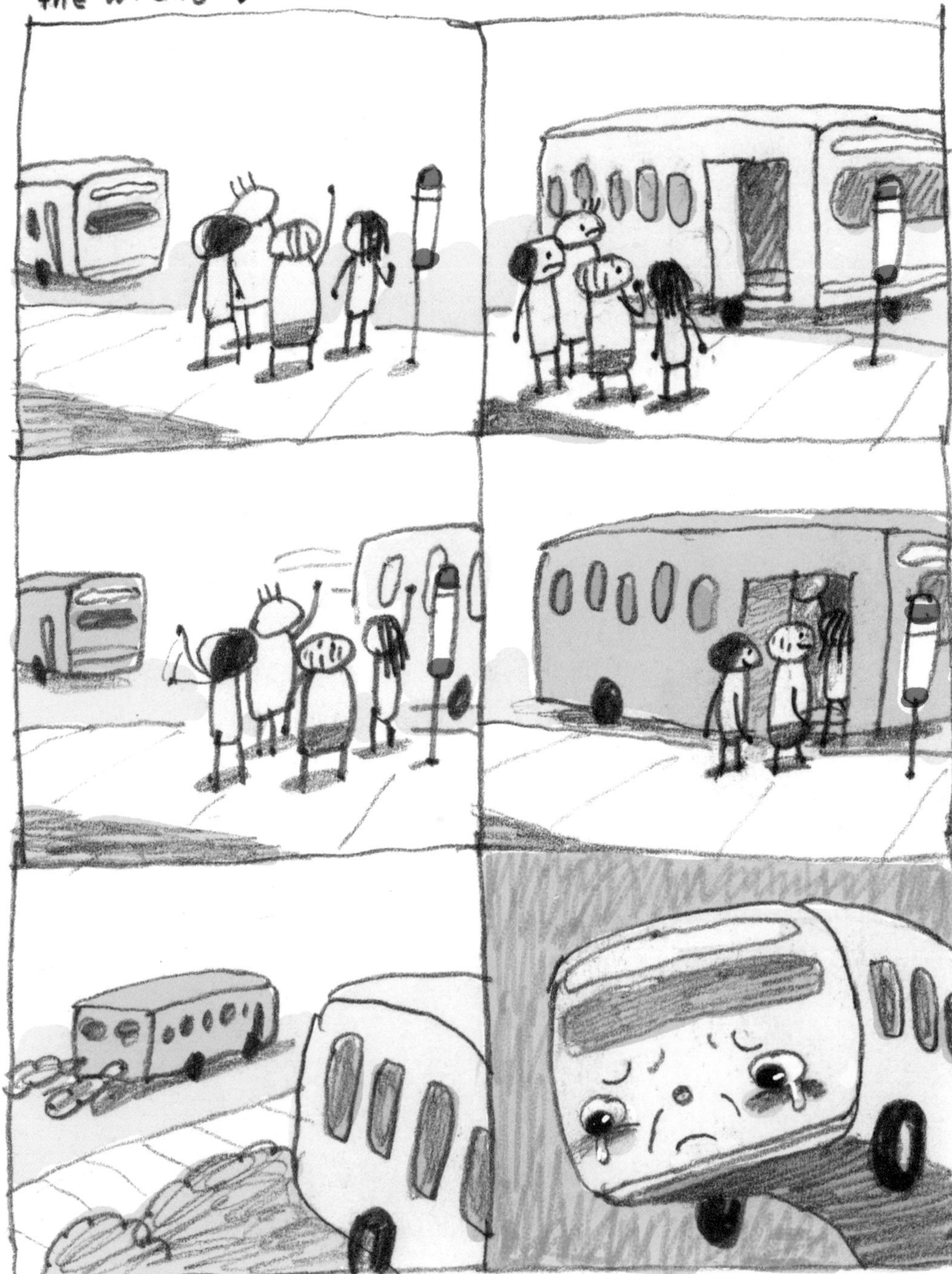

seo kim

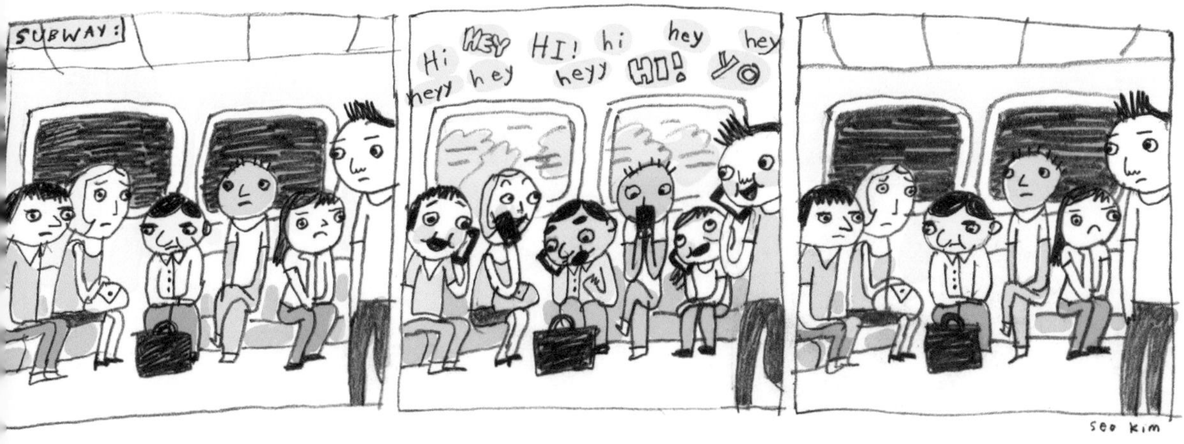
SUBWAY:
Hi
HEY
HI!
hi
hey
hey
heyy
hey
heyy
HI!
yo
seo kim

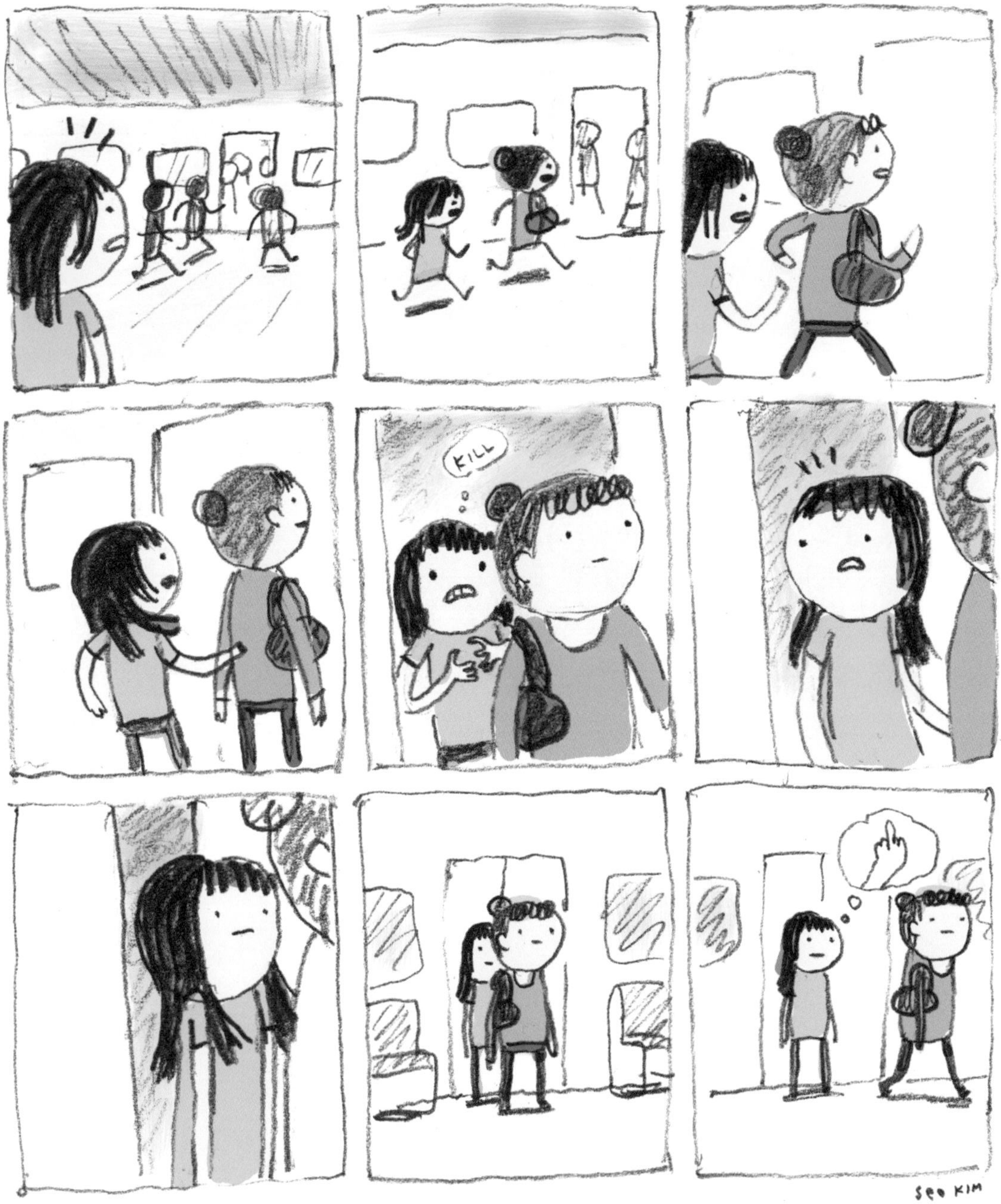
KILL

SEO KIM

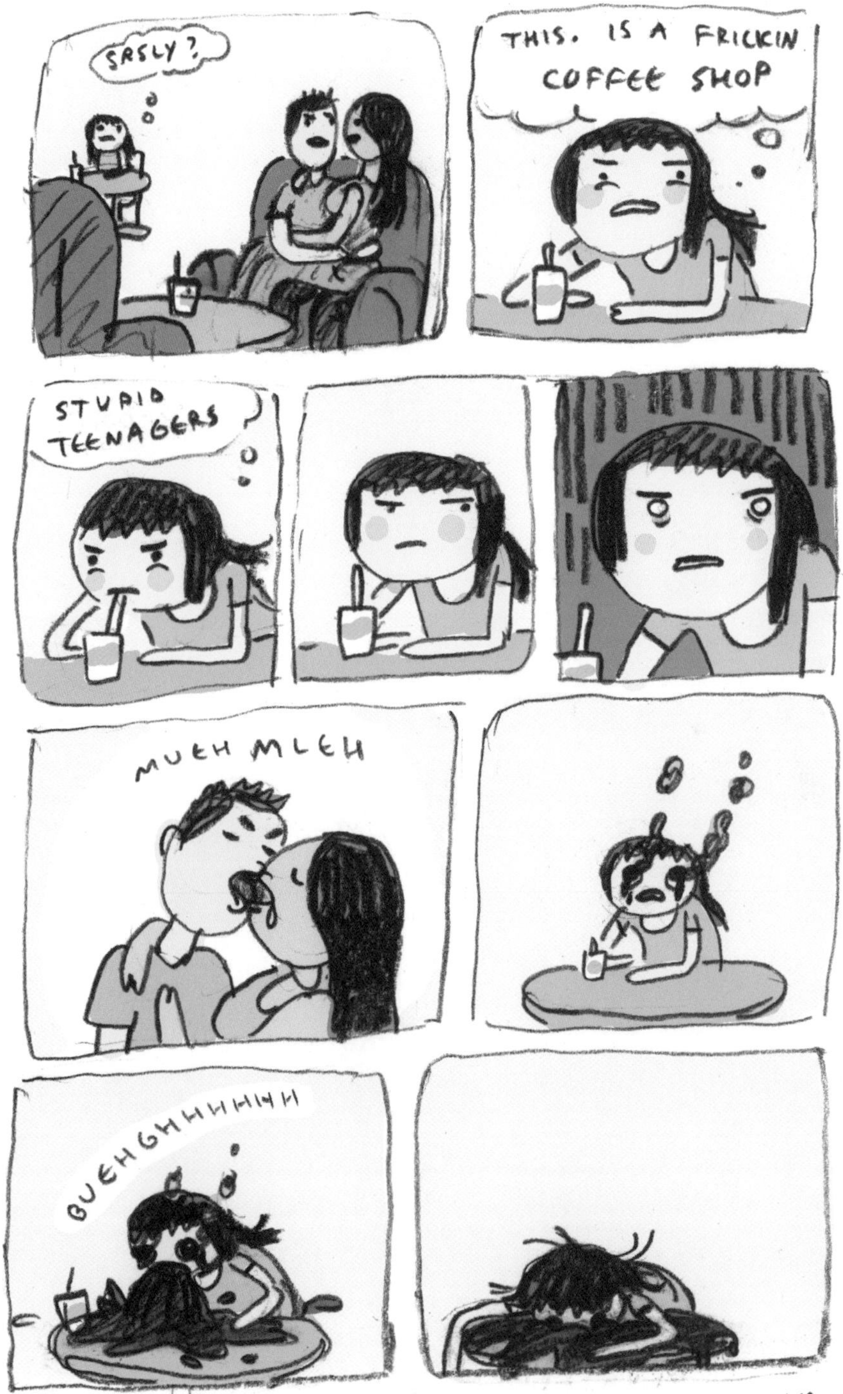
SRSLY?
THIS. IS A FRICKIN COFFEE SHOP
STUPID TEENAGERS
MUEH MLEH
BUEHGHHHHHHH
SEO KIM

EDDIE & ME

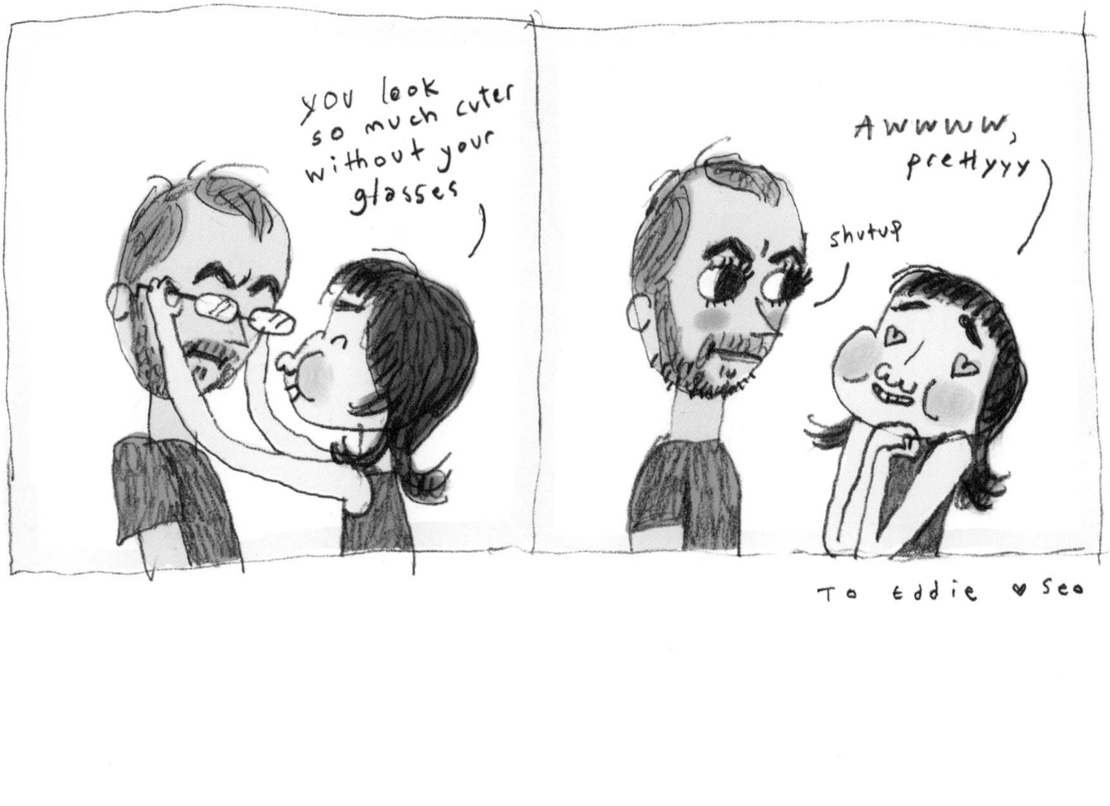
you look so much cuter without your glasses
Awwww, prettyyy
shutup

To Eddie ♥ Seo

LONG-DISTANCE RELATIONSHIP COMICS

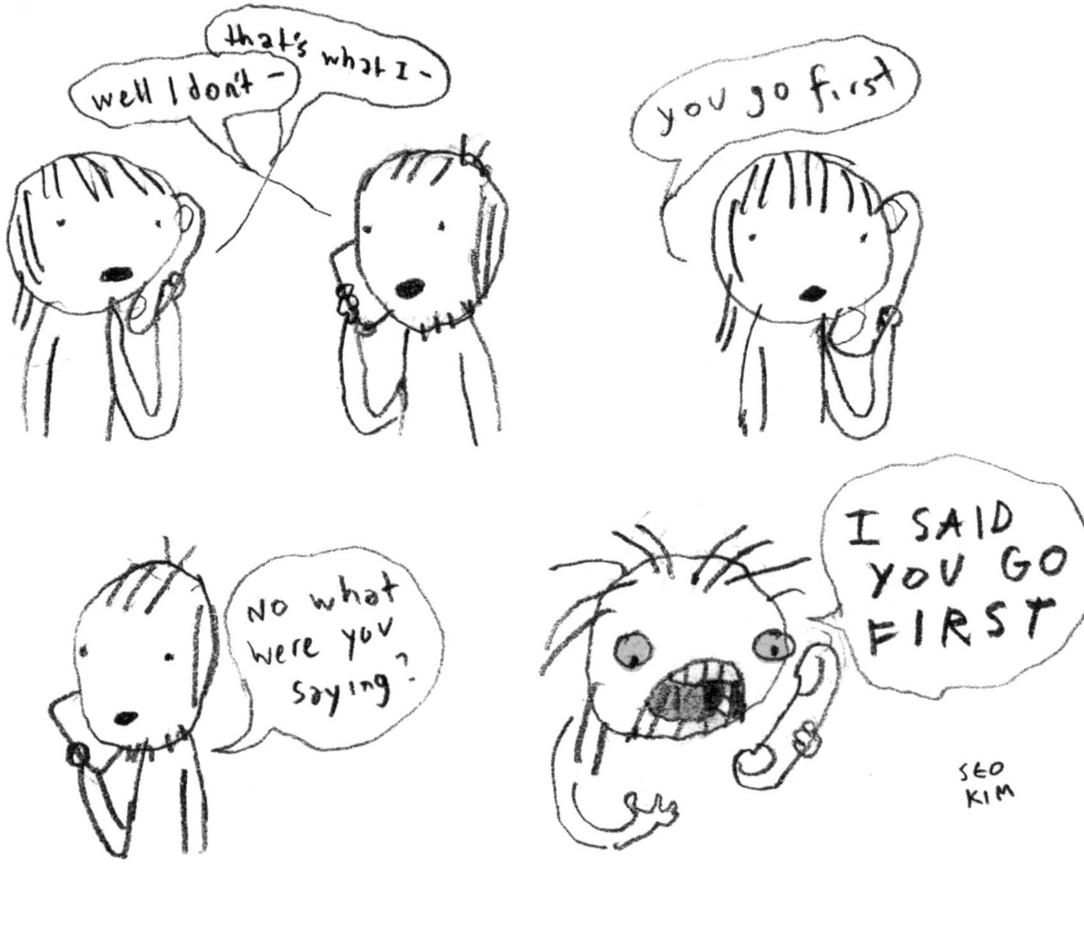
well I don't -
that's what I -
you go first
No what were you saying?
I SAID YOU GO FIRST
SEO KIM

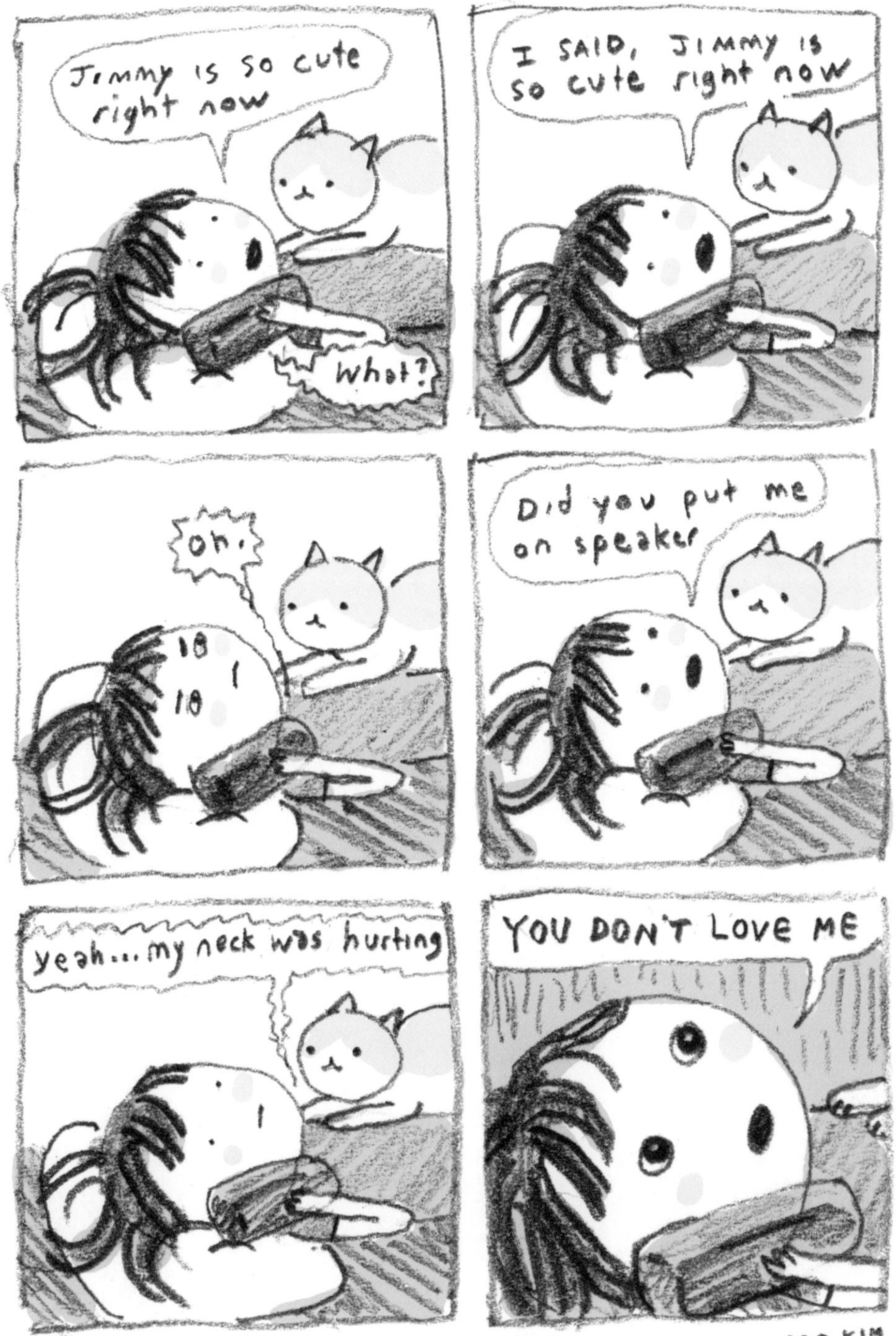
Jimmy is so cute right now
What?
I SAID, JIMMY IS so cute right now
Oh.
Did you put me on speaker
yeah... my neck was hurting
YOU DON'T LOVE ME

SEO KIM

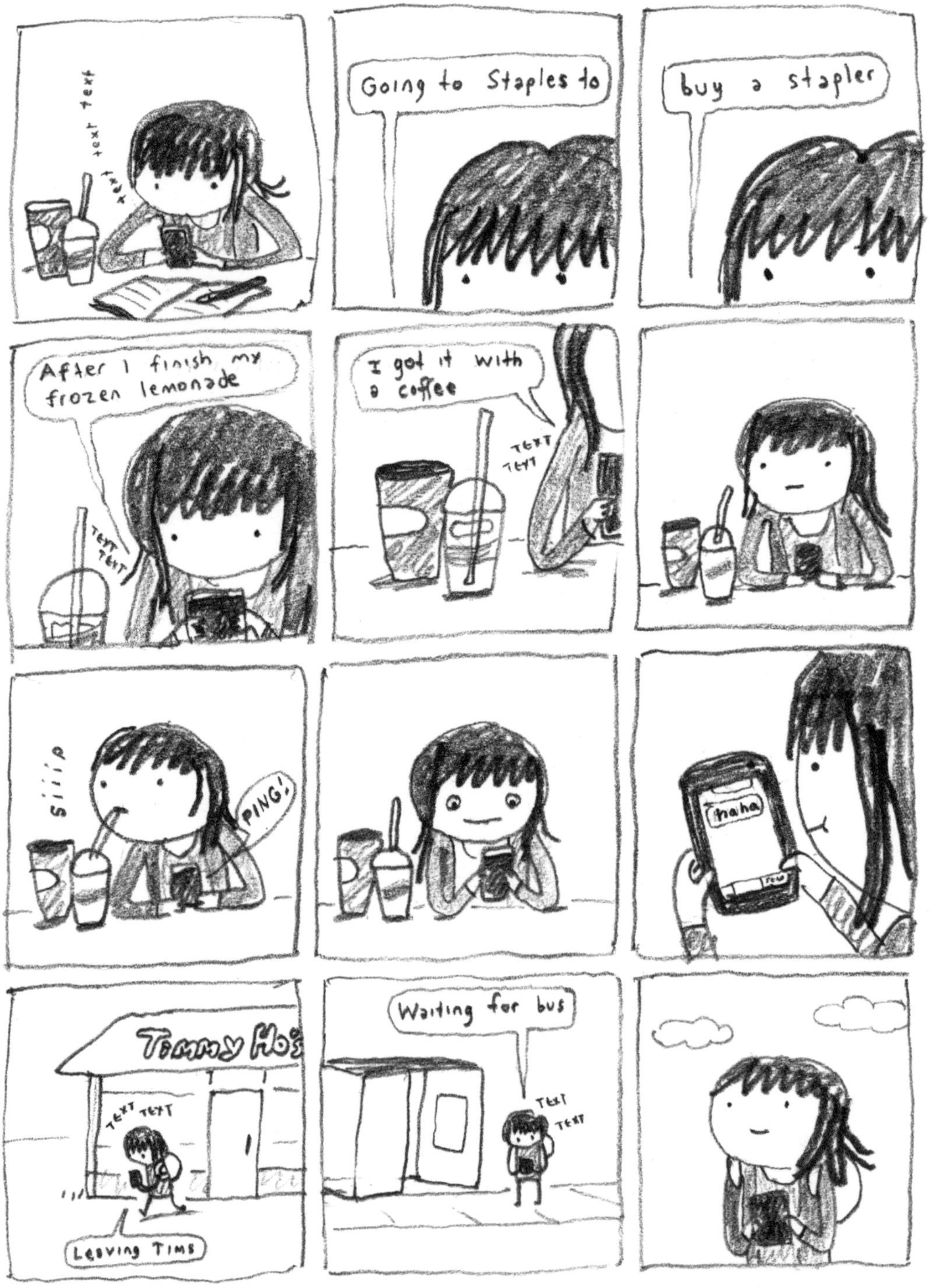
text
text text
Going to Staples to
buy a stapler
After I finish my frozen lemonade
TEXT TEXT
I got it with a coffee
TEXT TEXT
siiip
PING!
haha
Tommy Ho's
TEXT TEXT
Leaving TIMS
Waiting for bus
TEXT TEXT

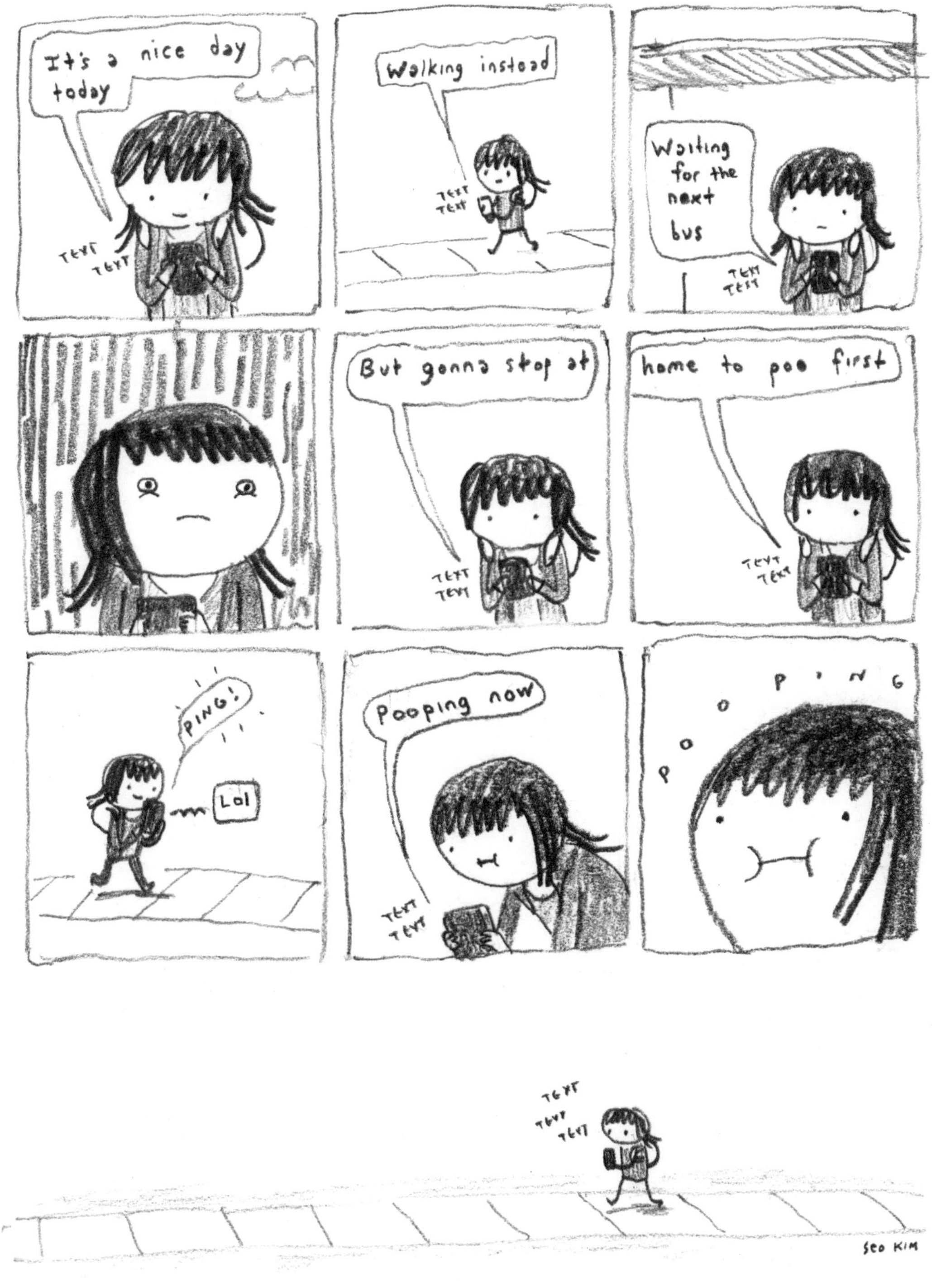
It's a nice day today
TEXT TEXT
Walking instead
TEXT TEXT
Waiting for the next bus
TEXT TEXT
But gonna stop at
TEXT TEXT
home to poo first
TEXT TEXT
PING!
Lol
Pooping now
TEXT TEXT
P O O P I N G
TEXT TEXT TEXT
SEO KIM

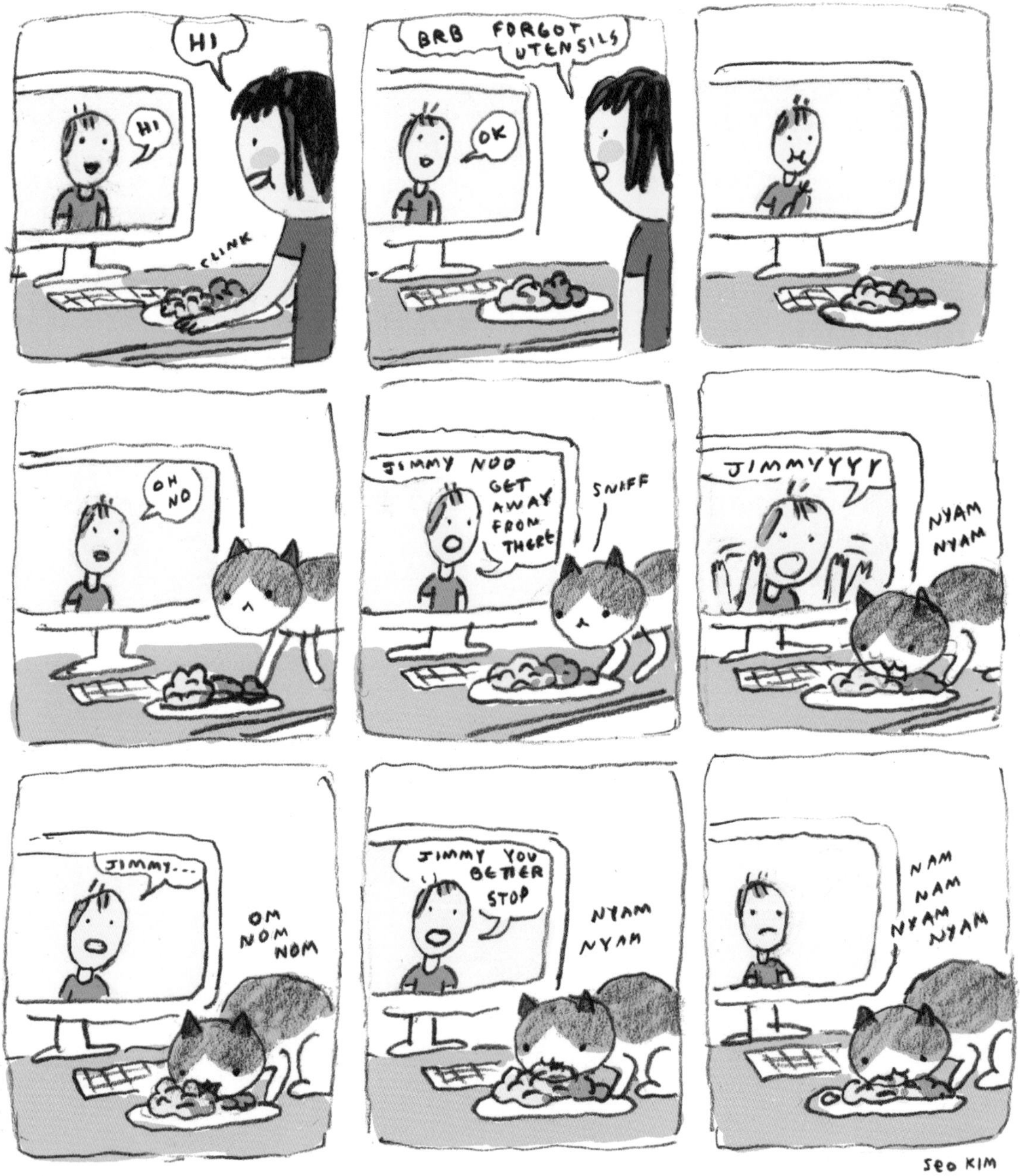
HI
HI
CLINK
BRB FORGOT UTENSILS
OK
OH NO
JIMMY NOO
GET AWAY FROM THERE
SNIFF
JIMMYYYY
NYAM NYAM
JIMMY...
OM NOM NOM
JIMMY YOU BETTER STOP
NYAM NYAM
NAM NAM NYAM NYAM

SEO KIM

I MISS SAD KFC.
YEAH, ME TOO...
FLASH BACK
BUAHHHHHHHHH
SIGH~
SEOKIM

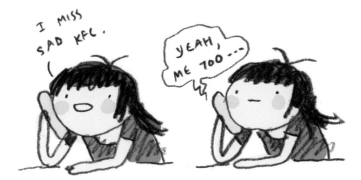

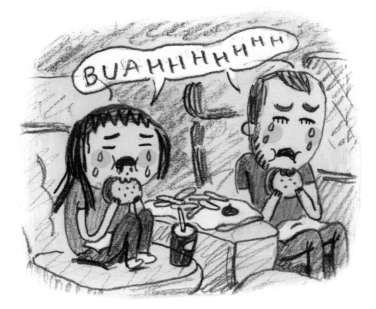

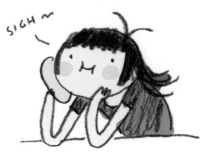

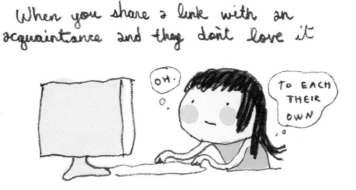

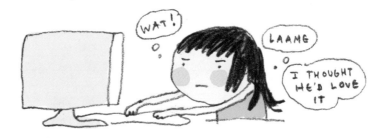

When you share a link with an acquaintance and they don't love it
OH.
TO EACH THEIR OWN
When you share a link with a friend and they don't love it
WAT!
LAAMG
I THOUGHT HE'D LOVE IT
When you share a link with boyfriend and he don't love it
DID YOU EVEN WATCH IT.
WATCH IT AGAIN.
SEO KIM

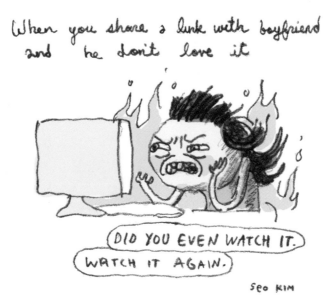

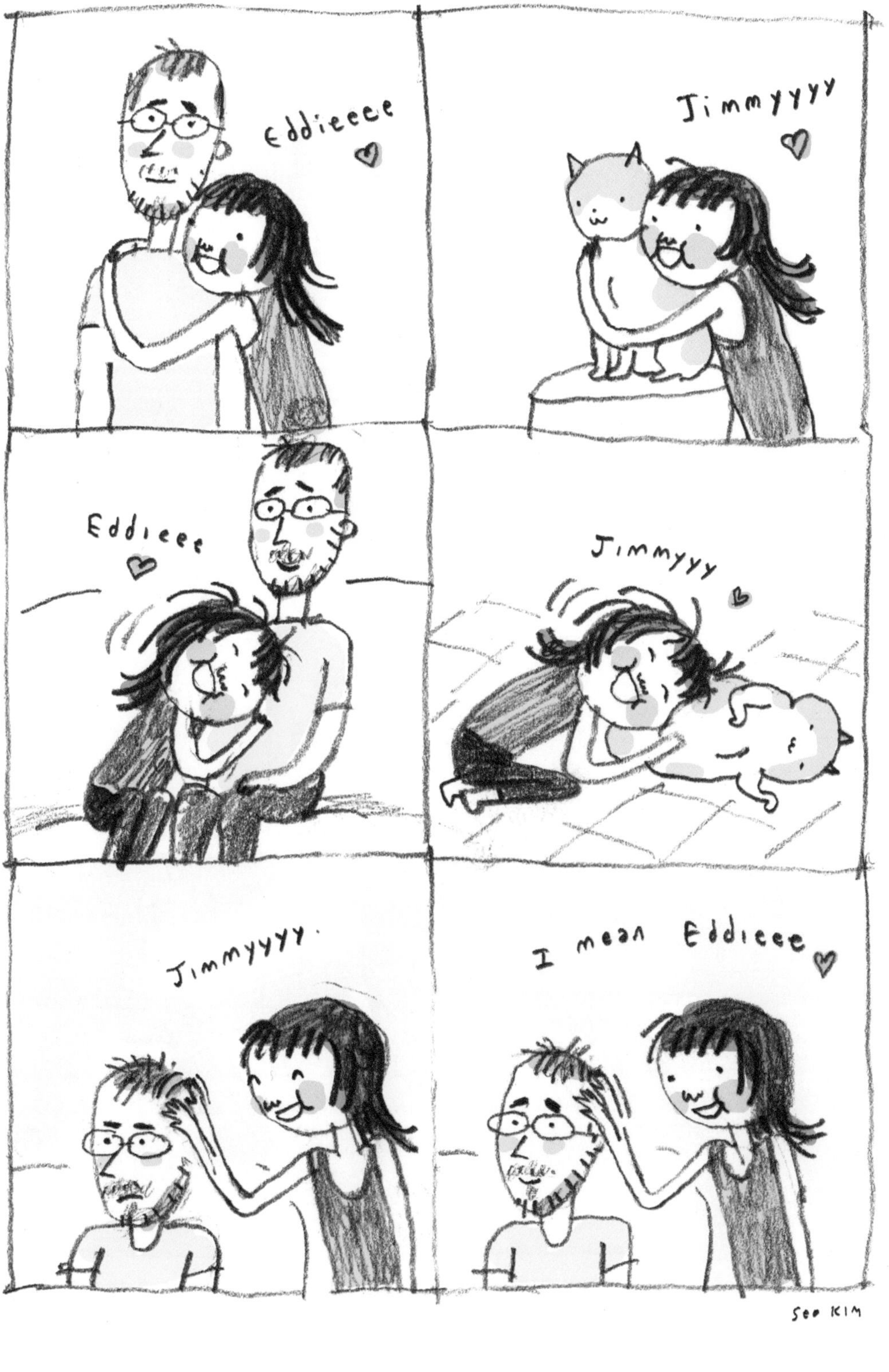
Eddieeee
Jimmyyyy
Eddieee
Jimmyyy
Jimmyyyy.
I mean Eddieee
See KIM

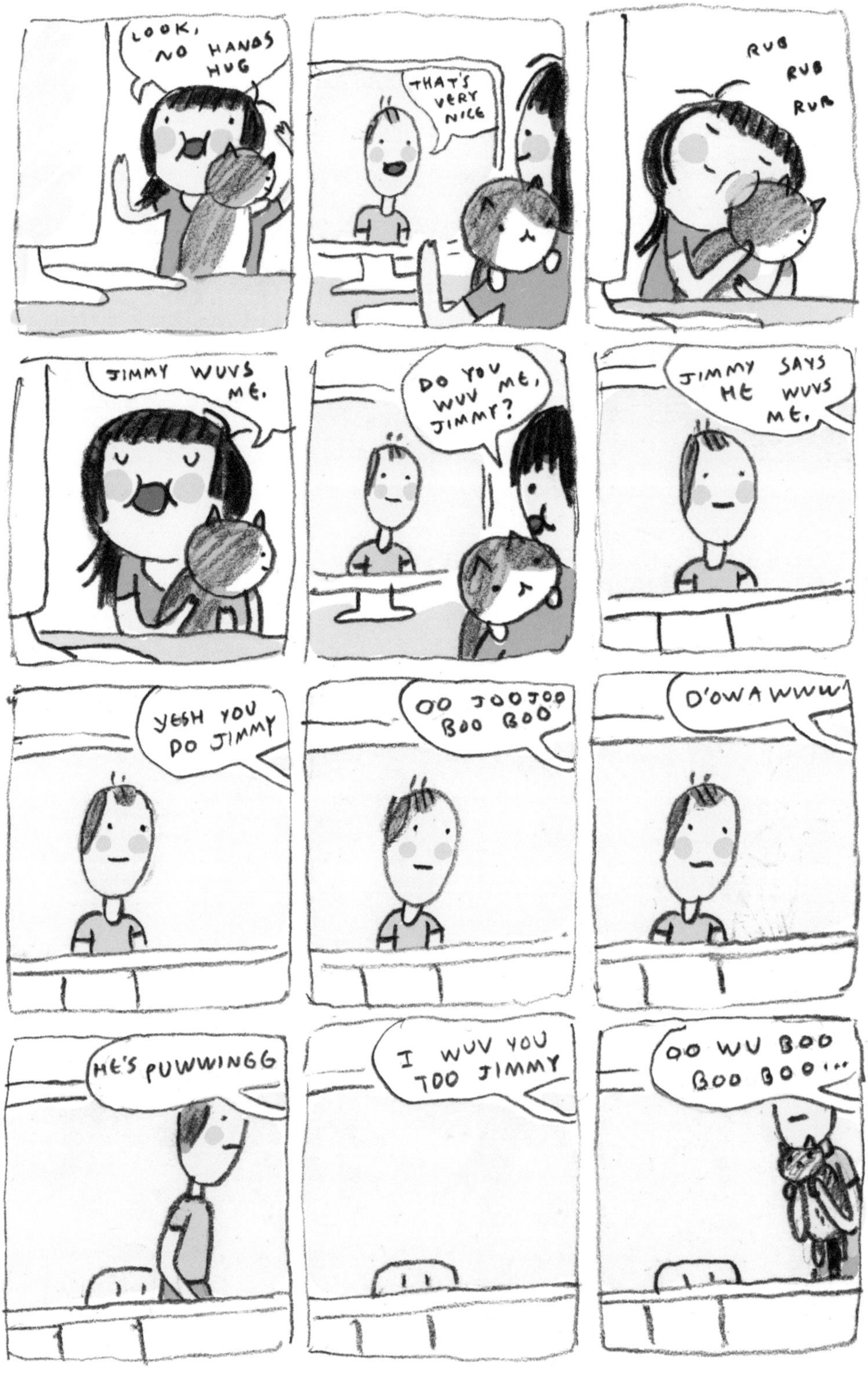
LOOK, NO HANDS HUG
THAT'S VERY NICE
RUB RUB RUB
JIMMY WUVS ME.
DO YOU WUV ME, JIMMY?
JIMMY SAYS HE WUVS ME.
YESH YOU DO JIMMY
OO JOOJOO BOO BOO
D'OWAWWW
HE'S PUWWINGG
I WUV YOU TOO JIMMY
OO WU BOO BOO BOO...

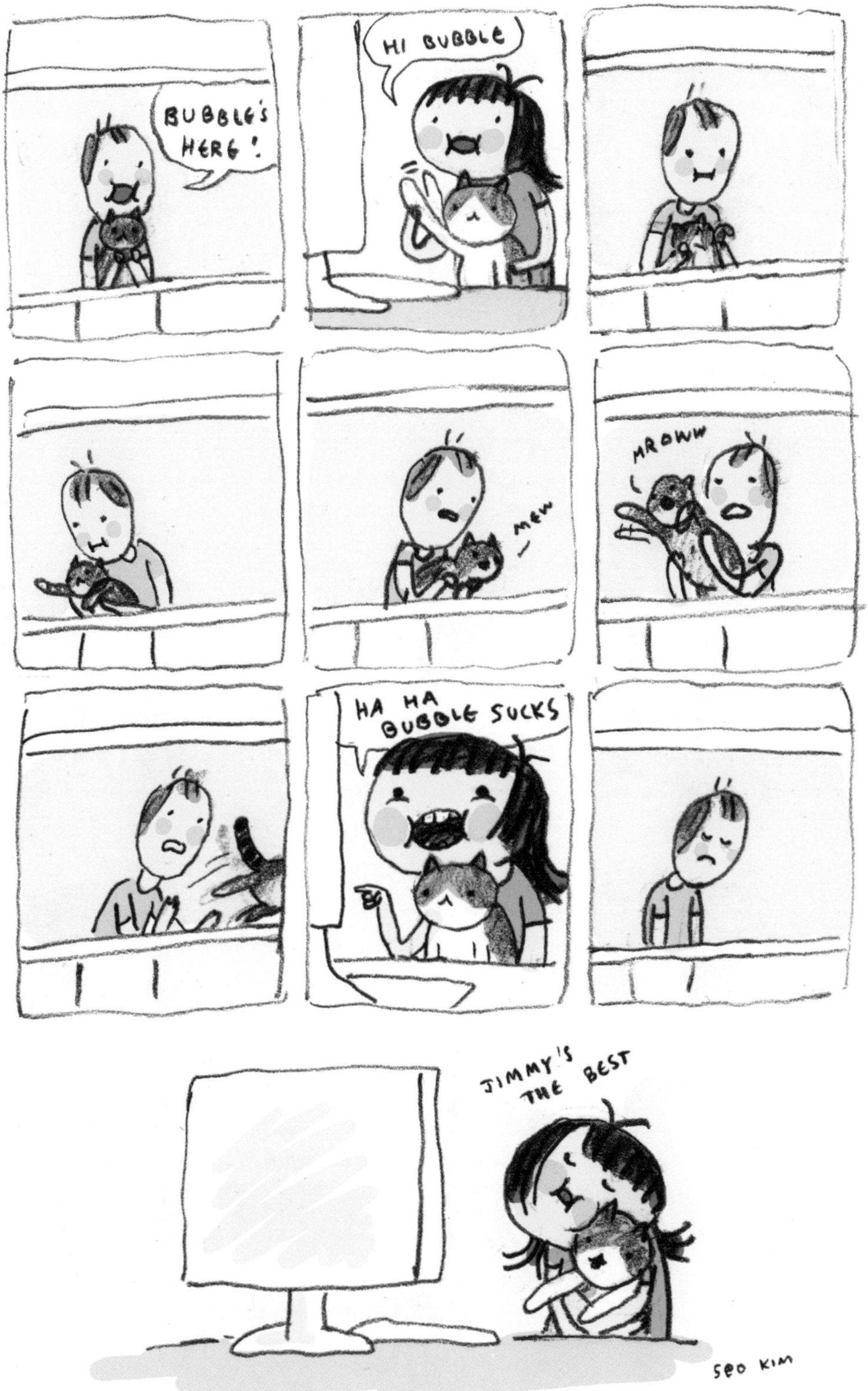
BUBBLE'S HERE!
HI BUBBLE
MEW
MROWW
HA HA BUBBLE SUCKS
JIMMY'S THE BEST
SEO KIM

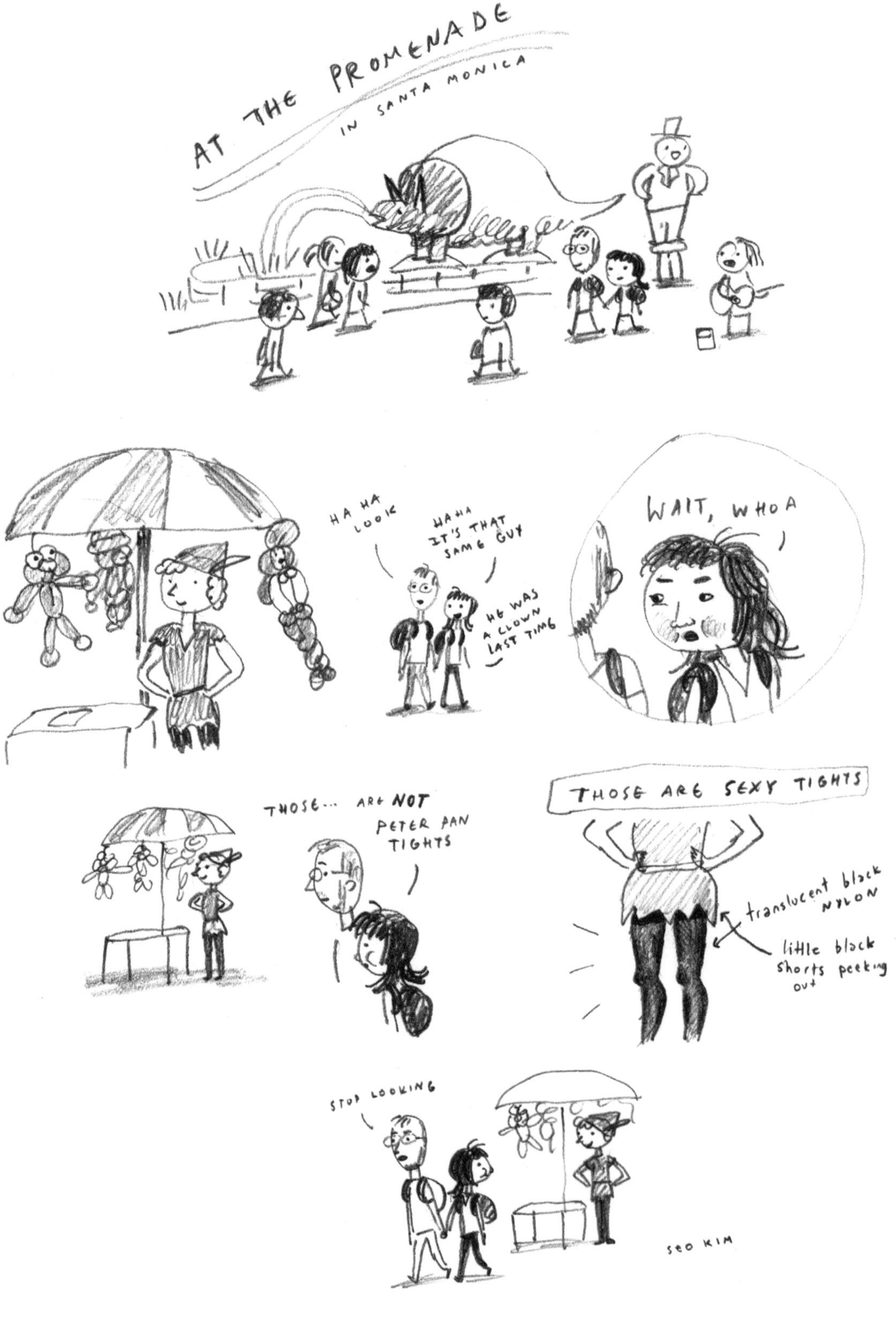
AT THE PROMENADE
IN SANTA MONICA
HA HA LOOK
HAHA IT'S THAT SAME GUY
HE WAS A CLOWN LAST TIME
WAIT, WHOA
THOSE... ARE NOT PETER PAN TIGHTS
THOSE ARE SEXY TIGHTS
translucent black NYLON
little black shorts peeking out
STOP LOOKING
SEO KIM

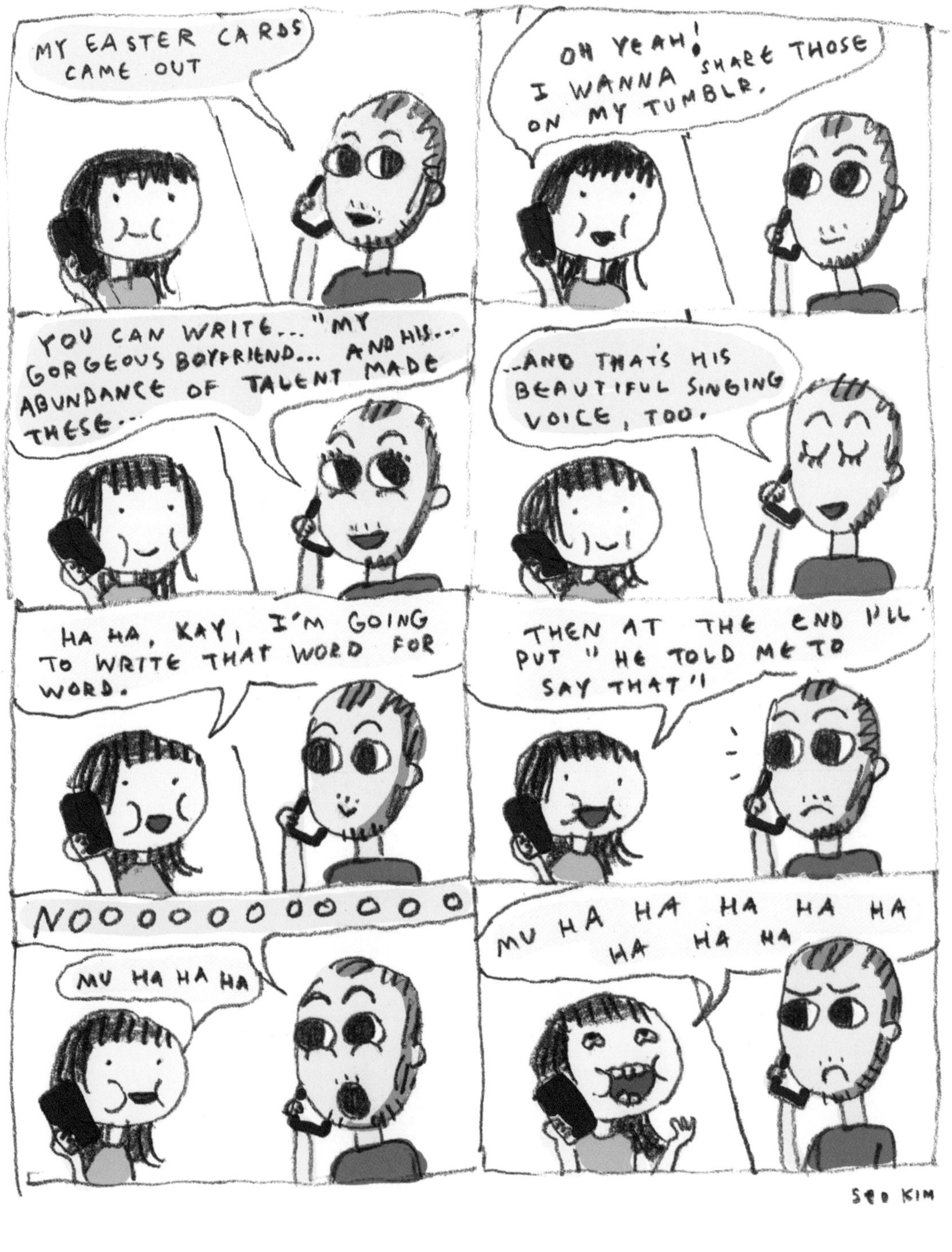
MY EASTER CARDS CAME OUT
OH YEAH! I WANNA SHARE THOSE ON MY TUMBLR.
YOU CAN WRITE... "MY GORGEOUS BOYFRIEND... AND HIS... ABUNDANCE OF TALENT MADE THESE...
...AND THAT'S HIS BEAUTIFUL SINGING VOICE, TOO.
HA HA, KAY, I'M GOING TO WRITE THAT WORD FOR WORD.
THEN AT THE END I'LL PUT "HE TOLD ME TO SAY THAT"
NOOOOOOOOOOOO
MU HA HA HA
MU HA HA HA HA HA HA HA HA
SEO KIM

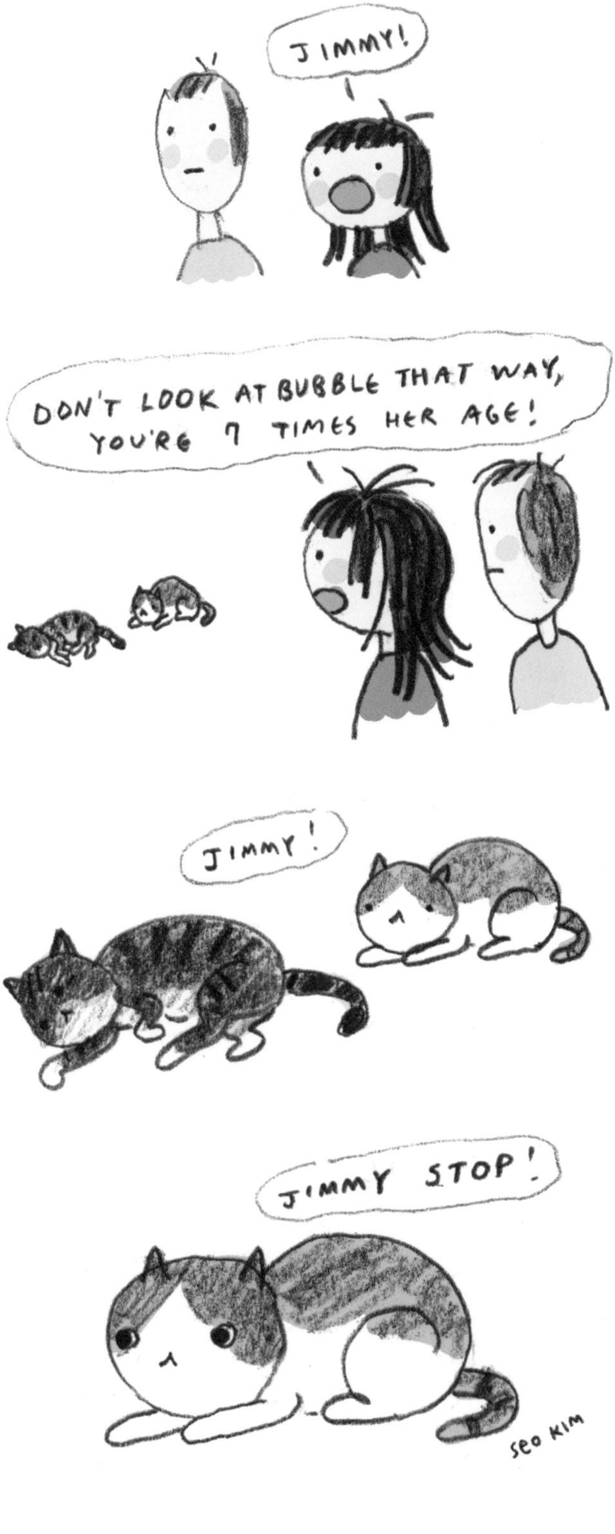
JIMMY!
DON'T LOOK AT BUBBLE THAT WAY, YOU'RE 7 TIMES HER AGE!
JIMMY!
JIMMY STOP!
SEO KIM

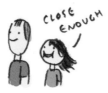

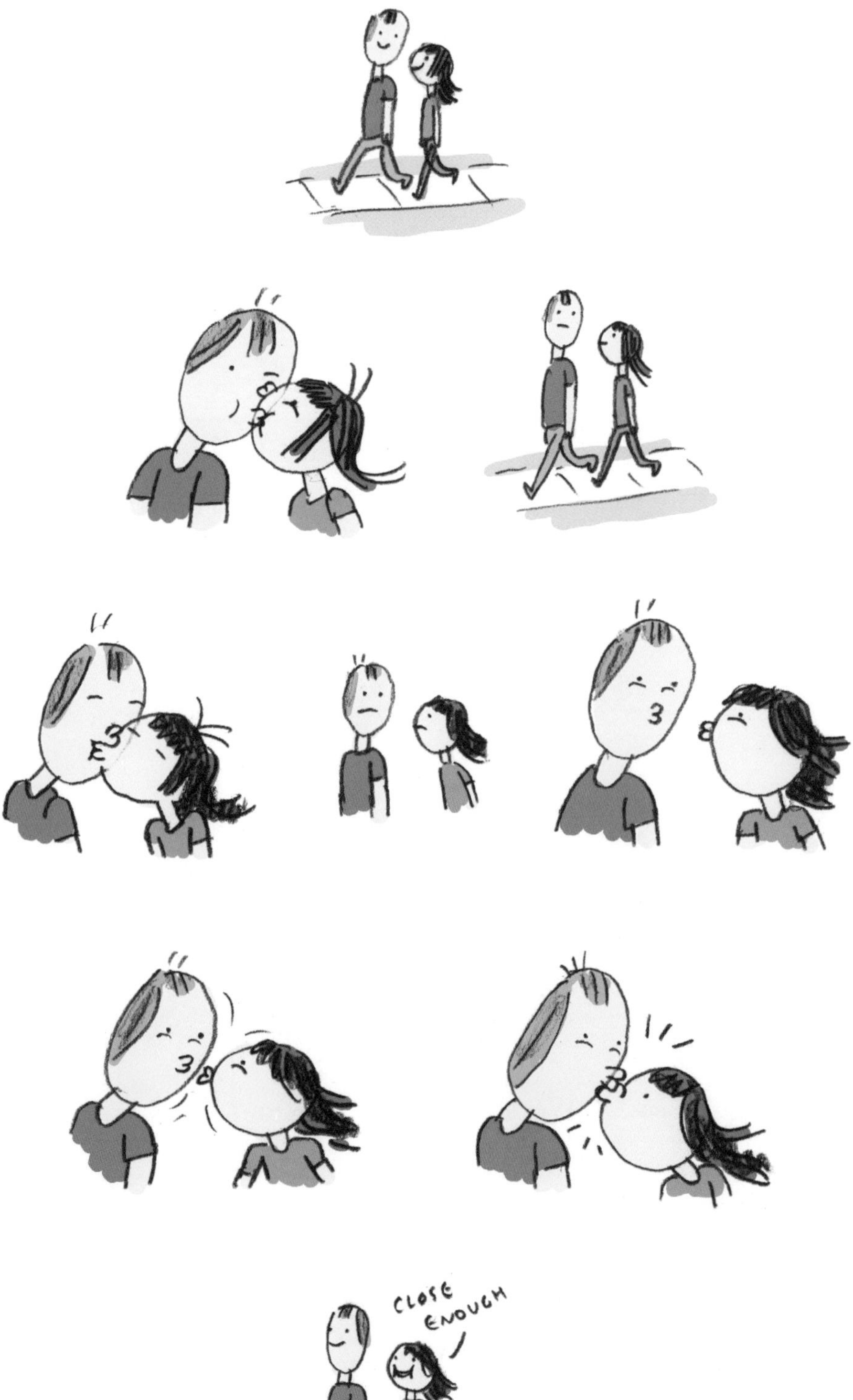
CLOSE ENOUGH
SEO KIM

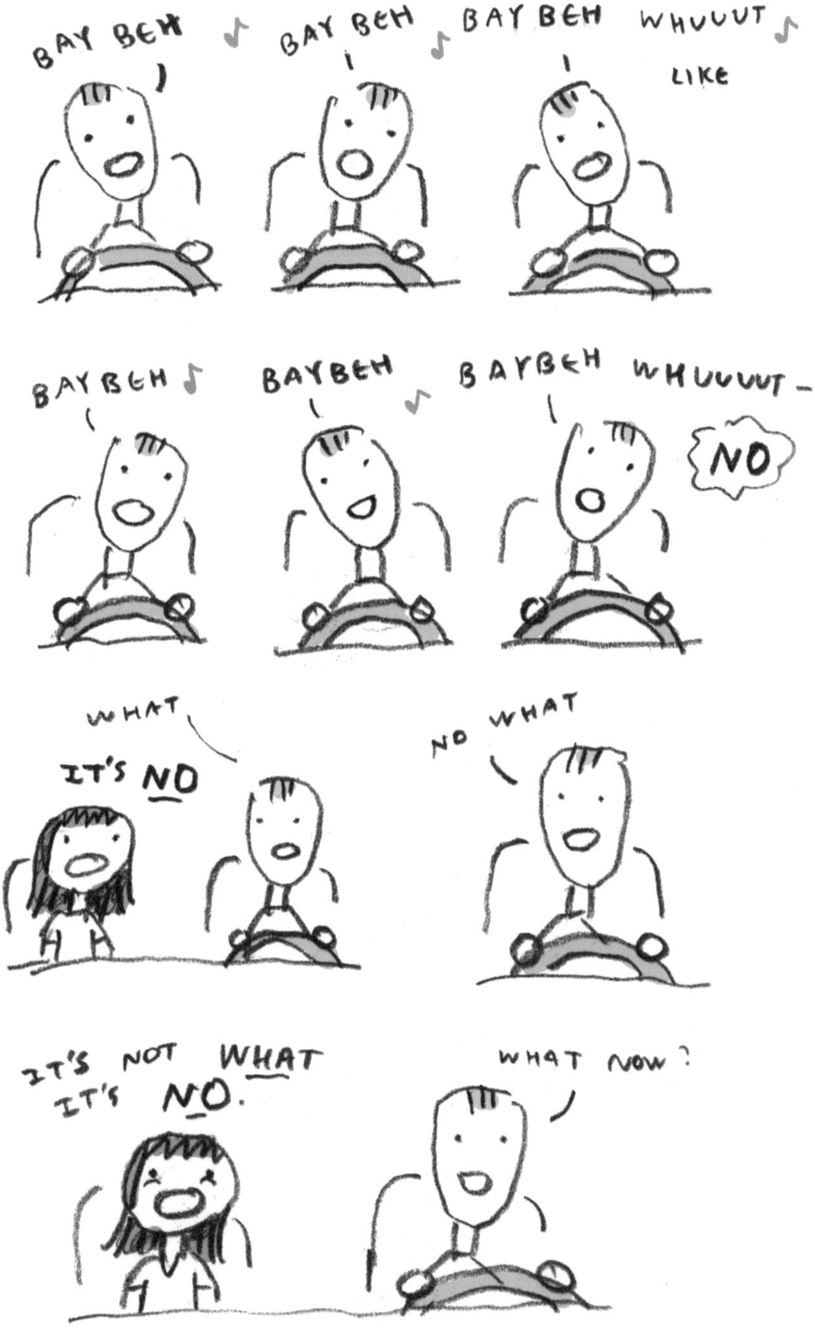
BAY BEH
BAY BEH
BAY BEH WHUUUT
LIKE
BAYBEH
BAYBEH
BAYBEH WHUUUUT-
NO
IT'S NO
WHAT
NO WHAT
IT'S NOT WHAT
IT'S NO.
WHAT NOW?

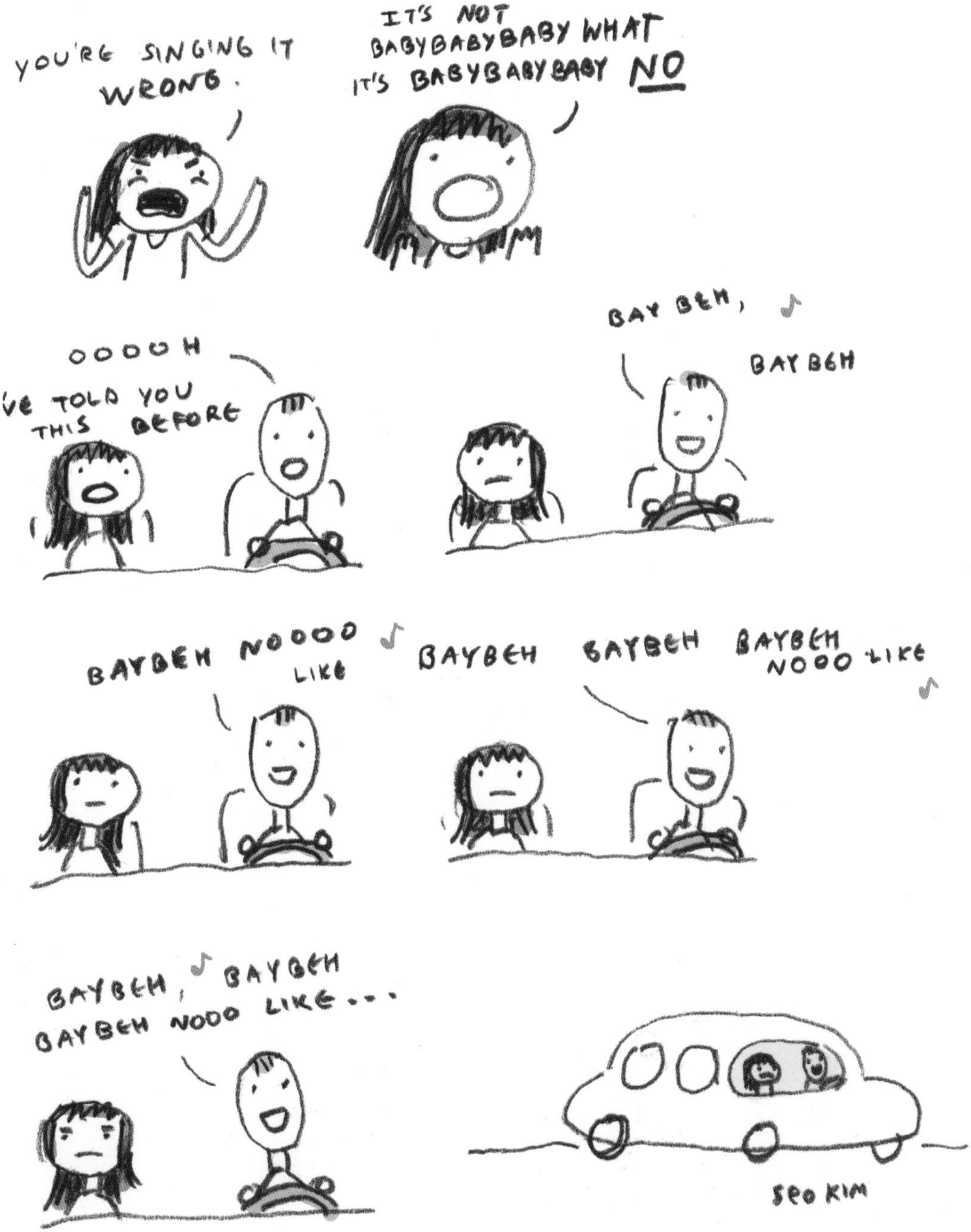
YOU'RE SINGING IT WRONG.
IT'S NOT BABYBABYBABY WHAT IT'S BABYBABYBABY NO
OOOOH
I'VE TOLD YOU THIS BEFORE
BAY BEH, BAYBEH
BAYBEH NOOOO LIKE
BAYBEH BAYBEH BAYBEH NOOO LIKE
BAYBEH, BAYBEH BAYBEH NOOO LIKE...
SEO KIM

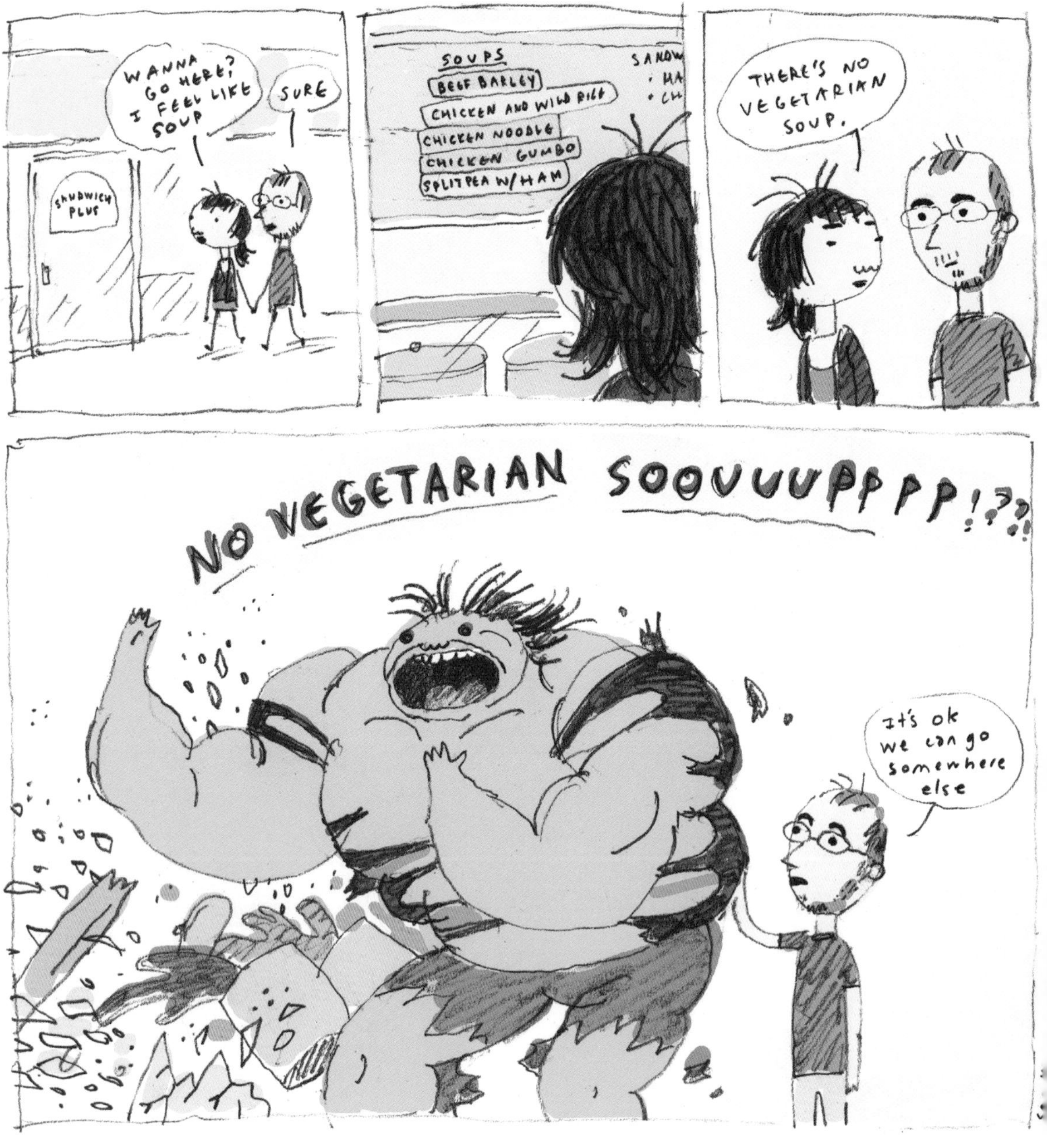
WANNA GO HERE? I FEEL LIKE SOUP
SURE
SANDWICH PLUS
SOUPS
BEEF BARLEY
CHICKEN AND WILD RICE
CHICKEN NOODLE
CHICKEN GUMBO
SPLITPEA W/HAM
THERE'S NO VEGETARIAN SOUP.
NO VEGETARIAN SOOVUUPPPP!??
It's ok we can go somewhere else

MISC.

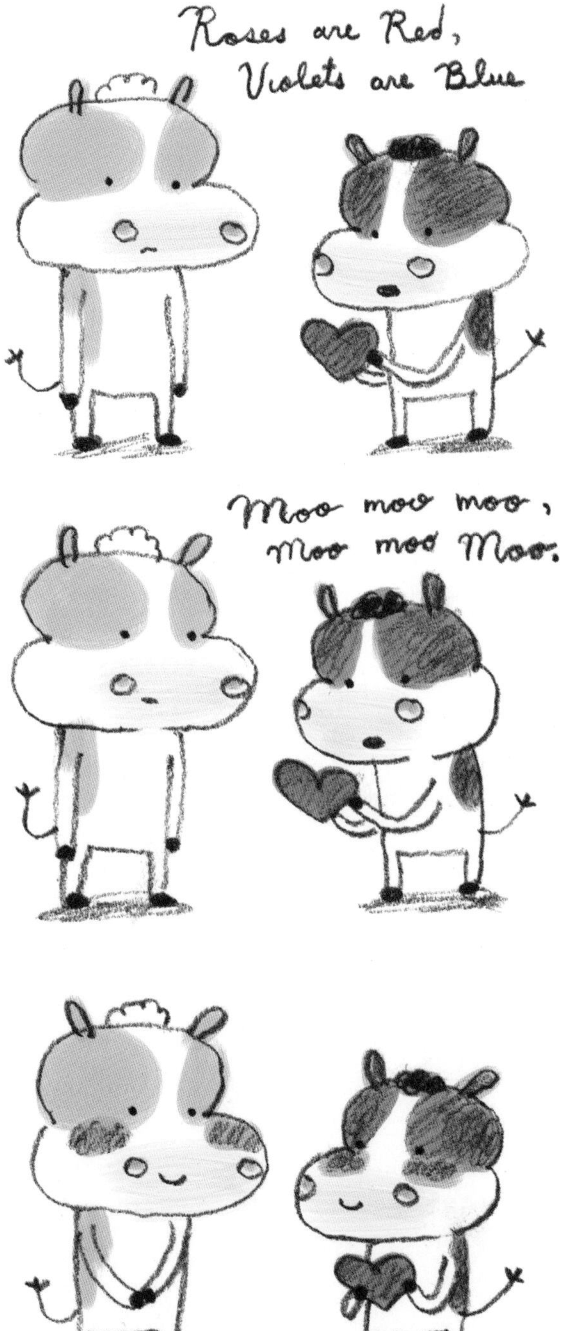
Roses are Red,
Violets are Blue
Moo moo moo,
Moo moo Moo.
seo kim

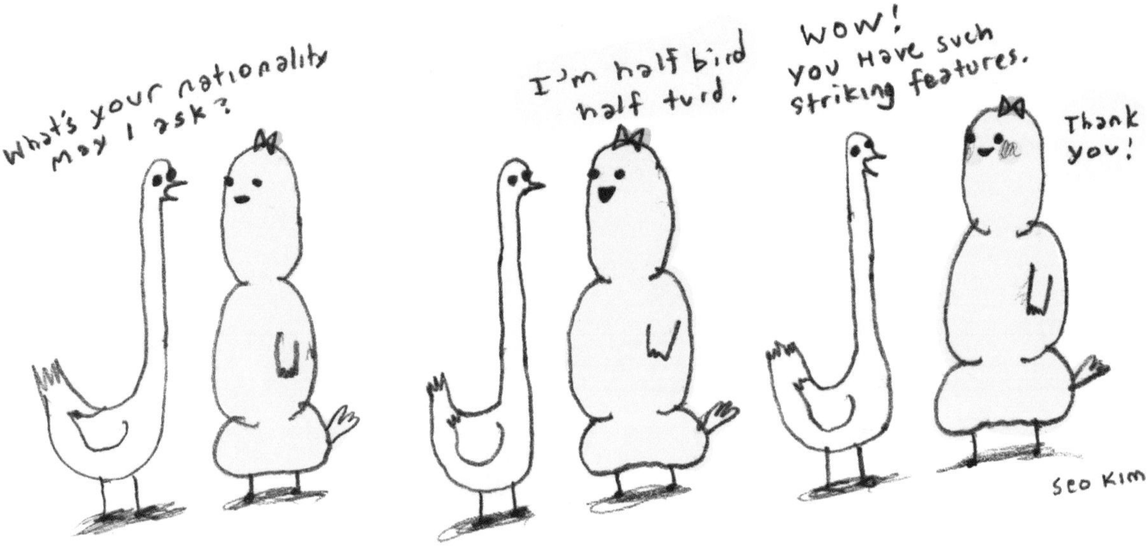
What's your nationality
May I ask?
I'm half bird
half turd.
WOW!
You Have such
striking features.
Thank
you!
Seo Kim

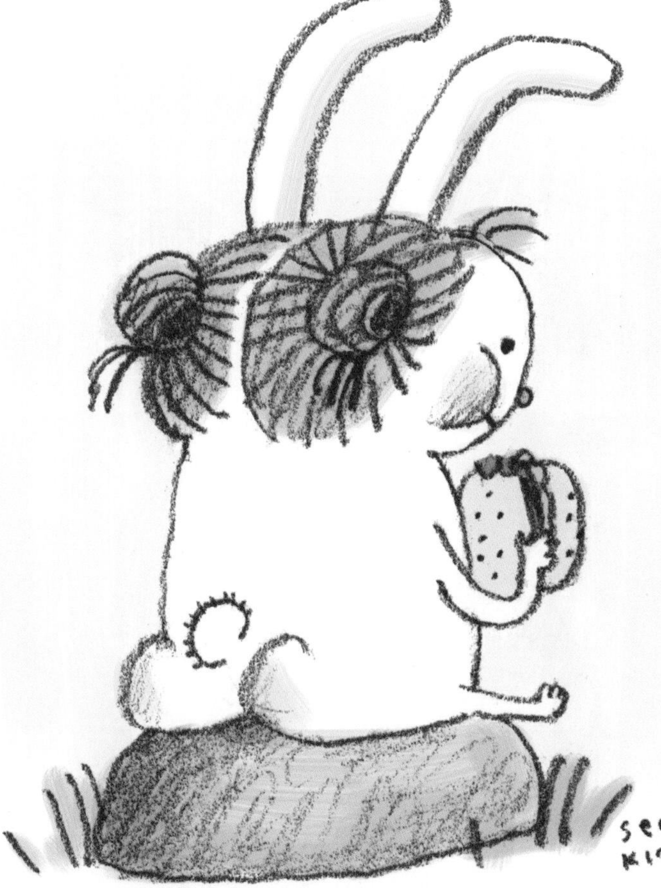
seo
kim

buns

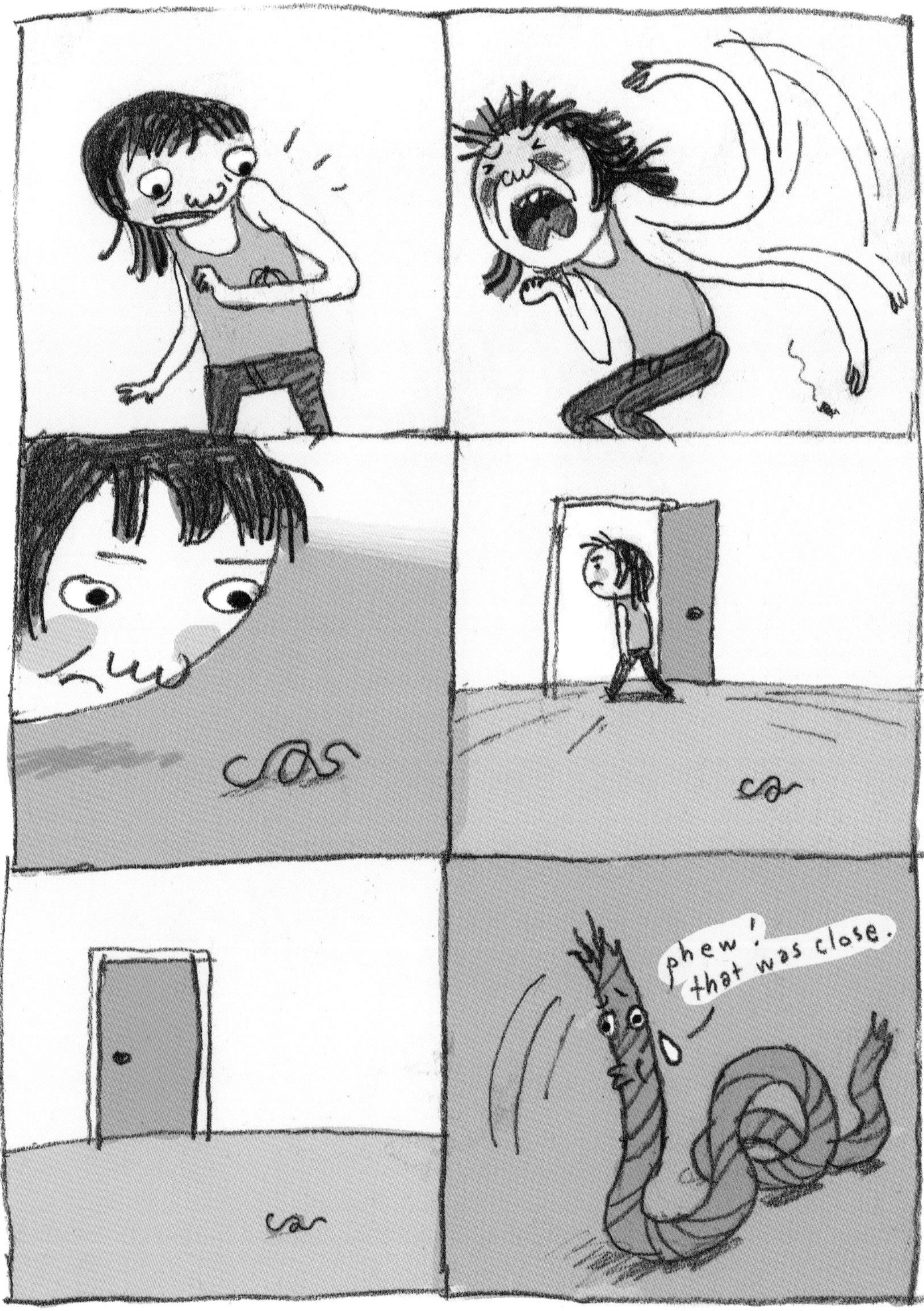
phew! that was close.

SEO KIM

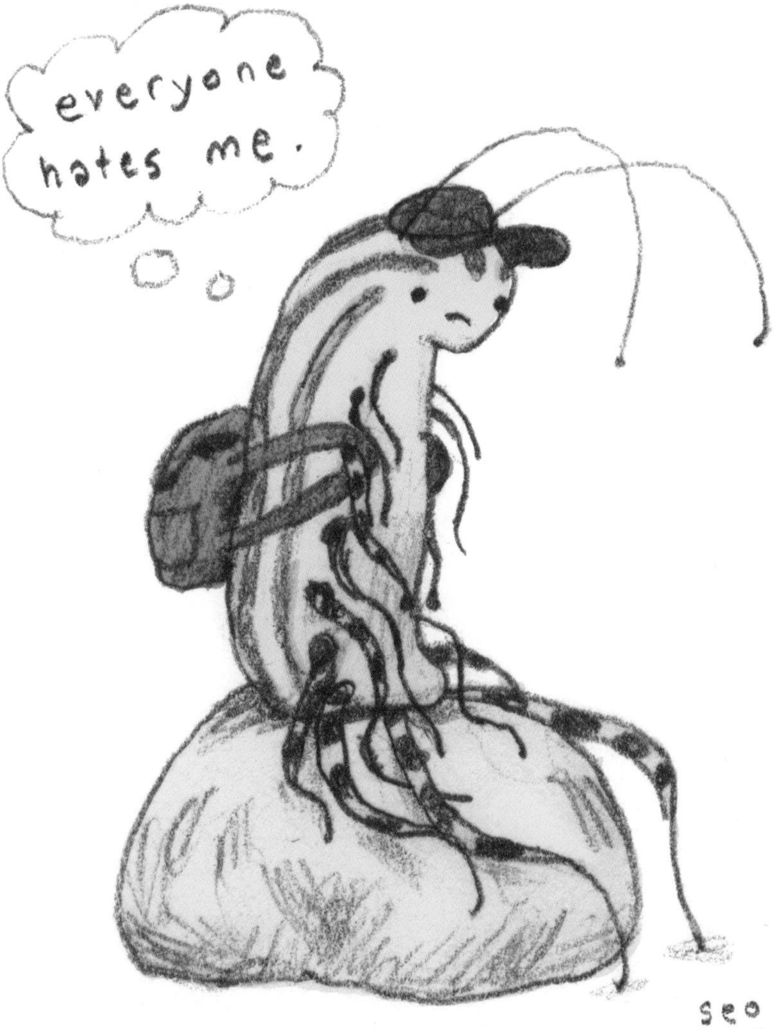
everyone hates me.
seo kim

Chocolate Chip Cookie Disease

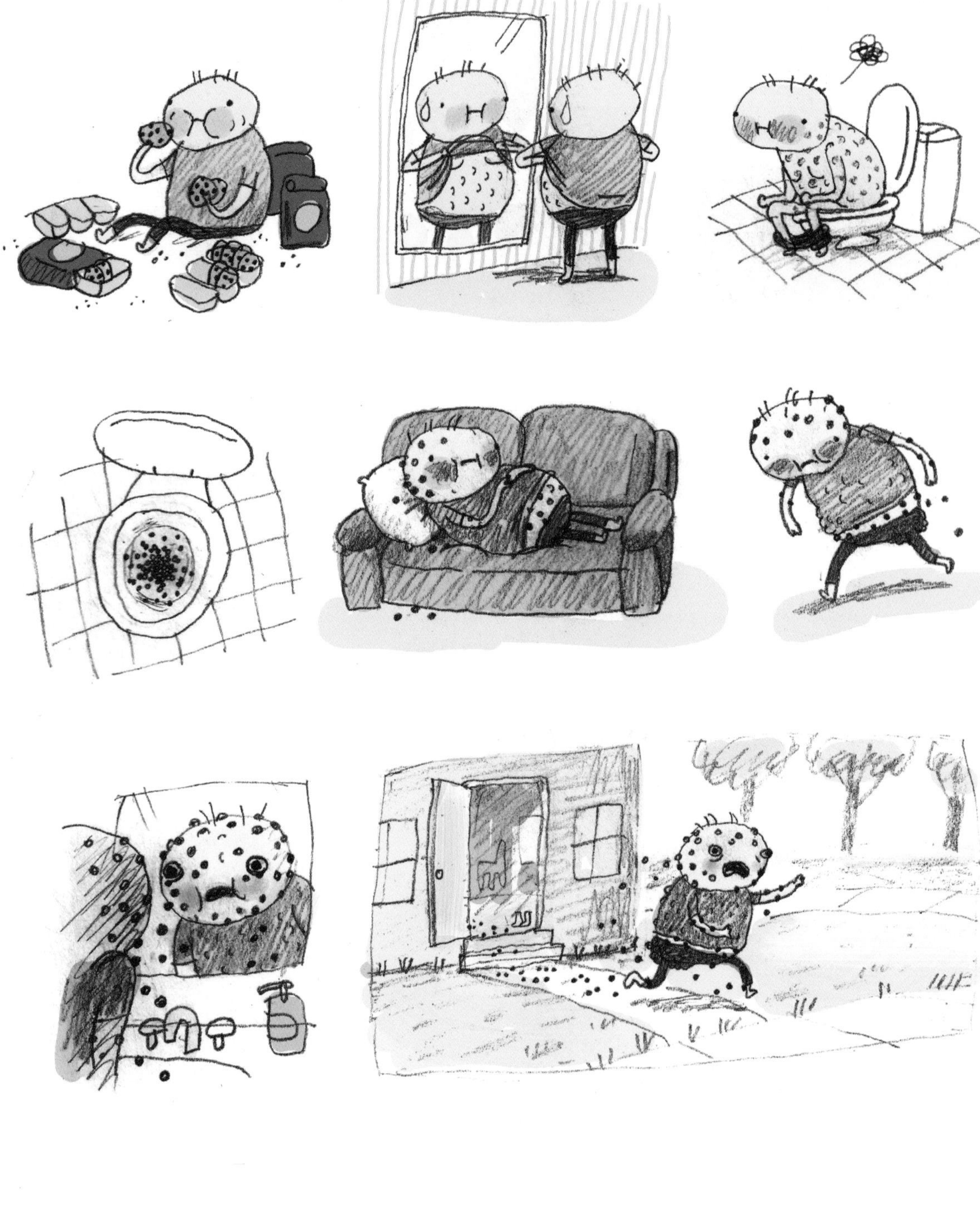

SEOKIM

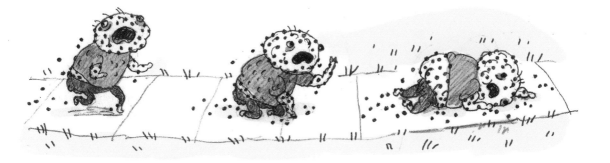

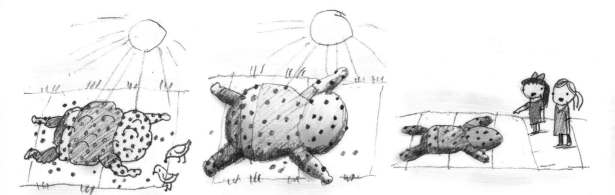

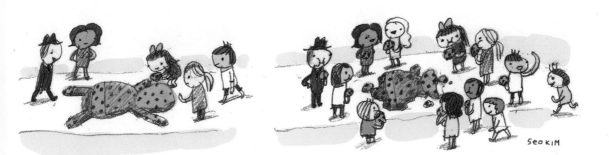

NICE FRO, YO!
THANKS, FRO-YO.
SEOKIM

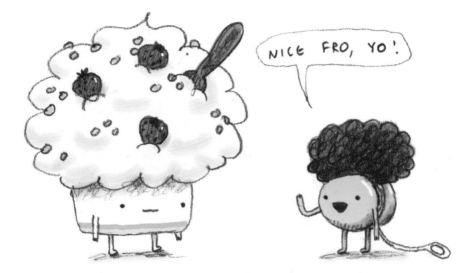

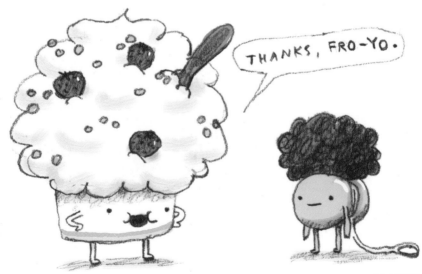

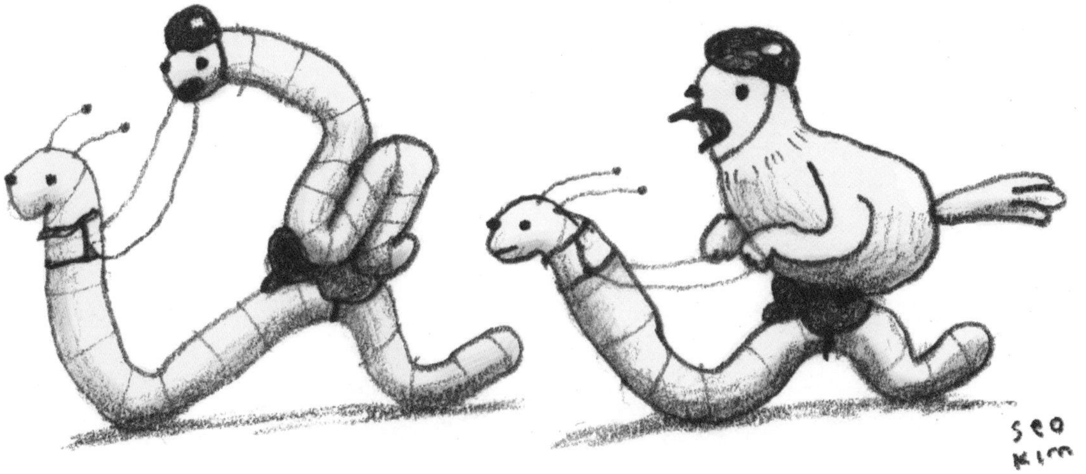
seo
kim

WORM VS. BIRD

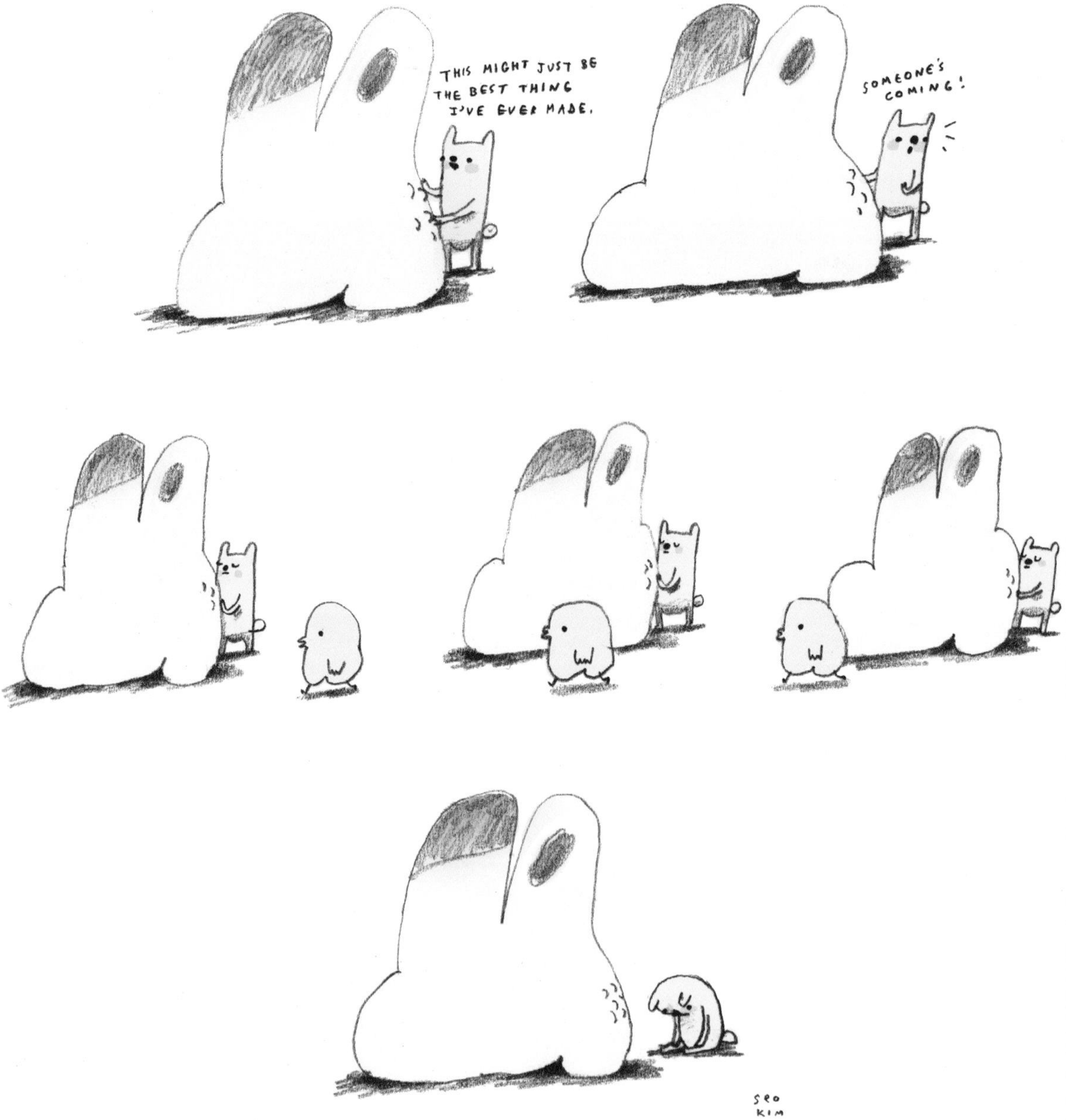
THIS MIGHT JUST BE THE BEST THING I'VE EVER MADE.
SOMEONE'S COMING!
SEO KIM

THIS IS MY JAM!
MEH
SHE DON'T KNOW SHIT ABOUT JAM.
SEO KIM

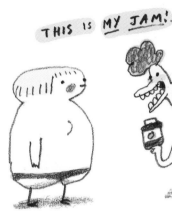

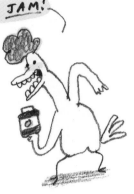

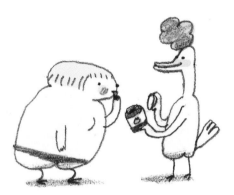

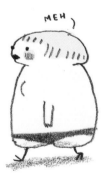

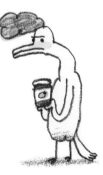

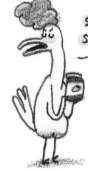

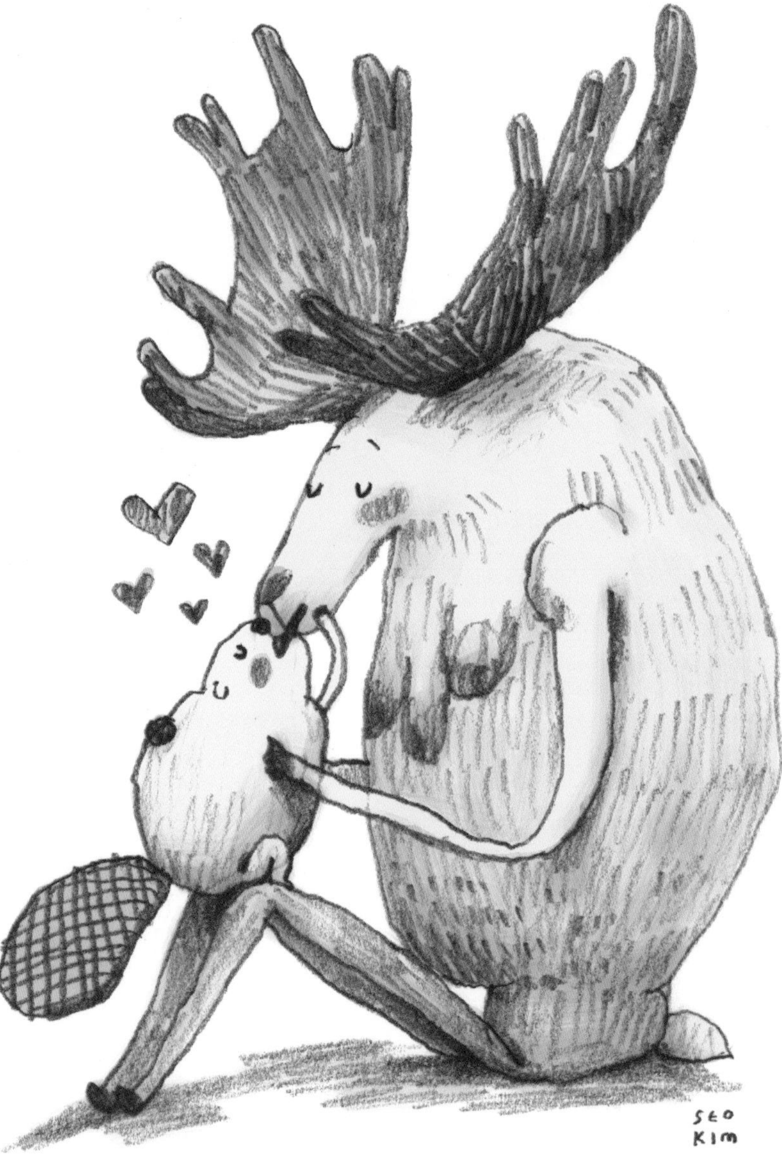
SEO
KIM

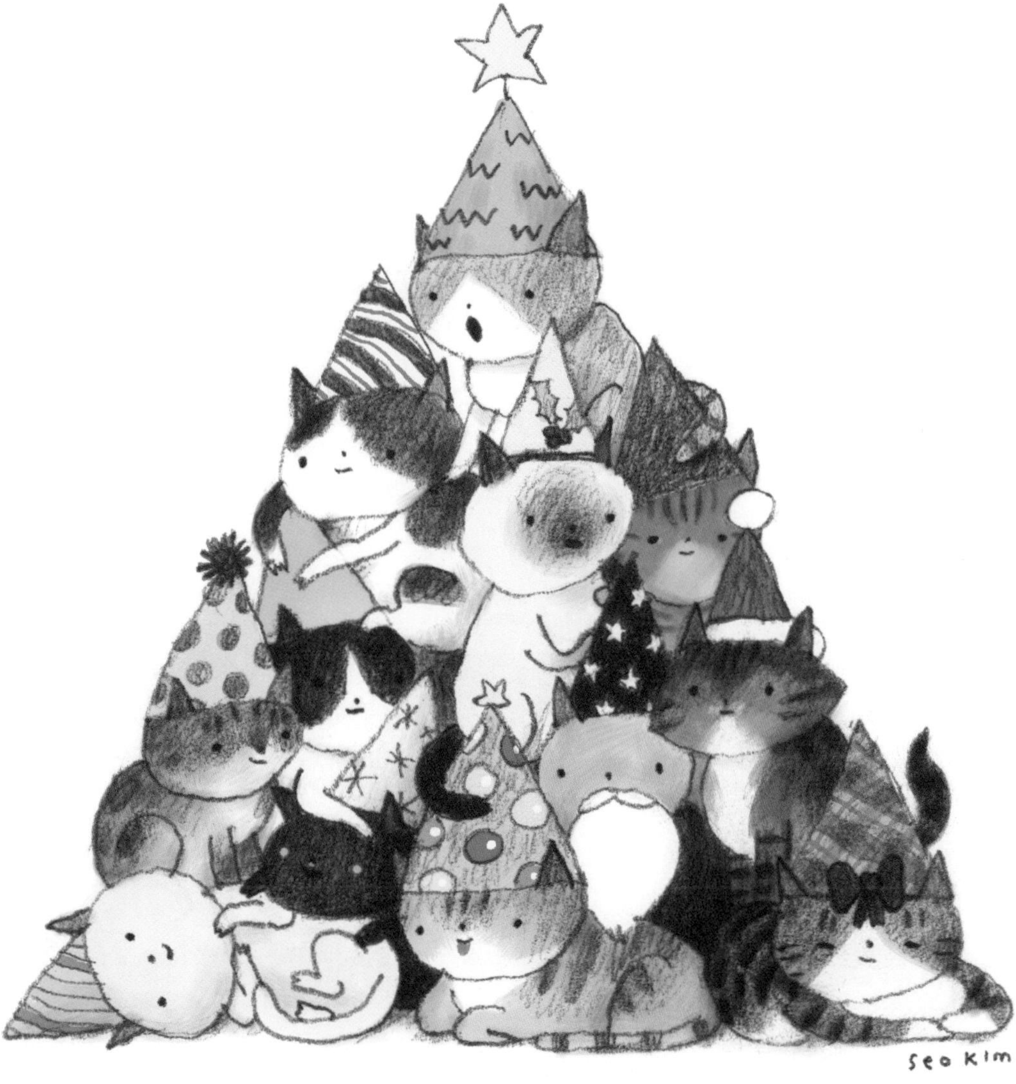
seo kim

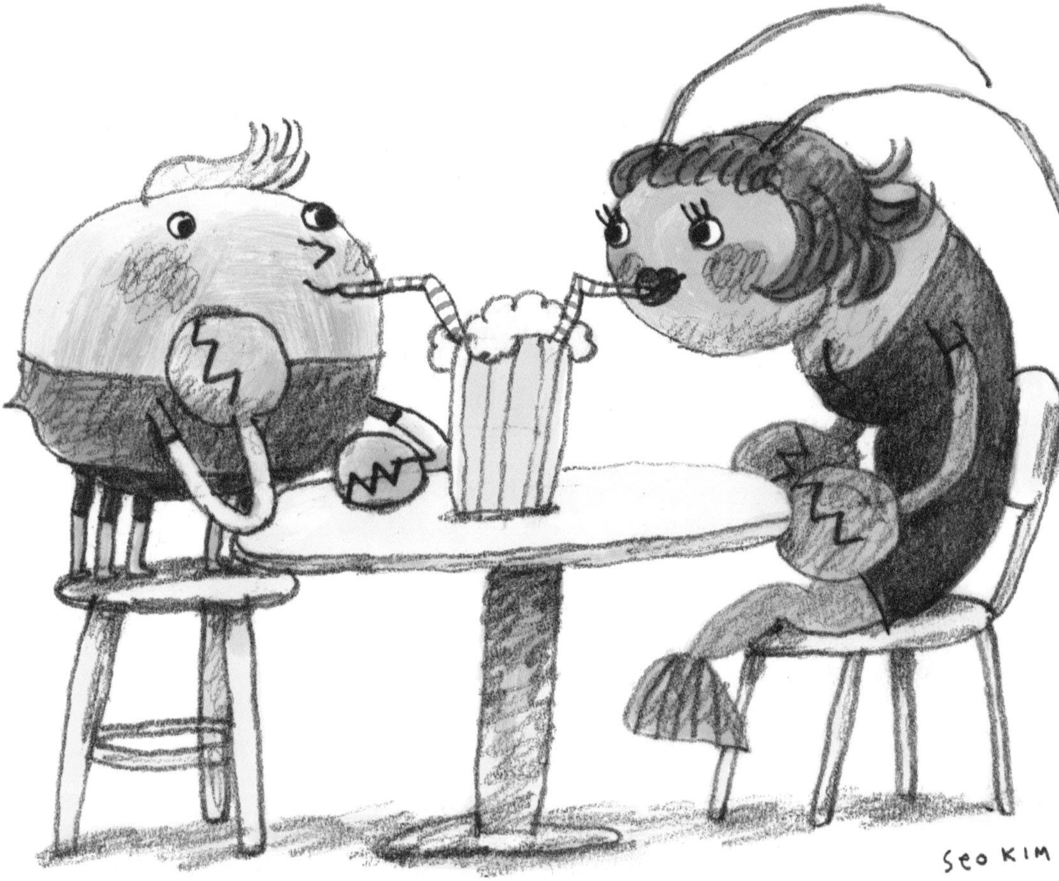
SEO KIM

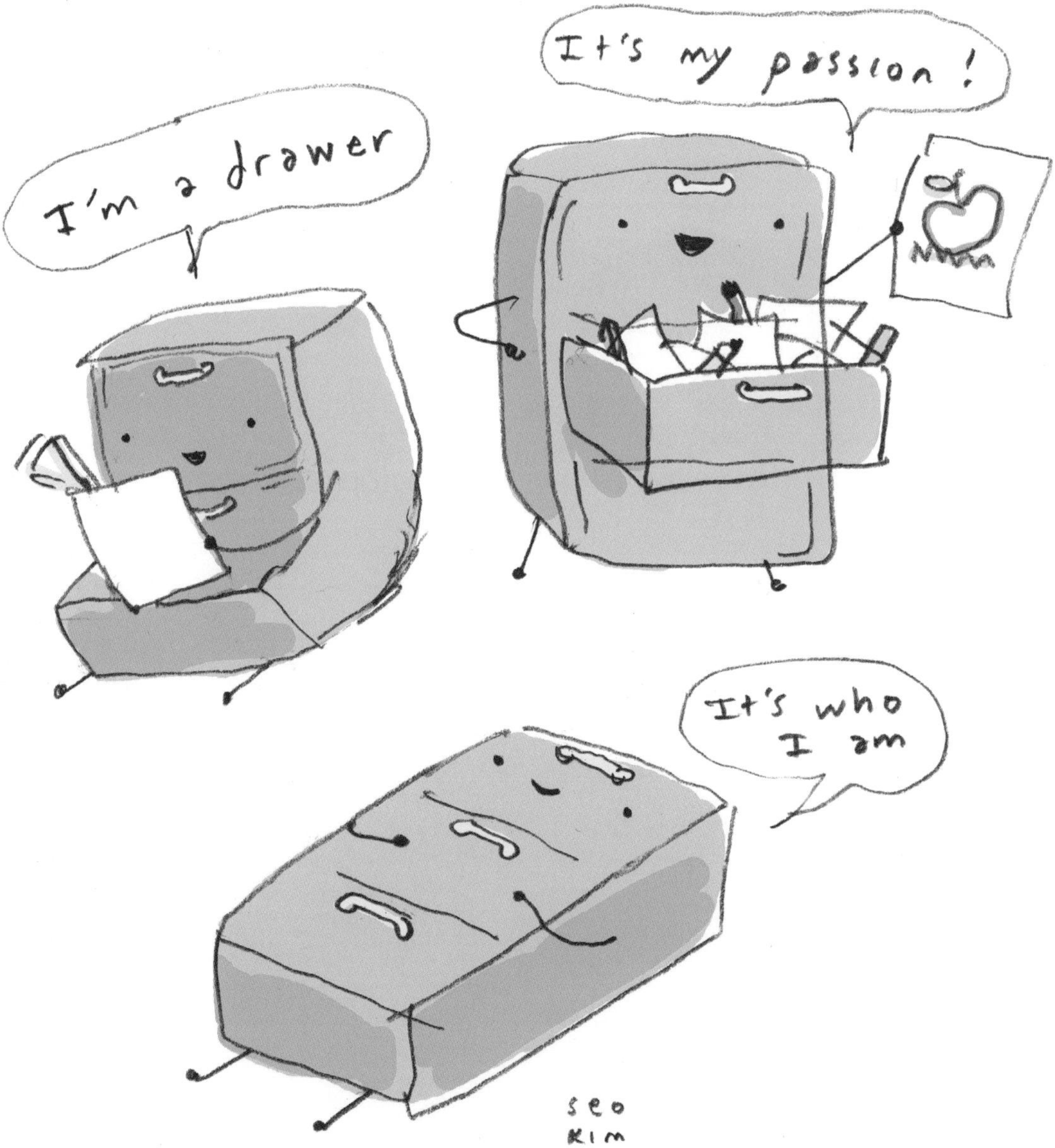
I'm a drawer
It's my passion!
It's who I am
seo kim

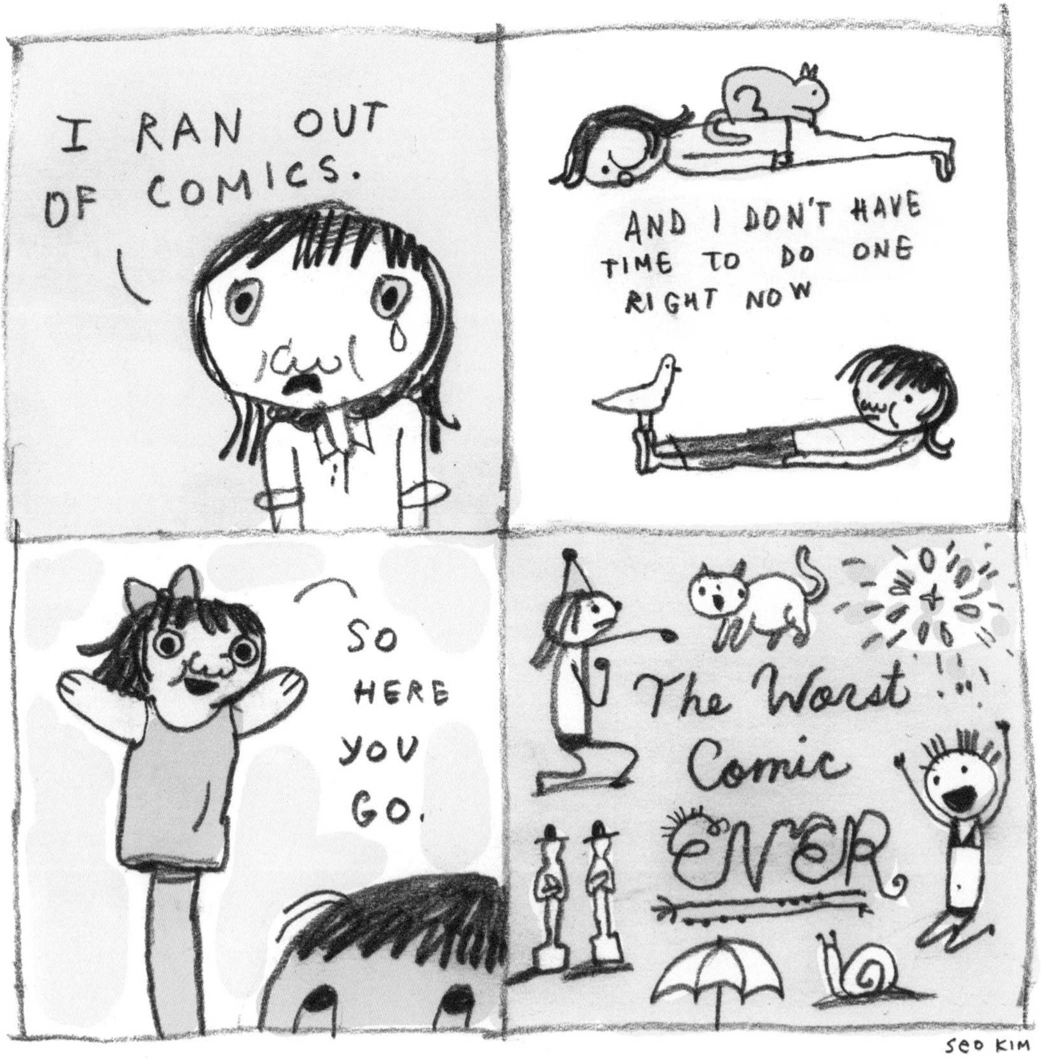
I RAN OUT OF COMICS.
AND I DON'T HAVE TIME TO DO ONE RIGHT NOW
SO HERE YOU GO.
The Worst Comic EVER
SEO KIM

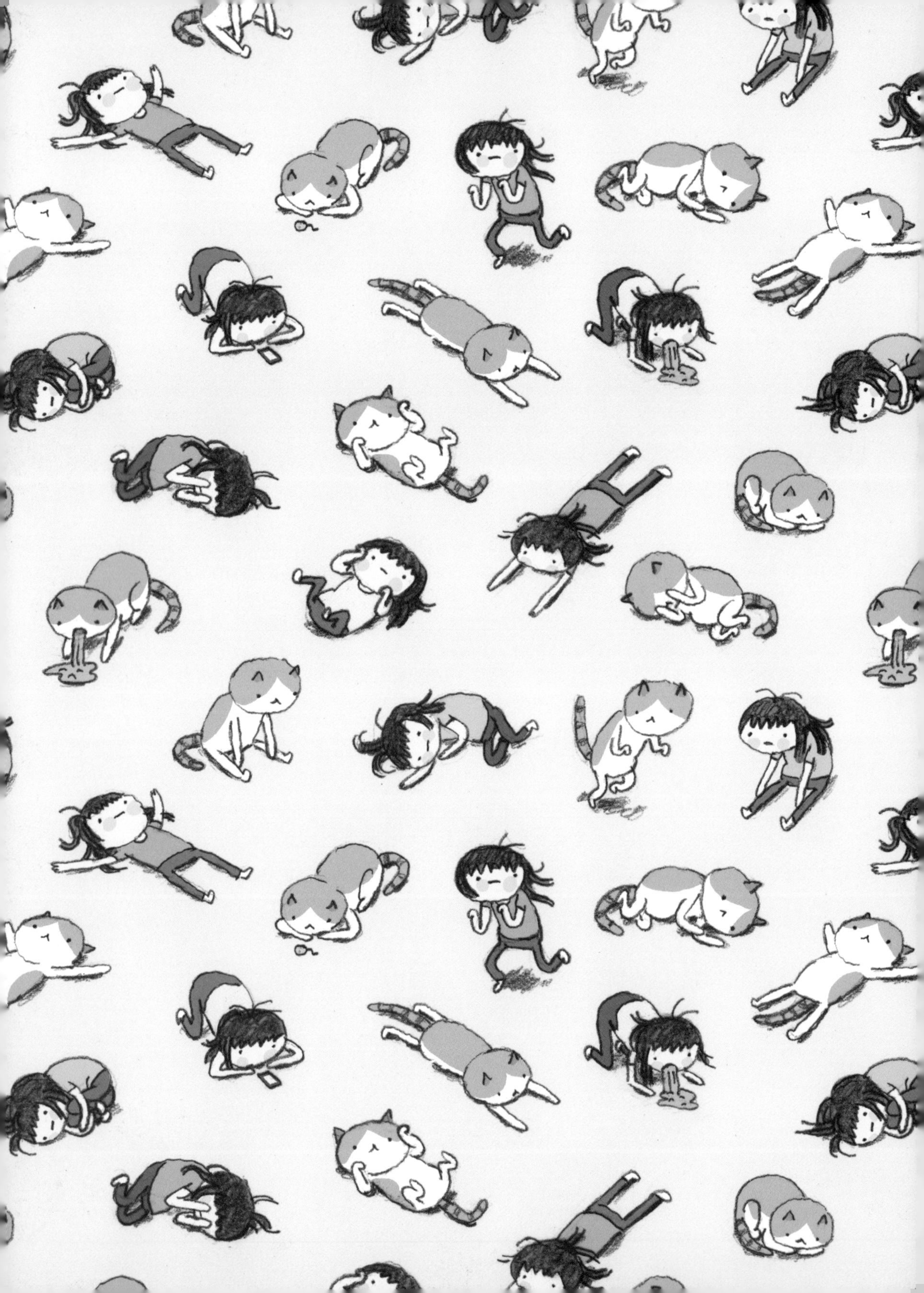